BASTARD POLITICS

SUNY series in Contemporary French Thought
―――――――
David Pettigrew and François Raffoul, editors

BASTARD POLITICS
Sovereignty and Violence

NICK MANSFIELD

Published by State University of New York Press, Albany

© 2021 State University of New York

All rights reserved

Printed in the United States of America

No part of this book may be used or reproduced in any manner whatsoever without written permission. No part of this book may be stored in a retrieval system or transmitted in any form or by any means including electronic, electrostatic, magnetic tape, mechanical, photocopying, recording, or otherwise without the prior permission in writing of the publisher.

For information, contact State University of New York Press, Albany, NY
www.sunypress.edu

Library of Congress Cataloging-in-Publication Data

Name: Mansfield, Nick, author.
Title: Bastard politics : sovereignty and violence / Nick Mansfield.
Description: Albany : State University of New York Press, [2021] | Series: SUNY series in contemporary French thought | Includes bibliographical references and index.
Identifiers: LCCN 2020016066 | ISBN 9781438481654 (hardcover : alk. paper) | ISBN 9781438481647 (pbk. : alk. paper) | ISBN 9781438481661 (ebook)
Subjects: LCSH: Derrida, Jacques. | Sovereignty. | Democracy—Philosophy. | Political violence. | Philosophy, French—20th century.
Classification: LCC JC327 .M29 2021 | DDC 320.1501—dc23
LC record available at https://lccn.loc.gov/2020016066

10 9 8 7 6 5 4 3 2 1

For Nicole Anderson and Elaine Kelly

CONTENTS

Acknowledgments ix

Introduction 1

One   Sovereignty: The Law of Misrule   13

Two   Bataille and Sovereignty: The Apotheosis of Violence   43

Three   Divine Violence and Justice   69

Four   Derrida on Sovereignty   99

Five   Sovereignty and Hospitality   121

Six   Bastard Politics: Sovereignty and Violence   141

Conclusion 171

Notes 175

Bibliography 185

Index 191

ACKNOWLEDGMENTS

Part of chapter 2 was originally published in *Lo Sguardo: rivista di filosofia* (13 [2013]: 143–62). Part of chapter 3 was originally published in *Cultural Studies Review* (18, no. 2 [2012]: 129–46). Part of chapter 5 originally appeared in *Derrida Today* (11, no. 1 [2018]: 49–59).

A big thank you to my generous bosses Jim Piper and Sakkie Pretorius for their indulgence and encouragement (even if I didn't always explain very clearly what it was all about). To my family also, especially my partner Bonny, for their patience and irrepressible excitement!

This book is dedicated to Nicole Anderson and Elaine Kelly. The continental philosophy world, especially the world of Derrida studies, owes a huge debt to Nicole for her commitment, dedication, and unstinting insistence on rigor and quality. I owe a great debt to her personally for her support and friendship over too many years to number. Elaine has read and reread drafts of this manuscript and offered unflinching support, encouragement, and insightful advice at all stages. But above all, I want to acknowledge Elaine's warmth, humor, and deep humanity, both in her work and her friendship. She is an inspiration to all of us.

INTRODUCTION

Sovereignty is NOTHING.

—Georges Bataille, *The Accursed Share:
An Essay on General Economy*, 1993

We are seeing a rebirth of rebellion. In recent years, the debate has been dominated by two grand narratives: one ideological—the neoliberal consensus—the other, a warning about where we are heading: climate change apocalypse. Both of these narratives are marked by a deep ambiguity: they are simultaneously narratives of activity and passivity, of human destiny and frustration of the will. For neoliberalism, on the one hand, we have no choice but to allow the market to be the judge of all things, because it is only in the market that we are able to prove ourselves most resolutely. In the face of rampant climate change, on the other hand, we await unknowns that will threaten our very existence, while at the same time, we expect ourselves to follow the science and make overarching collective plans about how the planet should be managed sustainably. Thus, climate change is something that will happen to us, yet we see ourselves as both thinking and managing the global climate future in its totality. What characterizes our sense of where we are in these two narratives is both a sense of command—we must act—and of vulnerability—things happen to us, whether we like it or not.

The aim of this book is to try to reconfigure this double logic by renewing the discourse of sovereignty. It argues, firstly, that the two discourses previously mentioned are inadequate as ways of grasping the future intentionally. The neoliberal faux-consensus rests on the idea that human life is theoretically unconditioned, opening potentially infinitely without either environmental constraint or determining historical legacy; the second assumes human life should go on while remaining almost totally agnostic about why that should be. These views are not wrong in any simple way, but they disguise another deeper question: Why is it that our life seeks to continue itself and our philosophies, both casual and systematic, consent? Is it just a further instance of the liberal orthodoxy that people should be allowed to live on freely according to any logic or meaning they choose if that's what they want to do? Such an assumption makes our philosophy unphilosophical. It answers the great ethical questions without recourse to any ethic. Or is it that there are not too few, but rather too many reasons to live, and there will never be consensus about what they mean, let alone which to prefer?

I do not intend to identify a version of what the will to life is or should be, but I do believe it is here that we need to start if we are to talk about the way forward. There is an assumption of human living-on that is either supposedly expressed in the grand narrative of neoliberal consensus or set aside as the incontestable question that the grand narrative of climate change apocalypse cannot or does not need to address. Whichever we choose, both of these grand narratives have lying behind them something larger and more insistent that they either take for granted or are incapable of addressing. I argue that this taken-for-granted thing is best considered using the language of sovereignty, for two reasons. Firstly, sovereignty provides a language for the human insistence on itself. Secondly, it is our ambivalence toward sovereignty, our complex double-drive to both fetishize and anathematize it, to celebrate and distrust it, to invest in it and fear it, to see it as both the guarantee of autonomy and freedom, and the greatest driver of straitening, homogenization, and oppression, that explains the doubleness I identified previously in our supposed grand narratives, their simultaneous recourse to drive and will, on the one hand, and vulnerability and passivity, on the other.

As we will see, there is an irreducible relationship between sovereignty and violence, and this is where sovereignty is at its most problematic. This is enough for some to see sovereignty as irredeemably contaminated, as irrecuperable for any positive political agenda. To others, violence is the tool that sovereignty is required to use in order to stabilize social order and defend its right. I will argue that neither of these positions is valid: on the one hand, sovereignty should not simply be excoriated because it is always open on violence. To abdicate sovereignty for this reason is, I will argue, to abandon the political altogether and, thus, to give up on life's commitment to the social future. On the other hand, sovereign violence is not simply a calm rational instrumentalism. The violence of the sovereign is, in the literature, first and foremost, the violence of God, what Walter Benjamin calls "divine violence."[1] As such, it is both unknowable and possibly infinite, refusing transparency, logic, order, and potentially all restraint. It threatens, firstly, those it would seek to rule, but also it then ends by putting everything at risk, including itself. Sovereignty, when allowed to fully express itself, is self-challenging. It is because of this deconstructive logic to sovereignty that my account inevitably ends with a detailed discussion of sovereignty in Jacques Derrida. Derrida's discussions of sovereignty represent a deep reflection on the genealogy of sovereignty in the political and other philosophy of the West. It focuses on the most important modern treatments of sovereignty, most explicitly those of Walter Benjamin and Carl Schmitt (and by corollary, Giorgio Agamben), and less explicitly, but perhaps more importantly, that of Georges Bataille, who never forgot sovereignty's generality and its wildness, and Martin Heidegger. Derrida famously said in the last interview before he died: "Deconstruction is always on the side of the *yes,* on the side of the affirmation of life."[2] As we will see, this is not a sentimental or simply benign commitment. In his last lectures, his discussion of the Heideggerian theme of *Walten* characterizes "life" as always already invested with the danger, promise, and violence of the sovereign. The deconstructive account of sovereignty stands, therefore, as the culmination of the Western discourse of sovereignty, looking back at its uneasy history but also considering its continuing and irrepressible claims. In my account, politics is sovereignty in action. Politics is not simply a way to get things done, to administer systems and plot incremental improvements in the quality of life. The deconstructive logic of life as always already animating the sovereign reveals sovereignty in its immanence in all human things, in its rampant generality. It shows how sovereignty is the language, above all, of human insistence.

In sum, therefore, this book aims to use an account of the concept of sovereignty in the work of Derrida to develop a new understanding of sovereignty in contemporary political thinking. It starts with a survey of canonical discussions of sovereignty in Western political thinking from Jean Bodin and Thomas Hobbes to Schmitt and Agamben to show that Derrida's rethinking of sovereignty develops from the key themes inherited from the tradition, while severely testing and challenging them. Importantly, it will conclude that there is a key role for a positive construction of sovereignty in critical political thinking. Recently, political philosophy has, on the one hand, taken sovereignty as an inevitable given in the logic of states, something that cannot be transgressed in international negotiations, for example; or on the other hand, it has treated sovereignty as a form of unaccountable power, an obstacle to human rights and social justice. By providing a double, deconstructive account of sovereignty, this book will argue that sovereignty is both a promise and a threat. It can both inspire and frustrate political innovation. It therefore provides the terrain we must negotiate to pursue new political ambitions while remaining aware of the dangers of political authoritarianism and violence.

Derrida's discussions of politics deal with the key issues now confronting us in the era of climate change, for example, whether law can be a vehicle for social justice, whether democracy can continue to provide us with an inspiring political horizon, and whether regimes of hospitality can still honor an openness to the other. I argue that each of these key political issues in Derrida involves important questions about the nature and role of sovereignty, an issue that increasingly preoccupied Derrida, and which in late work such as *The Beast and the Sovereign* lectures, was developing into a general account of the deconstructive impetus. Many post-Derridean accounts of sovereignty use deconstruction to challenge the autonomy and self-identity of powerful institutions, presenting the sovereign as something to be treated with suspicion. I argue that it is a fundamental misunderstanding of Derridean thought to see any identity in such a uniform way. The deconstructability of sovereignty reveals its instability as a concept but without simply demolishing it. The challenge of deconstruction, therefore, is to negotiate the way between interrogating sovereignty and learning not only how to cope with it but also how to live it.

Canonical accounts of sovereignty start by attempting to explain the authority of kingship. In these accounts, the sovereign monarch is both a version and an agent of God's power, both the image of God and God's "lieutenant." Since the fundamental attributes of the sovereign God are his unconditionality, autonomy, and self-identity, the human sovereign is automatically in a contradictory situation. To be like God, the sovereign must also be unconditional and autonomous, yet to be God's lieutenant, its authority derives from another sovereignty higher than and other to itself. Ironically, therefore, worldly sovereignty always relies on something larger and different to model and motivate its autonomy and self-sufficiency. The sovereign always remains threatened by its need to go beyond itself toward something always larger and absent.

In this way, sovereignty is grounded in something that cannot be contained or even clearly identified. It is perched above an abyss. Traditionally, this lack of definition has been papered over by giving it the name of God or by defining sovereign authority as something incomprehensible to human beings, an exception to human logic and accountability. From Bodin's theocracy to Schmittian exceptionality, sovereignty is understood as something divine and miraculous, beyond human rationality. It is Bataille who provides the most wide-ranging understanding of sovereignty as abyssal. I propose that to understand the full meaning of Derrida's accounts of sovereignty, it is necessary to appreciate Bataille's influence on deconstructive thinking. This is an important connection in an era where Bataille's importance is being acknowledged again by critical work in environmental philosophy.

Derrida's political thinking clusters around a set of doublenesses: law and justice, democracy and democracy to come, and absolute and conditional hospitality, for example. On one side of each of these doublenesses, we have a fixed and knowable institution or identity that relies on its pair for its meaning and value. Law, for example, is derived from the irrepressible and open-ended call to justice. Justice makes law possible, but because of its inexhaustible demands, justice is insatiable, unreachable, and thus impossible. Law can never satisfy the demands made on it by justice. Justice constantly violates law by requiring it to go beyond itself, to be more and more just ad infinitum. Justice, therefore, opens an abyss beneath law, allowing and explaining the meaning of law while endlessly undermining and ruining it. Justice, on the other hand, is nothing without law. Law is the only way by which justice can come into the world. These Derridean doublenesses are analogous to the relationship between the sovereignty of the king and God's sovereignty. God's sovereignty allows and licenses that of the monarch but exceeds and violates it at the same time. Sovereignty opens up an infinite abyss beneath any identity.

This abyss can be understood as a potentially infinite divine violence, the violence of God. Walter Benjamin connects this divine sovereign violence with revolution in an argument that Derrida, in his discussion of the violence of the law-justice complex, sees as dangerous. This threat of infinite violence looms behind sovereignty as its potential destination and ultimate risk. In a further argument, Derrida outlines the Heideggerian account of the dynamic of ontological difference—the emergence of beings in relation to a Being that cannot in turn emerge as itself—as fundamental to the development of all identities. I argue that the Derridean doublenesses like the law-justice complex are themselves examples of this same logic of a violent emergence in which sovereignty is always already at issue.

We have, therefore, a picture of sovereignty as providing the logic by which all identities emerge in relation to a potentially infinite violence that always exceeds them but that orients them too. The challenge is to propose a model of sovereignty that recognizes it as a risk while acknowledging its necessity. Sovereignty will always contain within itself the risk of absolute violence, but it is also the means of human aspiration. I will argue that by always proposing the possibility of the human rising higher than itself, sovereignty is the means by which the human will to self-overcoming and to freedom and justice become available to us. The challenge of sovereignty is to pursue the trajectory of this possibility while managing the risk of sovereign violence. Sovereignty, therefore, is both the authoritarianism that needs to be checked and the possibility that needs to be pursued.

Chapter 1 analyzes canonical accounts of sovereignty from Bodin to Giorgio Agamben to identify what is fundamental to the Western discourse of sovereignty. The aim of this discussion is to exhibit the unstable nature of sovereignty, which modern and contemporary accounts work to exploit. One issue we have already mentioned: how human sovereignty is commonly represented as either a version of God's sovereignty or as its instrument. This creates a complication in that one of the key elements of the sovereign is its supposed completeness, self-reliance, and autonomy. If the human sovereign is dependent on God for its authority, then it cannot be complete in itself or self-reliant. It cannot therefore be sovereign. What brings the sovereign closer to God makes it less like God. On the other hand, if God's sovereignty is enacted by way of another lesser form of sovereignty, then it is not indivisible, as Bodin claimed.

Sovereignty's reliance on God is merely one instance of the way in which sovereignty is represented as relying on something unsignifiable or beyond human understanding. This unknowable abyssal quality of the sovereign may take the form of the divine, as in Bodin or Hobbes; it may be the enigmatic genius of the lawgiver in Jean-Jacques Rousseau, or it may be the unaccountability of the sovereign who decides on the exception, as we find in Schmitt. God has been the most common name given to this undefined thing that grounds the sovereign, but this term doesn't capture—indeed may be an attempt to hide from—the irreducibly excessive and abyssal quality of the sovereign. By exposing itself to the unsignifiable and the excessive, the sovereign rests on a violence that is potentially infinite.

In chapter 2, we see how Bataille's extravagant account of sovereignty both subsumes and surpasses the earlier accounts analyzed in chapter 1. Bataille locates the sovereign as part of the limitless drive of energy that conditions human being. Here, the unaccountability of the sovereign and its openness on the divine become not a potential model of stable political order but part of the rampant force that drives all things. To Bataille, the means-and-ends logic of practical life is a mere segment of the larger drive of forces of energy toward excess and dissolution. Sovereignty is the name of the absolute freedom and license that represents the imaginary end of this drive. It is both irresistible and impossible, ineluctable and out of reach. Yet, it is the human drive toward sovereignty that defines our subjectivity as the orientation toward greater intensity, license, freedom, and strength. The traditional sovereign figure recognizes in us its inferior double, and we see in it the possibility of a higher life that will exempt us from being mere things. Through festivals of sexuality and death, our religions take us beyond this sovereign figure toward an infinite excess that we attempt to name as God but that is really the inexhaustible drive toward dissolution and thus an opening on the horror of absolute violence. As the combination of aspiration and danger, this infinite sovereign violence both lures and terrifies us, conditioning our subjectivity and social life in ways that are both magnetic and threatening. Bataille's account of the abyssal is one of the key antecedents of Derrida's thinking about sovereignty.

The focus of chapter 3 is on working out how sovereign emergence enacts divine violence and what this might mean for the heavily politically inflected terms of Derridean thinking. It deals with two instances of flirtation with divine violence: Benjamin's account of revolution as sovereign violence and the case of the medieval child killer Gilles de Rais. What these analyses show is that for Derrida, the absolute violence of sovereignty enlarges human possibility while remaining a source of danger.

For Benjamin, divine or sovereign, revolutionary violence supersedes conventional "mythical" law-making violence. Instead of encompassing only the narrow, petty world of basic human survival, divine violence offers a higher and richer conception of life. This violence's goal is not to demonstrate its own authority but to offer a superior way of being. Derrida builds on a critique of Benjamin to explain the relationship between law and justice. Justice for Derrida offers a broad awareness of what is owed to the other, but it also remains potentially terrifying. On the one hand, an overinvestment in justice like an overinvestment in sovereignty leads to cruelty and destruction. On the other hand, an underexposure to the enlarging nature of an excessive justice risks either dogmatism and institutionalized injustice or passivity. In Derrida, therefore, there must be a law that remains exposed to justice in all its irregularity and extremity and a justice that remains aware of the need to somehow deal fairly with the regular world of calculation and action. There is no simple choosing between these options or pretending that there is some transparent liberal legalism that can be pure of violence. Politics will always be a *bastard* thing (to use Derrida's term) made up of hybrids of different denominations of violence.

The case of Gilles de Rais is then compared to the story of Abraham in Derrida's *The Gift of Death*. Where Gilles attempts to live the full, wild, and murderous extravagance of sovereignty, Abraham enters into an aporetic relationship with the divine where it both inspires and exceeds him. He has to be both engaged with it but separate from it. It is this aporetic Godly non-Godliness that allows him to live on as a loving father. The case of Gilles shows that the attempt to live sovereignty ends only in failure, cruelty, and destruction.

Chapter 4 looks at the source of Derrida's seeming assumption of the irreducibly violent nature of self-identity. Here, we have to look into the way in which things emerge. This investigation leads us to the term Walten, which Heidegger uses to explain the violence implicit in the emergence of beings in relation to Being. Derrida discusses Walten in his last lecture series, entitled *The Beast and the Sovereign*. In Heidegger, *Dasein* emerges aware of itself as projected into the world as a whole as a being in relation to other beings and thus to Being in general. Beings emerge therefore as a version of something that seems to anticipate them and make them possible, which also remains in excess of them. We have already seen a similar logic in the emergence of the sovereign, as a version of the God that seems to precede and exceed it. The logic of sovereignty, therefore, is sewn into the very manner in which beings emerge, and it does so in relation to a violent "irruption" and "eruption," to use Heidegger's language. Dasein does not simply enact sovereignty, but is "gripped" by it, an instance of something larger that both allows it to emerge and threatens it. Dasein brings sovereignty into the world but also limits it, because it cannot simply become one with the drive of sovereignty to limitless violence. In Derrida's deconstruction of Heidegger, Walten marks all emergence with the irreducibly abyssal logic of différance, which thus lies within the doublenesses that characterize Derrida's political thinking, the doubleness of law and justice, for example, or conditional and absolute hospitality. Sovereignty and violence are thus at the heart of Derrida's treatments of the political.

The consequence for Derrida's thinking is that political values—right, democracy, and hospitality—form in relation to larger impulses that both extend and threaten them. Our discussion of Walten has shown that sovereignty is always already in play prior to the exact formation of any identity. As we have seen, sovereignty itself is a doubleness where the formation of political authority always takes place in relation to the infinity and impossibility of the abyss. Reflecting this structure, the doublenesses that characterize Derrida's discussions of politics are thus all denominations of sovereignty. Sovereignty is always prior to any other political identity and alive within it.

Chapter 5 more fully explains the relationship between Derridean political value-formation and sovereignty, with hospitality as an example. As with the law-justice complex, the doubleness of hospitality is invested by the violent complex of sovereignty itself. We have proposed previously that the key political issues of our time are the ones Derrida has most focused on: the possibility of justice, whether democracy still has a future, and hospitality in response to the movement of world populations, especially now that climate change will put further pressure on resources like water and arable land. The aim here is to show that these issues are not moral, theoretical, or administrative ones, to be solved by correct thinking or good planning, but are fundamentally political issues in which sovereignty is always already at play. In these examples, we see the dynamic of Walten at work historically. It is this dynamic we must understand if we are to deal with the political problems of our age.

We investigate the issue of hospitality in relation to the two cases from the Old Testament discussed by Derrida: the story of Lot and that of the Levite of Ephraim. Hospitality is important and exemplary here, but the meaning of these stories is not restricted to the ethic of hospitality alone. Hospitality is important in the story of Lot because it facilitates the enactment of God's will and power, firstly in punishing Sodom for its sinfulness but, over and above that, in enacting the covenant with Abraham's line. The story is about putting into place God's plan for the world, one in which his infinite and unquestionable power enters into human history by way of Abraham's family. Hospitality is subordinate to this larger meaning, which overwhelms it in significance. The story of Lot then is a story of God's sovereign rule, exhibited in acts that are simultaneously acts of love and acts of extreme violence. As we have seen in Benjamin, behind the complexity of law is the issue of sovereignty. Here, behind hospitality, sovereignty looms as the larger issue and more fundamental meaning.

Chapter 6 begins by developing a model for the complex dynamic of sovereign violence. We have already described the unstable relationship between sovereignty and violence as a bastard setup in which differing impulses of sovereignty and violence, sovereign violence and countersovereignty (both violent and not) inform, infect, and interpret one another. Here, we draw on Derrida's deconstruction of Levinasian otherness to present the dynamic of sovereignty and violence as an "economy of violence." Sovereignty cannot be seen as a simple or single thing. It is not simply the essence or root of political authority. It is less a theoretical concept than a persistent problem. It is not a metaphysically anchoring origin but an ineluctable part of the unstable means of all emergence. The emergence of the grand doubles Derrida uses to define politics cannot take place other than after and thus through and as versions of sovereignty, as subsovereignties or the enactment of a sovereign force that will never leave any emergence alone. When we address ourselves to these pressing political issues, sovereignty is always already at stake.

Yet, politics is nothing if it doesn't do things, if it lacks content. What would the content be of this sovereign politics? Chapter 6 concludes that because of the nature of sovereign emergence, there are three things inalienable from Dasein: sovereign insistence (the drive to prevailing that both pursues and questions sovereignty), freedom (the establishment of a domain within which beings can be), and justice (the fact that there can only be a multiplicity of beings, none of which has a right to priority). Sovereignty does not simply advance these three values. It may even inhibit them, but in the political context defined by the sovereign, they will always be at issue.

We make a mistake when we think of politics as about the right way to think, that all we have to do is get our thinking right and we will know what to do. In fact, politics is already at work before us, via Walten. We emerge in a world already conditioned by Walten to be a play of power. We can be sovereign, but only on the terms sovereignty delivers to us. Our subjectivity opens after Walten and therefore in sovereignty. The sovereign self is a real thing, but it arises after sovereignty. Our choice is thus not to defend or resist sovereignty. Our choices all have to be made within a sovereignty defined by the three themes of sovereignty: insistence, freedom, and justice.

The future is being made by sovereignty, whether we like it or not, as it simultaneously stabilizes and destabilizes itself in pursuit of impulses sometimes personal, sometimes material, sometimes aesthetic, and sometimes ideological. The clash of these impulses—multiple, self-fulfilling, self-challenging, fractional, unformulated, and decentered—both makes promises to us and threatens us. We have no choice but to pursue ourselves and our goals in relation to sovereignty, through it, even *as* it. The aim of this book is to do honor to the complexity of sovereignty, to warn against its danger and to reveal its promise.

CHAPTER ONE

SOVEREIGNTY
The Law of Misrule

Where does sovereignty come from? The answer, of course, is God. But what is the relationship between the sovereign and God? To Bataille, theorizing sovereignty after God is dead, the relationship was abyssal, but long before that, in Bodin, for example, the relationship between God and the sovereign was already problematic and unstable. Is the sovereign God's image or God's lieutenant, and what does that last word mean: Is the sovereign's representation of God an extension of God's power or an imitation of it? Is the sovereign the arm of God or his double? This chapter will survey canonical accounts of sovereignty, starting with these questions. It presents the genealogy of sovereignty account by account, in its messy history, rather than its thematic regularity. This is because these different accounts will remain a resource for the rest of the book and also to capture a sense of the disjunctions and inconsistencies that persist despite consistency in language and issue.

In Bodin, sovereignty is defined by its power to institute law. The sovereign is not subject to the laws it makes, nor does it need the consent of the governed to impose law: "The main point of sovereign majesty and absolute power consists of giving the law to subjects in general without their consent."[1] The sovereign receives its authority from no human source: "Persons who are sovereign must not be subject in any way to the commands of someone else."[2] No conditions can be placed on sovereign authority: "This power is absolute and sovereign, for it has no other condition than what is commanded by the law of God and of nature."[3]

Yet, Bodin recognized a set of limitations on sovereign authority. Sovereignty is not license. Rampant sovereignty is tyranny. He quotes Seneca approvingly: "Caesar, permitted all, is on that account permitted less."[4] The sovereign is not accountable to any greater human authority, or human constituency, but is bound by the commitments it makes. But over and above that, the sovereign is answerable to God. No earthly power can limit the sovereign, and the sovereign is not accountable to any human authority. If citizens must defend their actions to a magistrate, sovereigns must defend themselves before God, who is the most rigorous judge of all.[5]

The laws of God and Nature, therefore, are the only limit to sovereign power. Bodin makes this point repeatedly: "For he is absolutely sovereign who recognizes nothing, after God, that is greater than himself . . . a sovereign prince who is answerable only to God";[6] "this power is absolute and sovereign, for it has no other condition than what is commanded by the law of God and of nature,"[7] and so on. Yet, God does more than limit the power of the sovereign. The power of the sovereign comes from God's authority and is a version of it: "Since there is nothing greater on earth, after God, and since they have been established by Him as His lieutenants for commanding other men, we need to be precise about their status . . . so that we may respect and revere their majesty in complete obedience, and do them honor in our thoughts and our speech. Contempt for one's sovereign prince is contempt toward God, of whom he is the earthly image."[8] Here, the sovereign is both God's agent and a representation of him, both an instrument of his power and an image of it. This creates a tension, a possible instability that troubles the edges of Bodin's thought. As an instrument of God's authority, the sovereign enacts God-like power, bringing it into the world. In this way, the laws the sovereign enacts ultimately derive from God's mandate. This would explain why the sovereign transcends human institutions, even those that it institutes itself. It would also explain why the sovereign is a kind of perpetual foreigner in its own domain, in control, in power, but somehow always coming from elsewhere. From the Ptolemaic pharaohs to the Stuart and Hanoverian monarchs, the great Khans, Catherine the Great and the Manchurian emperors, even Napoleon, Hitler, and Stalin, foreignness is often an added mark of authoritarian leaders. Yet, even if it is to be God's arm, the sovereign cannot simply be part of God. This would make a part of him of inferior substance, and most importantly, it would divide God from himself, introducing an internal division in sovereignty, something Bodin has discounted altogether because "sovereignty is indivisible."[9]

If, on the other hand, the sovereign were the image of God, the substitute for God in the human domain, the sovereign would have to replicate God. This would create a rival to God's sovereignty, a second sovereign. The human sovereign couldn't be fully sovereign because God is a superior sovereign, nor could God be an absolute sovereign, because there would be a second and similar sovereign power. If the two were to be considered versions of one another, then the limitation that God places on human sovereignty would have to have some counterpart in God. There would have to be some limitation that God places on himself, which goes against the definition of God and, again, introduces division in sovereignty. In other words, if the sovereign is an image of God, then he cannot have the lesser power he must have as God's agent and servant because he would then cease to be like God. Similarly, if he is the servant of God, then he cannot be like God, who has nothing over him. He is in an irreducible contradiction, both like God and unlike him at the same time, and in the same aspect of his nature. What makes him like God makes it impossible for him to be like God.

The sovereign enacts God's power, even Godness, but is limited, constrained by the preexistence and priority of God: "Him beneath whose grandeur all the monarchs of this world should bear the yoke and bow the head in abject fear and reverence."[10] The impulse of sovereignty is always toward Godness, both giving the human sovereign authority but always withdrawing it. When the sovereign acts, its authority refers back to God. What gives law authority is not its legal or theoretical credibility, nor its moral purpose, but the fact it derives from sovereignty: "The law is nothing but the command of the sovereign making use of his power."[11] And this power again derives not from any inherent coherence or justification but simply because it replicates God's authority: "For if justice is the end of law, law the work of the prince, and the prince the image of God; then by this reasoning, the law of the prince must be modelled on the law of God."[12] We must bow to sovereign authority because it is the same as bowing to God. Treason against the sovereign is rebellion against God.

In other words, the gravity of the sovereign is God. It is because the sovereign can bring Godness into the world that we must respect it. Yet, the pressure this puts on the relationship between the sovereign and the divine pushes in both directions. Not only does divine power represent the limit of sovereignty but also sovereignty drives toward the divine as the natural trajectory of its elevation. This comes out in an important complaint Bodin makes about the excessive exercise of prerogative on the part of some monarchs:

> But as for the murderer by premeditation, "You shall drag him from my holy altar," says the Law [of God], "and you shall have no pity on him but shall put him to death, and then will I shed my great mercy upon you." Nevertheless, on Good Friday, Christian princes grant pardons only for things that are unpardonable. Yet pardons for such misdeeds bring with them plagues, famines, wars, and the ruin of states. That is why the law of God says that by punishing those who have deserved death, one removes the curse that lies upon the people. For of a hundred wicked deeds, not even two are brought to justice; of those that get there, half cannot be proven; and if proven crimes are pardoned, what punishment will there be to serve as an example to the wicked?[13]

The sovereign pardoning the unpardonable undermines divine justice. It expands the sovereign's exemption from being answerable into the divine domain and trespasses on the law of God, thus unleashing disaster. The drive of sovereignty, therefore, will always be toward the divine because this is the locus of its authority and the source of its meaning. Yet, this automatically places it in a contradictory position: both usurping God's power and being limited by it. It thus assumes a transgressive relationship to the divine. It is both the image and instrument of God, yet not God. The sovereign will always challenge God. This challenge will always take place in the domain of excess. The sovereign must attempt to resolve the aporetic position in which it finds itself by attempting to overcome the limitations placed on it by God. This is the logical consequence of the contradictory situation it is in. It has God's power but limits have been placed on the exercise of that power. To become more itself, it must become more God-like and thus push against God. To fulfill God's mandate, it must both imitate and defy God in one and the same act.

Pardoning the unpardonable is the pressure point where God's rule is both most fully enacted (in its unaccountability to reason or morality) and most at risk. It both conforms to and defies the meaning of both

God and the sovereign, by pitting the sovereign against the God that justifies and licenses it. God is always in excess of the sovereign, and the sovereign must reach toward this excess to fulfill God's will. The sovereign thus best pursues God's will by challenging it. An aporia opens between the sovereign's proper place defined by the mandate he has received to be God's agent and the reaching toward Godness, which the sovereign must undertake to fulfill the obligation to be like God. The impulse of the sovereign is always toward excess, yet this excess is already occupied by God. To be like God, the sovereign must always exceed, but God will not be exceeded, because he is himself the principle of excess. Both God and the sovereign are in contradiction with one another and with themselves.

We have seen how in Bodin, the contrast between sovereignty as the image of God and sovereignty as the arm of God creates a tension in which the human sovereign rises toward Godness while at the same time being excluded from it. This risks a contradiction in both the divine and the human sovereign. On the one hand, the sovereign divides sovereignty by taking on attributes of the divine and acting as the divine's instrument thus undermining sovereignty's essential and necessary unity. On the other hand, the divine places limits on the sovereign by always exceeding it hence dooming it to be incomplete and not absolute and thus no more than a failed version of the divine, or else in a permanent and essential state of insurrection against God. A simple hierarchy cannot thus be established between the divine and the sovereign, hence leaving both unresolved in their definition and their relationship always one of transgression.

On the one hand, what is the divine but that asymptote toward which the sovereign tends but that is unknowable except as that absent model dimly imaged in the sovereign, even at its most capricious? God is the King of kings. The language in which God is known locates him as a barely perceptible extension of the king in our midst, the prince's spectral prosthetic, an absolute or ultimate version of whatever power we know. On the other hand, what is the sovereign but a pale imitation of that greatness to which our faith and prayers tend and to which our duty and loyalty must be directed? God is in excess of the sovereign, but because that excess is a necessary part of the definition of God, it is an ineluctable tendency within the sovereign itself. God looms as that aspect of the sovereign that the sovereign must but cannot be. Is the sovereign the image of God? Yes, because it replicates the authority and charisma of God, but also no, because God preexists the human sovereign, is greater than it, and always limits its power. This means the human sovereign cannot be absolute and cannot be an image of the totality and unity of God.

Is the sovereign then the agent of God? Yes, because it is the way divine power arrives in the world and acts there, but on the other hand, no, because by being simply an agent of God, the sovereign is just a fleeting embodiment of the divine intention, which would mean it is not enduring or omnipotent, which contradicts its claim to being God's image. The sovereign is supposedly the image of God, but if the sovereign is limited (albeit by God), then it cannot be an accurate image of God. By being the thing God has power over, it is completely unlike the God of whom it is an image. On the other hand, God cannot be absolute if it can only be realized in its agent, the human sovereign, who represents it and acts on its behalf. This divides it, and it thus loses the absolute unity that is its definition.

No hierarchy or order can be established to make this problem simple. If we could provide clear demarcations between God and the human sovereign, and a simple relationship between them, the crossover between them—the charge—that gives the sovereign its authority and that makes the divine real, that licenses the sovereign to act and allows God to appear in the world, would all be ruined. The confusion and (non) disjunction between them is what makes this complex work. As Ernst Kantorowicz pointed out eloquently, the king "was both above and under the Law, both greater and lesser than himself."[14] Without this doubleness, neither the divine nor the human sovereign could make sense. The threat to both the divine and the human sovereign inhabits both of them. This is what makes them capable, but it also provides them with the tension and indefiniteness that energizes their charisma and makes them both effective and beautiful.

In Hobbes, we see an analogous tension, but it is even more complicated. God is the essence of sovereignty, but sovereignty is also a social and political construct, a contract in fact. Subjects constitute the sovereign by ceding prerogative to it, and therefore its acts are identified explicitly by Hobbes as acts of the subjects themselves. Sovereignty here becomes a version of God constituted by human beings. For Hobbes, God is the "sovereign of sovereigns." Not only does Christian revelation institute a religious order for the human race but also it gives rise to laws, which are themselves part of the divine dispensation: "But where God himself, by supernatural revelation, planted religion; there he also made to himself a peculiar kingdom; and gave laws, not only of behavior toward himself; but also toward one another; and thereby, in the kingdom of God, the policy and laws civil, are a part of religion; and therefore the distinction of temporal, and spiritual domination, hath there no place."[15] The laws of nature tend in a variety of directions for Hobbes. Sometimes, he identifies the "general inclination of all mankind" as "a perpetual and restless desire of power after power," which "ceaseth only in death."[16] Elsewhere, "the first and fundamental law of nature . . . commandeth men to seek peace."[17] Nature pits human beings against one another most famously in a presocial space where nothing is guaranteed, neither property nor justice, with life as a result risking becoming "nasty, brutish and short";[18] yet at the same time, "justice, that is to say, performance of a covenant, and giving to every man his own, is a dictate of the law of nature."[19] The law of nature "is the eternal law of God,"[20] and at the same time, it is enfolded in the social law: "the law of nature . . . is a part of the civil law of all commonwealths of the world. Reciprocally also, the civil law is part of the dictates of nature."[21]

How is this complex model of divine, natural, and social laws to be understood? Nature encourages human beings to act out their desires and their will to power, yet at the same time, God has implanted in them an inclination toward justice and social cooperation. Law must be this complex because it needs to explain both the violent impulses toward competition and fragmentation that possess us before we establish political order and also the opposite impulse that makes us want to overcome anarchy and make peace with one another under the agreed rule of the sovereign. In other words, Hobbes' understanding of nature must include both the lust that sets us at each other's throats and the determination to control and limit it. Both of these impulses inhabit us in our presocial state, creating the problem and proposing the solution at one and the same time, and they both must reside together in our hearts before there is a constituted society to speak of. The divine must both make us mad and cure us of our madness.

In Hobbes, the sovereign initially occupies the same complex position we have already encountered in Bodin. The sovereign is both an image of God and his lieutenant. One important idea implied in Bodin is made more explicit in Hobbes: instead of the worldly sovereign being an image of God and thus explained and made real to us as a lesser God, God is most readily known by way of sovereignty. God is an image of the sovereign. The figure of the sovereign not only is justified by its likeness to God but also explains God to us. Without the sovereign, we would not know what God is like. In this way, Hobbes elevates the conception of sovereignty to another level, and this also advances the thinking about the sovereign's role as God's agent or lieutenant. The sovereign is an agent of God, because it mediates between the human and God. He writes: "For there is no covenant with God, but by mediation of somebody that representeth God's person, which none doth but God's lieutenant, who hath the sovereignty under God."[22] Here again, we have the doubleness of the sovereign: both image of God and the thing that acts on God's behalf, thus bringing God into the world. We saw in Bodin how by becoming God's agent, the sovereign risked dividing God's power, which as the unconditional and absolute cannot be divided by definition. Similarly, by relying on God's power for its justification, sovereignty could not be an undivided power either. It therefore can only be sovereign by way of the thing—its relationship to the divine—that stops it from being complete and singular, God-like and thus sovereign. In Hobbes, this problem doesn't go away, but the ground has shifted. God is an extension of sovereignty. The key place is occupied by the sovereign itself, which becomes the only way that God can be known. It is not possible to have a relationship with God, except by way of the sovereign, who puts in place—effectively *is*—the covenant with God. The sovereign in Hobbes takes on a much more intense being. Instead of being merely an agent of God, and his image, the sovereign becomes the realization of God, the way God is known, and the only possible way we can relate to God.

This elevation of the sovereign elevates the human, but it humanizes God. This humanization of God takes a more important form in the political dynamic by which the sovereign is instituted. The formalization of the sovereign in Hobbes' model of the social contract is well known. In the natural state, human beings are driven by their desire. This desire is ultimately a desire for power, no matter whether it expresses itself through a desire for riches, knowledge, or honor. Yet, we cannot be confident in our grasp of any of these things, since there is no law to guarantee ownership. There is neither justice nor injustice, since there is no way in which these can be formulated or justified. Individuals take and hold what they can by force but in turn lose it when overwhelmed by superior strength. Our disposition, however, tends not only toward self-protection and self-assertion but also toward justice and fairness, so in the chaotic, doomed, and brutal world of nature, we imagine a system that would guarantee the security of persons and property. How is this system to work? It requires we cede power to a single, unified entity: the sovereign. The sovereign may take a variety of forms, but no matter whether it is corporate or individual, whether a council, parliament, or king, it is singular and unified. It makes laws but is not answerable to them. It underwrites civil relationships with law and oversees social exchange with force. The sovereign protects us from the vicious and unregulated competition of nature while allowing us to fulfill our desire safely. It offers us the possibility of satisfying our longing but in a way that is protected from that longing's rapaciousness.

The sovereign is separate from us, but at the same time, it is a product of our own will and work. Hobbes is quite explicit about this point. The sovereign may be separate from the regular citizen. It may not be under the law in the way the subject is. It acts to limit and control the social, though is itself not subject to limit and control. But crucially, its actions are not alien. The sovereign is not another species. It may be an image and an agent of God, but it is not otherworldly. Its unity and absoluteness separates it from us, but it is ours. Whatever acts it performs, it performs on our behalf. It is us in action: the citizens who institute the sovereign act through it. The sovereign is the citizens in action corporately. Whatever it does, we do: "The law is made by the sovereign power, and all that is done by such power, is warranted, and owned by every one of the people";[23] or "nothing the sovereign representative can do to the subject, on what pretence soever, can properly be called injustice, or injury; because every subject is author of every act the sovereign doth, so that he never wanteth right to any thing, otherwise, than as he himself is the subject of God, and bound thereby to observe the laws of nature."[24] We have seen how human beings are subject to God's natural law, and the civil laws that they institute are part of God's law. For this reason, when we establish sovereignty as our founding social principle, we are implementing natural law. We are fulfilling God's plan. Yet, Hobbes is quite explicit. God's agency—the lieutenancy of God—which Bodin saw as vested in the sovereign, truly rests with the human. Human beings take on God's agency. The sovereign mediates between God and the human, but its actions are fundamentally social actions. Both the event that institutes sovereignty and the ongoing actions of the sovereign are firstly the acts of the corporate human subject. Humans institute the sovereign, and what the sovereign does is their action. The sovereign is God's image and lieutenant, the mediator between God and the human, but he is also a human invention and a human agent. In fulfilling God's law, the human makes the sovereign, who is God's agent. In fulfilling God's law, the human takes on an attribute of Godness. It becomes the animating principle of sovereignty. To enact God's law, it has to become like God. The sovereign is a contrivance of the human, emerging historically in response to the problem of social order, individual desire, and the security of property. In other words, it emerges on a human scale to solve human problems on human terms, not simply because God requires it. We may be fulfilling God's plans, but only indirectly, and not simply to do what God requires.

In turn, we only know God by way of the sovereign. God is the sovereign's sovereign. He is an image of the sovereign. The thing we institute as an act of corporate self-constitution and preservation, as the means by which our desires will be satisfied, is our only point of access to and way of understanding God. We are ourselves instituting Godness as a form of our own agency. Yet, the supremacy of God, unimaginable outside of the identity and shape of the human as it may be, is never directly challenged. God's law encloses our social acts without question. As the source of law, God will always exceed the human. Yet, what this law requires is that the human establishes the sovereignty that both reflects and structures God's nature. And this thing acts for humans on human terms to satisfy human needs and solve human problems. God's law may enclose the human, but the human encloses, defines, and animates that thing which is most God-like. God exceeds it as the law but is lesser than it, because the human creates God's agency—the sovereign is the clearest exhibition of God's agency—as its own agency. We take on God's prerogative.

The structure being outlined here is also aporetic. We are not discussing a clear and transparent system. Hobbes asserts both the supremacy and the absoluteness of God, but God is only known on human terms by way of something human beings establish. The most important manifestation in the human world of God's will is a creature of human will—indeed, human will made into a "man," the sovereign. On top of this, this man is the image of God. We only understand God as the ultimate version of this sovereign prince, King of Kings yet still a king, knowable only as a king is known. The sovereign mediates God for us, but the God we discover by way of this mediation is an image of what we have made. God is made in man's image. God is the alien thing within the human that the human enacts but that remains over and above the human. It is the thing the human makes, though it will always exceed the human. Sovereignty is simultaneously lesser and greater than God but also that in the human which is both lesser and greater than the human. In turn, God becomes both lesser and greater than the human: we only know what is great by way of what is less than great. We are only interested in what is less because of the greatness within it. We both follow and challenge God. Our defiance of God arises by way of our attempts to be most faithful to him. As our argument progresses, we will see the persistence of this logic: sovereignty is the impulse toward Godness in the human. This will-to-Godness is both the greatest possibility of human aspiration and the greatest human risk.

In Hobbes, the sovereign is not answerable to the laws it makes. This unaccountability is a consistent theme through canonical accounts of sovereignty and reaches its fullest expression in Schmitt's sovereign exceptionality. In Rousseau, this exemption of the sovereign from its own laws splits human individuals between their role as a part of a corporate sovereignty and their identity as private citizens. No rule can bind the sovereign people: "There neither is, nor can be, any kind of fundamental law binding on the people as a body, not even the social contract itself."[25] The sovereign, here as in Hobbes, gives the law to itself, and therefore, it acts only in the interests of the individuals who constitute it. Therefore, by definition, it cannot do them any damage: "As the sovereign is formed entirely of the individuals who compose it, it has not, nor could it have, any interest contrary to theirs; and so the sovereign has no need to give guarantees to the subjects, because it is impossible for a body to wish to hurt all of its members and . . . it cannot hurt any particular member."[26] The sovereign then is incontestable. Its logic here is purely self-referential, even tautological: the sovereign is the people; it must by definition work in their interests. It is "like a private person making a contract with himself."[27] Since the sovereign can only legitimately take the form of the people, whatever it does must be in their interests. "The sovereign by the mere fact that it is, is always all that it ought to be."[28]

But tension remains. Individuals submit to the sovereign as an expression then of their submission to their own belonging to the collective. Any rule or law imposed on them, they impose on themselves. They compel themselves to obey themselves. The relationship they have with themselves is not a simple one of self-identity and absolute coordination. The collective works in the individual's interests, but the individual tends to experience the collective as a constraint. The individual's relationship to the collective is one of submission. The people submit themselves to themselves: "In order that the social pact shall not be an empty formula, it is tacitly implied in that commitment—which alone can give force to all others—that whoever refuses to obey the general will shall be constrained to do so by the whole body, which means nothing other than he shall be forced to be free."[29] No consensus can reduce the problematic nature, or the intensity, of this last phrase.

The social covenant therefore relies on a divide between the will of the individual as individual and "the general will he has as a citizen."[30] These two may be different from or even contrary to one another. The relationship between the two sides of this fractured subject remains problematic. Private individual freedom is preserved but not as it was in its natural state. It is reinvented after the social bond, on sovereignty's terms. Initially, the social bond arises by way of "the total alienation by each associate of himself and all his rights to the whole community."[31] So, individuals must put every aspect of their being at the disposal of the collective. In turn, later, when they exercise some private will, it is nominally a continuation of what they were in nature but as something only available in society, under the auspices of the sovereign and on the sovereign's terms: "Each man alienates by the social pact only that part of his power, his goods and his liberty which is the concern of his community; but it must be admitted that the sovereign alone is the judge of what is of that concern."[32]

Natural individuals must first alienate their rights to the sovereign, totally. If, as they emerge in the social field, they preserve any of their property and freedom, they do so only under the auspices of the sovereign. They lose everything but only to regain it later, somewhere else, in another form altogether. The natural quality of the natural person survives, but it has been reprocessed and reinvented as social. The natural becomes, therefore, postsocial. This creates an aporia. The private survives as a space outside of the social and sovereign but under its sway. The sovereign thus covers the entire human field—the world of both the citizen and the private individual—because it is the sovereign that defines what is and is not legitimately public and private. Yet, the private part of that field is beyond the sovereign. The private is both within the sovereign and beyond it, at one and the same time. The relationship between the person and the sovereign persists as problematic. It is and is not subject to the sovereign. This contradiction does not arise as a pattern of alternation in which different aspects of the individual's life are separated from one another, some public, some private, the former ruled by the sovereign, the latter not. The situation for the individual is aporetic because it is in its most intensely private moments that the individual most acts out its belonging to the sovereign, which is the only thing that can define what the private is allowed to be. The subject is most subject to the sovereign when it occupies the space the sovereign designs for it as outside the sovereign.

How does this contradiction arise? How does it happen that the citizen is split in this way? The answer lies in the process by which the social is founded. As we know, Hobbes imagined a drama in which humans, lost in the chaos of violent and unregulated natural life, get together somehow to institute a power before which they will submit. This meant that Hobbes had to see in the natural human both a disposition to violent competition—otherwise nature would not be the undesirable insecure state it is—and a counterbalancing disposition toward peace and cooperation—otherwise there would be no inclination to solve the problem of violence and institute sovereignty. Hobbes did not actually believe this drama happened as a clear, identifiable historical event, but the arrangement had always already been made somehow. In Rousseau, the functions here are more clearly peopled, and as a consequence, the event is more historically identifiable. The institution of the sovereign in its place as the centerpiece and engine of all political legitimacy takes place not in a vague or mythic, imaginary event, whose consequences we can see but whose unfolding we can't narrate. The sovereign has its place made for it by the heroic, albeit ambiguous, figure of the *lawgiver*. The lawgiver creates the space in which the sovereign can be established. In so doing, he puts the human through a transforming fire that remakes everything, and after which nothing will ever be the same again. It is this violent process of transformation, this residually Christian belief in a rebirth through violence, that makes the subject irreducibly aporetic forever.

Lawgivers have no place in society. They are outside of both the sovereign and the government. They may make these possible but don't belong in the ongoing mundane world of ordinary history that they institute. The lawgiver then is otherworldly, an impossible figure, whose role is to transform the natural into the social. Here, the situation becomes far more complex than earlier formulations would seem to imply. The human subject that is transformed by the lawgiver from natural to social is not simply split between the public citizen and the private self. It is reformed by the institution of law so that everything that it is afterwards comes to it out of the fiery furnace of socialization:

> Whoever ventures on the enterprise of setting up a people must be ready, shall we say, to change human nature, to transform each individual, who by himself is entirely complete and solitary, into a part of a much greater whole, from which that same individual will then receive, in a sense, his life and being. The founder of nations must weaken the structure of man in order to fortify it, to replace the physical and independent existence we have all received from nature with a moral and communal existence. In a word, each man must be stripped of his own powers, and given powers which are external to him, and which he cannot use without the help of others. The nearer men's natural powers are to extinction or annihilation, and the stronger and more lasting their acquired powers, the stronger and more perfect is the social institution. So much so, that if each citizen can do nothing whatever except through co-operation with others, and if the acquired power of the whole is equal to, or greater than, the sum of the natural power of each of the individuals, then we can say that lawmaking has reached the highest point of perfection.[33]

Before society is instituted by the lawgiver, the individual lacks nothing. She or he is "entirely complete." The lawgiver incorporates this complete thing into the social whole, remaking it so that its very being comes from its belonging to the collective and not from its solitude, as it had been before. By way of this integration into the collective, the individual gains its moral being. Here, the social is not a compromise, where the fully fledged individual makes some sort of practical accommodation with the collective for purely pragmatic reasons. The individual only gains its deep and authentic, legitimate being by way of its membership of the social.

This transformation is violent. It strips away everything that composes the individual, not simply offering it another way of life, but reducing it to zero in order to remake it as something new. The social individual is not simply the human being recast, but reborn, reconstituted from a reopened nothingness. This process destroys as much as it gives and Rousseau emphasizes its violence: "What makes the task of the lawgiver so difficult," he writes, "is less what has to be established than what has to be destroyed."[34] The lawgiver presides over the death and rebirth of the entire social enterprise. The state is born again "from its own ashes, and leaps from the arms of death to regain the vigor of youth."[35] The intense, apocalyptic nature of this drama is what has allowed lawgivers to compare themselves with the divine and to be seen as Gods: "This sublime reasoning, which soars above the heads of the common people, is used by the lawgiver when he puts his own decision into the mouths of the immortals, thus compelling by divine authority persons who cannot be moved by human prudence. But it is not for every man to make the Gods speak, or to gain credence if he pretends to be an interpreter of the divine word. The lawgiver's great soul is the true miracle which must vindicate his mission."[36] We have seen how the private nature of the individual under sovereignty is a transformed version of the autonomy and integrity—the completeness—of the presocial self. Yet, this selfhood only persists with the permission of the sovereign. The sovereign constructs a zone of privacy that it licenses. Yet, it can only create such a private space outside of itself. The result of this paradox is that the outside of the sovereign only exists under the sovereign's auspices. It is an inside outside. This contradiction is the result of the violent, notionally divine act of the lawgiver, who remakes the individual on social terms, destroying it and then giving back to it whatever it continues to have as an individual, but now as a social thing. The transformation that makes this possible is a violent one, perpetrated by a being who has no place in society, acts by violence, and is notionally connected to the divine. What makes and remakes us in the double domain of the sovereign is the dark chaos of divine violence.

As we will see, Walter Benjamin also understood sovereignty as enacting divine violence in the form of revolution, but it is Carl Schmitt who provides the most compelling modern analysis of sovereignty. Schmitt's emphasis is on the charismatic nothingness at the heart of sovereignty. Sovereignty for Schmitt rests on the prerogative to identify when a hole in due process, in constitutional order, and even in defensible logic, is to become the defining condition of the moment. Here now, sovereignty, unaccountable to law, to the proper function of responsibility and even to truth and correctness, announces and enforces the authority of what cannot be represented. The sovereign decision opens over the abyss of the exception, but the decision is itself also exceptional, because it can only be a decision by stepping outside of the regular established order of properly constituted meaning. It identifies the exception by being itself exceptional.

It seizes the moment, interrupting the logical sequence of events. It identifies the crisis and responds to it by leaping into the dark and acting in a way that defies explanation. The exception is alien to regular order, and the sovereign decision is alien to regular understanding. To Schmitt, it recalls the Christian miracle. It is part of the theological implication and spellbinding mystery of authority. Schmitt was a fool for dictatorship but not out of personal weakness or mindless conformity. There was in fact something weirdly renegade about him: divorce put him outside of the Catholic Church and perceived opportunism outside of the Nazi Party. To Schmitt, inexplicable and unaccountable authority was the lodestone of political power, and it was this that is most graphically exhibited in the sovereign decision. By being compared to the divine, the sovereign belongs to another order of being. To Derrida, Schmitt only went part of the way, because the decision's openness on the abyss is an openness on the wholly Other and, as such, brings the fixity and ascendancy of the sovereign itself undone as well. This means sovereignty is subverted as it is exercised, but such doubleness doesn't fit with Schmitt's account. Schmitt insisted on unaccountability: to him the sovereign belonged to a greater other self we cannot understand. By definition, it cannot be questioned.

"Sovereign is he who decides on the exception."[37] For Schmitt, sovereignty comes into its own and becomes most visible in atypical circumstances, yet this does not mean it is only relevant in a state of emergency. What happens in extreme circumstances simply reveals what is essential about the sovereign. Sovereignty as exercised in crisis gives us insight into the essence of political authority. It is not an extreme measure, but "a general concept in the theory of the state."[38] What this means is that the norm is demoted, or at least its priority is reversed. Instead of living in a system where the norm rules and we simply call on the sovereign in extremis, the sovereign identifies the crucial moment when the norm has no jurisdiction or authority. The sovereign does not rely on the norm for its meaning and cannot be judged by it. Sovereignty is a hole in the fabric of constituted order, which is subordinate to it. What the sovereign reveals is that the norm may operate, but in the end, it does not rule. Only when the norm breaks down does the true nature of power become apparent.

An emergency arises. According to Schmitt, the "concrete application" of sovereignty is needed in a "situation of conflict."[39] The norm sunders, creating an unmapped zone in which the sovereign is necessary. Something extraordinary happens, and the norm reaches its limit, thus creating the opportunity for sovereignty. But sovereignty does not only occupy a hole in the norm. It is a hole itself. It is not accountable, nor can it be understood in logical terms. It fills a hole with a hole. Schmitt writes: "The precondition as well as the content of jurisdictional competence in such a case must necessarily be unlimited."[40] Both the situation and its remedy are excessive by nature. Both the problem and its solution know no bounds. The sovereign both "decides whether there is an extreme emergency as well as what must be done to eliminate it."[41] Yet, it is this abyss at the heart of order that must save order, and to that extent, it is faithful to it, while defying it. It destroys the logic of order while defining and, in the end, sustaining it: "Although he stands outside the normally valid legal system, [the sovereign] nevertheless belongs to it, for it is he who must decide whether the constitution needs to be suspended in its entirety."[42]

Sovereign exceptionality opens a gap then in the logic of rule and order through which the essence of political certainty appears. This certainty derives from our necessary subservience to and exclusion from the unsignifiable mystery of unaccountable authority. Because the exception is a blank spot in the texture of political reality and the decision is itself implicitly exceptional, the nature of the situation and the logic brought to bear upon it defy interrogation. In their very vacancy, the two aspects of the decision and exception complex require obedience. Not only is this fixed point the pivot on which political events turn, it is also the resting point of the meaning of the order itself. This brings to it a level of awe and fascination that bubbles beneath Schmitt's prose. In the end, it is not just the seduction of political authority itself, to which Schmitt is drawn, but beyond that is his very interpretation of life itself, in its vacuous, *real* energy: "The exception is more interesting than the rule. The rule proves nothing; the exception proves everything: It confirms not only the rule but also its existence, which derives only from the exception. In the exception the power of real life breaks through the crust of a mechanism that has become torpid by repetition."[43] This openness on "real life" is the hole in the texture of legal order. No legal principle can substitute for the vacuity of real life. The moment of the decision is a "moment of indifference"[44] to Schmitt, a time when the fine discriminations of legal meaning have no value, when action trumps explanation, and the brute impact of the deed erases any refined and accessible weighing of knowable alternatives. The decision responds to the "necessity to judge a concrete fact concretely,"[45] not to make sense of it. Yet, the decision does not wreck rational legal meaning. The latter finds its only certainty in the moment of its failure, where the decision overrules it.

The authority of the decision rests then on its guaranteeing the order of legal logic by rupturing it. It guarantees meaning by way of meaninglessness. The consequence of this is that the sovereign decision defies any judgement or priority. It is indisputable. It is right even when it is wrong. The decision, Schmitt says, is "absolute and independent of the correctness of its content."[46] All the aspects of the decision in Schmitt's account, its being beyond calculability, order, accountability, reason, meaning, the logic of correctness, and so on can be summarized by the one statement: the decision "emanates from nothingness."[47]

This nothingness to Schmitt is not nihilistic. It is analogous to the unknowable heart of theological mystery. This is because to Schmitt, societies replicate their theology in the political form they adopt: "The metaphysical image that a definite epoch forges of the world has the same structure as what the world immediately understands to be appropriate as a form of its political organization."[48] In the seventeenth-century theory of the state, therefore, "the monarch is identified with God and has in the state a position exactly attributed to God."[49] The exception is the worldly form of the divine miracle[50] conjured out of a nothing that cannot be represented in the world and which the world cannot understand, in an act that defies credence, reason, and logic. In deism, the modern constitutional order abhorred the miracle as it abhorred every threat to reason and a logically constituted system of law. The exception in turn was just as anathema. "The rationalism of the Enlightenment rejected the exception in every form."[51] It was the "conservative authors of the counter-revolution who were theists" who argued again for the "personal sovereignty of the monarch"[52] because they saw it as consistent with theology. Sovereignty, to Schmitt, then has a significance well beyond its political efficacy. As with earlier thinkers, the sovereign represents the point where divine logic comes into the world. Even in a secularized context, the logic of counterrevolution requires that the mundane acts of the world be seen to have a theological significance. The sovereign is not simply ordering a society in response to crisis. It is not just dealing with problems in the smooth running of an effective organization. It is fighting evil, and a cosmic *radical* evil at that, hence, the impatience with which Schmitt insists on a sovereignty we cannot understand and should not try to rationalize, but merely obey. "In the face of radical evil," he says, "the only solution is dictatorship."[53]

The state of emergency then is not merely a crisis that requires immediate and resolute action. It is the opening for the deep and hidden truth that defines the essential nature of the political order to come to the surface and reveal how things are and how they must be. This depth is not mysterious simply because it is only accessible to the sovereign monarch or dictator but because it opens onto the unconditional and unsignifiable zone of the theological to which we must bow in our incomprehension. This zone of the divine exception disrupts the neat and logical texture of legal order, history, social accountability, transparency, and the signifiable, sundering it with a dark and intense, "feverish" interruption. This gap we know only as a gap. It does violence to order and rules us by violence. In Schmitt's account, sovereignty guarantees order by administering violence on it. This violence is not only its logic of interruption but also its necessary reaching into the dark of the abyss of exceptionality and decisionism. The abyss extends the violence of the sovereign toward the infinite. This infinite violence is implied in everything the sovereign does. There is a trace of violence in every tiny gesture of the sovereign. That is its charisma and why we are in thrall to it. When Schmitt says that the only way of dealing with radical evil is dictatorship, he is not arguing on the basis of evidence that only highly centered power can deal with difficult practical situations. He is investing his faith in infinite violence as a solution in and of itself. This violence is itself irresistible, and as such, it is the truth, regardless of whether it is correct or not. To say that sovereignty is exceptionality, then, is to say that sovereignty is violence and not just in a pragmatic way as a last resort in a difficult situation. Sovereignty is an imitation of, and a tribute to, the infinite violence of God. This is what places it beyond our understanding and beyond question. God is the limit to our right to question, and God's infinite violence is the abyss of his incomprehensible judgement into which we fall. The sovereign arrogates this violence to itself, because in our ordinariness, it remains beyond us and greater than us, something we cannot exercise and to which we must submit.

We have seen a connection between sovereignty and the violence of the undifferentiated. The unconditional always threatens to pull into the abyss any logic of identity and order. This is why Schmitt is the essential thinker of sovereignty. He sees the sovereign as defined by its prerogative in not only identifying the moment in which the legitimate order is to be suspended but also deciding without accountability what is to happen in that moment. The exceptionality of the sovereign is thus double. The sovereign decides when a hole has appeared in the neat fabric of social order, and then what should be done about it. Neither of these decisions adheres to any constituted order, responsibility, or logic of right or truth. The sovereign doesn't need to be right. It identifies disruption and thus owns it, telling us when order has broken down, even when we can't see it ourselves. It then responds to that breakdown with an act predicated on a nothing that we cannot understand. It knows when violation has occurred and answers violation with more violation. This total unaccountability opens history and politics onto the unknowable and potentially infinite, in other words, on what will always exceed and which will not let anything rest. What always exceeds also always undoes, always positing something else or something more. In its lack of definition, this excess becomes abyssal, promising a disruption without end. In Derrida, we will see that this openness must also unsettle sovereignty itself, requiring that sovereignty be turned against itself by the decision recognizing that its openness on the abyssal is not a mystery, as it is in political theology, but the unclosable openness on otherness, an otherness always notionally peopled. Yet, as we will see, this otherness is not always benign. It offers itself in a tangled economy of violence, where sovereignty and countersovereignty challenge one another, compete and even blend at times into complex historical dynamics of danger and force. Prior to this, the openness on the abyss has always been read theologically thus identifying God with the sovereign, the sovereign with the abyss, the abyss with violence, and thus God with violence.

Michel Foucault has provided an influential account of the way in which sovereignty has given way to other models of power, such as discipline and ultimately biopolitics. How does this account help us with understanding the relationship between sovereignty and violence? To Foucault, modern political thinking since the Middle Ages has focused on the issue of what form of constituted order is or is not legitimate. "The problem of sovereignty is the central problem of right in Western societies."[54] Foucault himself is interested in investigating another arrangement of power that is not simply reducible to sovereignty.

> From the nineteenth century until the present day, we have . . . in modern societies, on the one hand, a legislation, a discourse, and an organization of public right articulated around the principle of the sovereignty of the social body and the dele-

gation of individual sovereignty to the State; and we also have a tight grid of disciplinary coercions that actually guarantees the cohesion of that social body. Now that grid cannot in any way be transcribed in right, even though the two necessarily go together. A right of sovereignty and a mechanics of discipline. It is, I think, between these two limits that power is exercised. The two limits are, however, of such a kind and so heterogeneous, that we can never reduce one to the other. In modern societies, power is exercised through, on the basis of, and in the very play of the heterogeneity between a public right of sovereignty and a polymorphous mechanics of discipline.[55]

Foucault outlines the contrast between these two models of power.[56] Sovereignty is built around an axis that runs from dominant to subordinate subject. It is unitary and depends on a clearly identified legitimacy. Disciplinary power, on the other hand, manufactures subjects that suit its "actual relations of subjugation."[57] Instead of a fundamental unity, these "relations of domination . . . assert themselves in their multiplicity, their differences, their specificity [and] their reversibility."[58] Finally, unlike sovereignty, these relationships are not to be understood in terms of their legitimacy, which pales in significance compared to "the technical instruments that guarantee that they function."[59] So, on the one hand, for Foucault, is the traditional model of power as ascendancy, centrality, and right. On the other hand is a power function, operating by way of heterogeneous relationships that are so mobile they easily diversify, fragment, and reverse themselves. Their nature is fundamentally objective, not personal, and their justification is their technical efficiency and rational purpose.

This discussion leaves unclear the exact relationship between the principle of sovereignty and the operations of this alternative, disciplinary power. This is the key question Agamben goes on to theorize. The issue for Foucault at this stage, however, is slightly different: "How can we pursue our analysis of relations of domination? To what extent can a relationship of domination boil down to the notion of a relationship of force? To what extent and how can the relationship of force be reduced to a relationship of war?"[60]

Can war function as a model of social relations? Is peace coded war? Did Clausewitz get it the wrong way round: is social peace really simply a continuation of war by other means? He goes on: "War can be regarded as the point of maximum tension or as force-relations laid bare. Is the power relationship basically a relationship of confrontation, a struggle to the death, or a war? If we look beneath peace, order, wealth, and authority, beneath the calm order of subordination, beneath the State and the State apparatuses, beneath the laws and so on, will we hear and discover a sort of primitive and permanent war?"[61] The short answer is yes, but a more significant point is being made. The main point of Foucault's analysis is to replace a model of power defined by fixed points between which relationships form and to which those relationships are subordinate, with one in which the relationships are themselves primary. As Agamben will go on to argue, the exact nature of the relationship between sovereignty and disciplinarity is unclear, but it is clear that Foucault wants to see them as somehow in coordination. The disciplinary relationships of domination are part of the apparatus of sovereignty and can be described as war. What does this say about the relationship between sovereignty and violence?

There seem to be three possible answers to this question. The first is whether or not the institution of sovereign right, the State, is merely a cover for the violent war going on in society. Foucault is attempting to resuscitate a history long neglected by what he considers the Roman style of history long dominant in the West, which explains and justifies legitimate power. There is another approach to history, however, perhaps influenced more by the apocalyptic Jewish tradition in which the law is not the triumph of right. This history "is interested in the battle-cries that can be heard beneath the formulas of right, in the disymmetry of forces that lies beneath the equilibrium of justice."[62] In this alternative account, the State cloaks the violence that constitutes it, pretending to provide stability and peace. "The State is nothing more than the way that the war between the two groups in question continues to be waged in apparently peaceful forms."[63] Sovereignty is violence's disguise.

The other two possible readings of the relationship between sovereignty and violence emerge in a further elaboration of alternative histories that see society as riven between two contending parties: "The introduction of the theme of national dualism . . . made it possible to conceptualise two things that had not previously been inscribed in either history or public right. One was the problem of whether or not the war between hostile groups really does constitute the substructure of the State; the other was the problem of whether political power can be regarded both as a product of that war and, up to a point, its referee, or whether it is usually a tool, the beneficiary of, and the destabilizing, partisan element in that war."[64] Is sovereign power a prize of the social war? Does the war produce that power so that sovereignty is actually what is at stake in the war between competing parties? Sovereignty here is not a clearly formulated, theoretically justified, and morally right system. It is the ascendancy of the victor over the vanquished, and the discourse of right is simply a contemptible and cynical rationalization of the right of conquest. Finally, is sovereignty merely a tool, an implement that can be used to the benefit of one side or the other in the social war? Does one side merely use the discourse and machinery of sovereignty—the law, the police, the army—as its weapons, which the logic of constituted order facilitates and justifies?

In sum, then, sovereignty can be either the cover for violence, the prize of violence, or an implement of violence. Of course, it is mere intellectualism to disentangle these three denominations of sovereignty in a simple way. The operation of sovereignty will always involve a complex integration and alternation of all three. They cannot be kept apart. From a theoretical point of view, however, the key finding here is the separation in Foucault's account of sovereignty and violence: violence uses sovereignty, violence wins sovereignty, or sovereignty disguises violence. Sovereignty is not intrinsically violent, in and of itself. It is separated from violence outside of the events that bind them together. We have seen in earlier accounts how sovereignty opens onto an abyss. Here in Foucault, we see a pragmatic account of politics that avoids what seems to be the key question. Is sovereignty implicitly a type of violence and inalienable from violence, not as its cloak or tool, but as a form of violence itself? It is Bataille who we will look to for an answer to this question, one that departs from and yet subsumes earlier accounts.

As I have mentioned, Agamben's account of sovereignty aims to clarify an issue that is seen as still unclear in Foucault's work, specifically the relationship between structures of power, on the one hand, and the modes of subjectivity instituted by disciplinary apparatuses, on the other, thus between "political techniques" and "technologies of the self."[65] For Agamben, it is sovereignty, understood according to Schmitt's definition, that provides the missing account of the intersection between "the juridico-institutional and the biopolitical models of power."[66] In fact, to Agamben, it is the lack of separation between these two styles of power that constitutes "the original . . . nucleus of sovereign power."[67]

Agamben's account is very well known, and my aim here is not to run through its key elements. However, what is of interest to our discussion is that for all its talk of clarification and its insistence on a definitive account of the essential attributes of sovereign power across the whole history of Western politics, I will argue that Agamben's account is undermined by its recourse to topographical metaphors that are clumsy and blurred. Primary among these is the repeated use, in a variety of contexts, of the phrase *zone of indistinction*. This zone may be between potentiality and actuality, between exterior and interior, or between law and violence. The phrase *zone of indistinction* aims to give some sense to the dynamics of sovereign power, specifically how it includes within the purview of the law those subject to it, by excluding them from the systematic and accountable operations of legal process. It is unclear why this process is understood topographically as a zone, rather than dynamically as a mechanism, or temporally as an event, or in any number of other ways. Topography may seem to offer the fixity of an enduring account of structured power. What is interesting in particular is the way this metaphor seems to be an attempt to withstand something much more energetic, dangerous, and unstable, which is touched on but not pursued in Agamben: an account of law as an abyssal violence.

Agamben develops the Schmittian definition of sovereignty as aporia:

> The paradox of sovereignty consists in the fact the sovereign is, at the same time, outside and inside the juridical order. If the sovereign is truly the one to whom the juridical order grants the power of proclaiming a state of exception and, therefore, of suspending the order's own validity, then "the sovereign stands outside the juridical order and, nevertheless, belongs to it, since it is up to him to decide if the constitution is suspended *in toto*" (Schmitt, *Politische Theologie*, p.13). The specification that the sovereign is "*at the same time* inside and outside the juridical order" [italics added] is not insignificant: the sovereign, having the legal power to suspend the validity of the law, legally places himself outside the law. This means that the paradox can also be formulated this way: "the law is outside itself," or: "I, the sovereign, who am outside the law, declare that there is nothing outside the law."[68]

The sovereign is the one who decides on the state of exception, where and to whom it may apply. In this way, the sovereign administers the law by defining who is outside of it. By identifying the "zone" in which the law doesn't apply, the sovereign shows that the key aspect of the law is that place that is beyond the law. The sovereign thus spans the limit of the law. It is both inside and outside the law at one and the same time. The spatial metaphorical language Agamben adopts then allows the statement that the sovereign is "outside" the law. The result of this is to reduce the volatility and dynamism of the situation. Instead, the metaphor implies that what we have here is an enduring and fixed constituted order, even if that constitution is informal, undisclosed, and pragmatic only. Agamben's aim is to provide an account of Western politics' enduring nature. Spatial metaphors imply fixity and continuity. Yet, what we have here is a situation not in which an overarching colossus stands astride an imaginary wall, but one in which two contradictory sanctions operate together, forming and shattering one another simultaneously, held in an irreducible tension wherein one perpetually both inspires and troubles the other. Conformity to the law is constantly ironized by awareness that the law can be exceeded, that it doesn't always have to apply uniformly and universally. The state of exception opens up in what at first seems unmapped territory. Yet, it remains forever vulnerable to being entrapped again and accountable to the reapplication of the law. In other words, by trying to represent the state of exception topographically, Agamben undoes the very logic of dynamic doubleness that his account of sovereignty attempts to explore. What is internally and dynamically riven, self-constituting, and self-decomposing in one and the same instant is flattened out into a model of political order.

Agamben thus proposes aporia but does not commit to it. The very self-consuming logic of aporia is established but only to be flattened out as if it can be somehow stable and enduring. Aporia, in other words, simply becomes paradox. So, what we have is a discourse that recognizes abyssal complexity and dynamism but that also risks everything by an enforced coherence. The truly problematic questions get argued away. The model that is supposed to provide an understanding of the essence of Western political logic is used to cover up instability, fragility, and impossibility. A formulaic description of doubleness freezes and thus betrays doubleness, because the credibility of the formula itself becomes more important than the politics it claims to describe.

What is being covered up by the formulaic account here? The simple answer is violence. In attempting to locate the exception at the point of the origin of the law, Agamben argues for irregular violence as the primal act in the constitution of regulating law:

The law has a regulative character and is a "rule" not because it commands and proscribes, but because it must first of all create the sphere of its own reference in real life and *make that reference regular*. Since the rule both stabilizes and presupposes the conditions of this reference, the originary structure of the rule is always of this kind: "If (a real case in point, e.g.,: *si membrum rupsit*), then (juridical consequence, e.g., *talio esto*)," in which a fact included in the juridical order through its exclusion, and transgression seems to precede and determine the lawful case. Then the law initially has the form of a *lex talionis* (*talio,* perhaps from *talis,* amounts to "the thing itself") means that the juridical order does not present itself originally simply as sanctioning a transgressive act but instead constitutes itself through the repetition of the same act without any sanction, that is, as an exceptional case. This is not a punishment of this first act, but rather represents its inclusion in the juridical order, violence as a primordial juridical fact (*permittit enim lex parem vindictum,* "for the law allows equitable vengeance" [Pompeius Festus, *De verborum significatione,* 496.15]. In this sense, the exception is the originary form of law.[69]

Here, the law must first open the space in the world where it can operate. It must therefore situate itself in relation to the specific case. It must retrospectively nominate a specific event, or "fact," that requires the law's response. The law then does not simply correct or cancel this transgressive fact by way of the certainty of its truth. It responds to transgressive violence by its own violence, in other words, by repeating it. But this second "legal" violence will not itself require sanction. This unanswerable, unsanctionable counterviolence does not only repeat originary violence. It makes originary violence the essence of the law, the "primary original fact."

Sovereignty as the institution constituted on this exceptional violence thus rests on what Schmitt saw as the unsignifiable, which is analogous to the Christian miracle. Agamben chooses a related but more blunt way of describing it: "The exception is to positive law what negative theology is to positive theology."[70] Beneath the order of the sovereign is the "unrepresentable,"[71] "the suspension of every actual reference,"[72] a miraculous nothingness whose enactment can only be understood as violence. Agamben refers to Pindar to formulate the link between sovereignty and violence: "The *nomos,* sovereign of all/ Of mortals and immortals,/Leads with the strongest hand/Justifying the most violent/I judge this from the works of Hercules."[73] The crucial thing that happens here is the loss of difference between violence and justice: "*Nomos* is the power that 'with the strongest hand,' achieves the paradoxical union of these opposites."[74] Agamben summarizes this move by conflating law and sovereignty: "*The sovereign nomos is the principle that, joining law and violence, threatens them with indistinction*. In this sense, Pindar's fragment on the *nomos basileus* contains the hidden paradigm guiding every successive definition of sovereignty: the sovereign is the point of indistinction between violence and law, the threshold on which violence passes over into law and law passes over into violence."[75]

Sovereignty then does not simply enact or use violence: sovereignty is the vanishing point between law and violence. But what is violence? Is violence the savage cut, the blow, the explosion, or killing? Is it the disruption of morality and order, the shattering of paradigms, or the provocative new thought? And what is the measure of violence? Is it the end or the beginning, the revelation or the obscuring? Is it one or two? Does it finish us off or expose us to everywhere and forever? Violence is itself without announced limit. Law is measured by what is before it, institution, purpose, or prejudice, but violence has no measure. The word itself is an abyss of indefiniteness, both physical and abstract, moral and futile, purposeful and wild. When we talk about violence, we are talking about the possibility that anything might happen, with or without either meaning or limit.

Sovereignty in Agamben is abyssal. It is no surprise then that he finds a (failed) colleague in Bataille. Agamben's comments on Bataille in *Homo Sacer* are very revealing. Quoting Bataille's crucial and famous remark: "The sovereignty of which I speak . . . has little to do with that of states," Agamben comments: "What Bataille is attempting to think here is clearly the very bare life (or sacred life) that, in the relation of ban, constitutes the immediate referent of sovereignty."[76] Agamben has often been criticized for pursuing his argument analogically. Rhetorically, here, he overcompensates for the gaping hole in this way of proceeding by a rather anemic insistence. The connection is not clear at all, even if you say it is. Bataille's comment on sovereignty and his account of sovereignty in general—or death for that matter—goes well beyond the logic of the sovereign ban. As we will see, sovereignty in Bataille refers to that drive to excess out of which all identifiable things are constituted, to which they all refer, and toward which they are all drawn inevitably. Indeed, they arise only in relation to this excess that makes them possible. Instituted human sovereignty, what we might call the sovereignty of states, or in Bataille, the sovereign figure is no different. It relies on a larger, more determining sovereignty, the one Bataille refers to that "has little to do with the sovereignty of states."[77] This is a sovereignty that is always excessive and ever irreducible. It is this sovereignty that we glimpse in the sacred and death, both always irresistible in their excess, even as horror. In many of the accounts of sovereignty we have already seen, this sovereignty is revealed in the mystical quality of the sovereign, its replication of the divine on Earth.

Agamben's ambition is to produce one of the defined accounts of sovereignty Bataille sees as limited. This is the function of the topographical metaphors in Agamben: spatial metaphors imply an enduring stability. Agamben wants to stabilize violence, not ontologically, but semantically, not in what it is, but in what it means. His account opens on a violence—a "life"—he wants to fix in place as part of his model of constituted order. By being situated topographically, this violence finds a place and thus ceases to be violence. The very insight Agamben offers—that an abyss of violence opens within the sovereign—is compromised by being locked into a fixed formulation.

Yet, this ambition to provide a stable account founders when the argument ends with an account of violence that acknowledges the abyssal but refuses to give in to what it means, in an act of what is obviously deconstruction but without courage. As we have seen, sovereignty has often been seen to rest on an unsignifiable or indeterminable something that can never be simply stabilized or fixed in its identity. This abyss provides the sovereign with its authority but also undermines its pretensions to fixity. Even when the abyss is named God, stability remains elusive. The human sovereign cannot replicate or enact God's power without either resting on his higher authority (and thus not itself having the completeness that sovereignty requires) or else by dividing God's sovereignty and, thus, automatically making it less than sovereign; therefore, sovereignty is aporetic. Yet, attempts to stabilize this abyss are attempts to be free of the problem the sovereign proposes. From Bodin's unambivalent attribution of sovereignty to God to Agamben's attempts to stabilize our understanding of sovereignty in a topographical model, political discourse about sovereignty has been in flight from sovereignty. Yet, it has always known implicitly that sovereignty is a locus of obscurity, risk, and unaccountable violence, even when it seems to offer the possibility of order, improvement, and human elevation. Sovereignty cannot be limited, hence, its function as a kind of endless and interminable energy, growth, and improvement and its aspiration to infinite strength and self-overcoming. This self-overcoming installs self-disruption into the heart of things. Hence, it must be seen as infinite, open-ended, and ineluctably violent, even to itself. The attraction of sovereignty to Bataille is not that it is good, nor that it is preferable or a program. Sovereignty as either preference or program would reduce it to the unsovereign domain of the daily struggle of meaning and purpose—things sovereignty might gear but will always exceed and shatter. We will see in Bataille's study of Gilles de Rais that sovereignty might be a locus of not only horror but also cowardice and feeblemindedness, thus undermining any sense that it is heroic. Therefore, sovereignty is not a goal, nor a value in Bataille, yet, it remains insistent. His account subsumes the accounts of sovereignty we have already seen, locating and shattering them. We now turn to this account with the aim of showing how it precedes Derrida's treatment of sovereignty, wherein Bataille's insights are recovered for a language of political possibility.

CHAPTER TWO

BATAILLE AND SOVEREIGNTY
The Apotheosis of Violence

The sovereignty I speak of has little to do with the sovereignty of States.

—Georges Bataille, *The Accursed Share*

This is not the sovereignty of God, it is not the sovereignty of a king or a head of state, but a sovereignty more sovereign than all sovereignty.

—Jacques Derrida, *The Beast and the Sovereign*, 2011

It would be a mistake to insist that the accounts of sovereignty presented in chapter 1 somehow reflect a single strand of thought. Yet, a number of consistencies do emerge, even if they cannot be combined into a single story. Most importantly, the sovereign is identified with God, and God is identified with the unsignifiable abyss. Sovereignty is consistently understood as a version of divine authority, either the way that divine authority is exercised in the world or as a version or image of that authority. There is nothing above the sovereign but God. Yet, the sovereign is an image of God. In the Hobbesian account, it is even the other way round: God is an image of the sovereign. This may seem merely rhetorical in Hobbes, yet it is made necessary by his need to see human sovereignty in contractual terms as the product of a human consensus. This means God's sovereignty must be constructed retrospectively, as the preexisting absolute that can only be understood and described after the formulation of the social contract, because it can only be understood on the contract's terms. This is a complication of earlier accounts but not a substantial deviation from them.

Another complication had arisen earlier because of the complex relationship between the two roles imagined for the human sovereign. The sovereign is seen as both representing God's power on earth and a version of it. In other words, the sovereign both enacts divine authority and is therefore subordinate to it, on the one hand, while on the other, it is the image of God and has, therefore, all the same attributes as God. The complication arises here because God is ostensibly unified with nothing superior to it. In Bodin's account, for example, the sovereign is like God: unified, possessed of an incontestable authority, and answerable to no one. Yet as God's agent, the sovereign is answerable to God. It is therefore subordinate. The sovereign is like God in its unity and superiority, yet not like God, precisely because its real source of authority is outside of itself. It is divided therefore and has at least God over it. It thus both is and is not God. Looked at from the inverse perspective, by being an agent of God, the sovereign divides God between his ontology and his action. Whichever construction you choose, God and the sovereign challenge each other or draw each other toward aporia.

Yet, a further complication arises when we see how these accounts define God. God by definition has nothing over him. Nothing preexists God, and there is nothing to which God can be held accountable. God is indeterminate and unconditioned by definition. The reference to God is a reference beyond representation into a space that cannot be specified or delimited. This effects the figure of the human sovereign as well, which takes on the divine's unaccountability. Sovereignty is the absolute other. The king is really a foreigner and always remains so. Rousseau's lawgiver cannot find an enduring place in the society he constitutes. The bringer of the law is cursed and alone as only gods can be cursed. In Schmitt, the sovereign exception is doubly unaccountable. It acts in the moment when no rationally formulated statute holds. Its opportunity arises when no rule can apply. On top of this, what it chooses to do in that moment is not accountable to any logic and requires no explanation. This is why Schmitt compares it to the miracle. It intervenes when real-world law fails and doesn't need to be justified. It is its own explanation. The act of the sovereign is almost purely self-referential. It is right not because it is the best or the most correct option nor because it is the most practical, or even the most powerful. It is right because it is the sovereign act. It doesn't matter whether it is right or wrong on any other terms: appropriateness, practicality, morality, ideology, humanity, and so on. It is right in a way that cannot be explained or even formulated. It doesn't need to be. Sovereignty is right for no other reason than it is sovereign.

Sovereignty opens onto the abyss of the divine. It is in the work of Bataille on sovereignty that the abyssal logic of sovereignty is most ruthlessly pursued. The violent and reckless nature of Bataille's thought pursues the unaccountability of sovereignty in the Western tradition to its logical end. This takes sovereignty beyond the political, however broadly defined, into a full account of human being. Sovereignty becomes both opportunity and danger, but it is a mistake to see romance in it, as Bataille himself was sometimes (almost) tempted to do. Sovereignty is the lodestone of the human, and it cannot be either chosen or spurned. It cannot be the source of a political program. Nor is it something we could ever abandon. It is not a tool by which we define our future freely and purposefully, but it is our future inevitably. It is to Bataille's account of sovereignty that we now turn.

In Bataille, sovereignty is abandonment to the abyss. The sovereign goes beyond anything that could be conventionally known as subjectivity because it tries to live the excess and intensity of the abyss even though in the end such a life is unlivable. Sovereignty is the horizon of human being and is thus an endlessly receding line toward which human life tends but that it can never reach. All human life refers to sovereignty and inevitably reaches toward it, but anything that could possibly be called the sovereign life leads to destruction, evil, and horror. For Bataille, religion traditionally attempted to engage with this excess and destructiveness, hence, its preoccupation with sexuality and death, its use of sacrifice as access to triumphal meaning, and its arrogation of violence to the divine. Christianity echoes all these preoccupations as much as any religion but is in denial of them, seeking in moral judgement some way of sublimating its own drive toward the abyss. This makes it the "least religious" of all religions, as Bataille remarked.[1] How does sovereignty emerge for Bataille? Bataille provides at least two important ways of representing this process. These two are analogous to one another and often appear together. The first draws on the language of economy, the second continuity and discontinuity.

Bataille intended that his writings on economics would engage with conventional discourses of economics. In this way, they represent an attempt to describe the human involvement with the material world in as broad terms as possible. The key dynamic in Bataillean economics is the inexhaustible wealth of the solar. The sun generates energy without pause. This energy expands relentlessly. It may be diverted or it may change its form, but it can never run out. The sun bathes the earth with energy. This energy takes on complex forms—life, for example—which shape energy into apparently self-contained and limited systems. These systems draw on energy as they fold in on themselves, becoming things. Yet, energy is not exhausted. It keeps arriving on the earth unstoppably. Each thing seems to set itself up against this rampant flow of energy, even though it is fed by it. Energy both fuels and defies systems. Even as the system becomes efficient because of the energy flowing into it, it must find some way to resist being overwhelmed. Energy just keeps coming, threatening to overheat systems with an excess of the very thing that makes them possible.

Bataille uses the terms *general* and *restricted* economies to describe this complex unfolding. The limitless field of ever-expanding energy flying out from the sun and hitting the earth with an inexhaustible force is the general economy of energy. The general economy never weakens or lessens in Bataille. Energy never lets up. It keeps on coming inexhaustibly. It always exceeds and overwhelms. The general economy sets no limits to its expansion spatially or temporally. Restricted economies, on the other hand, transform inflows of energy into minisystems with defined limits. They may form out of the rampant energy of the general economy, but for their limits not to be immediately shattered, they must find some way of resisting energy's excess. They turn against excess simply for their own survival. Yet nothing can stop the energy of the general economy, and nothing can resist it. Restricted economies keep receiving the energy they need to operate, but energy saturates and inevitably overwhelms them. The bounds within which they function inevitably shatter. They push outward until the uncontrollable and illimitable field of energy bursts them at the seams and ultimately overcomes them. You can put a plant in a pot, but it will continue to grow until the pot itself shatters.

The second way in which Bataille imagines sovereignty is in terms of continuity and discontinuity. This represents a translation of the same logic we have already met in the discussion of economics into another idiom. The world of energy is one of infinite transformations and transitions and of constant becoming. One thing cannot stop itself from becoming another. Any definition or delimitation we place on this open-ended process of becoming is merely an artificial attempt to arrest constant change or at least to make it pause long enough for it to be apprehended by thought. In this way, we allow it to appear and linger in the world of practical decision-making and language. Taken in its most untouched way, this is a world of uninterrupted continuity. Our attempts to control this world—necessary though they may be given our practical needs—are merely momentary interruptions in the drive of energy onward into endless change. We need to break the flow of continuous energy sometimes, but its impulse to resume flow and expansion always remains. Discontinuity is merely a momentary and forced pause within the drive to greater continuity.

These motifs in Bataille animate a proto-deconstructive logic. The general does not simply contradict the restricted economy nor is continuity the opposite of discontinuity. They are each two phases of one operation, or to be more accurate, two impulses in one double, self-threatening manifestation of force. On the one hand, a restricted economy, the momentary slowing and entrapment of energy turned toward a specific and limited goal does not contradict the general economy. It is merely one demarcated phase in its natural work. The general economy will always overwhelm and ruin any specific restricted economy, but it remains its source and wealth. There would be no practical means-and-ends operations without the general economy feeding and enlivening them and, in the end, looming over them, threatening and smashing them. On the other hand, the general economy only appears in the world and can only manifest itself in the form of the overwhelming of restricted economies. It has no other ontology. The general economy is the impulse toward excess and transformation within any restricted economy. It is the restricted economy's impulse toward self-overcoming. It is not separate from the restricted economy but is simply the inability of any restricted economy to contain itself or be limited to a fixed quantity of incoming energy. Conversely, the restricted economy is merely a moment—detectable, knowable, and namable—in the unstoppable through-flow of energy toward maximum dissipation. Discontinuity never stops the onward drive of continuity. It merely allows it to linger awhile. We focus on the restricted and the discontinuous because we cannot live in the whirlwind of the wild flows of energy of the general and continuous. Knowledge and language are not possible there, in the same way that signification takes place within the context of the extravagance and entropy of dissemination but must at least momentarily resist it.

Later, we will look at the complex doublenesses that characterize much of Derrida's work: the relationship between law and justice, for example, or conditional and absolute hospitality, enacted democracy and democracy to come, exchange and the gift, and so on. Suffice it to say here that what Derrida does in each of these cases is to provide a deliteralized, free-floating, and unreal adaptation of the Bataillean schema, less emphatic but still recognizably Bataillean. For example, as we will see, justice in Derrida's "Force of Law" is the infinite and overweening imperative to which law always aspires but that it can never reach. The law attempts to enact justice but will never be able to do so fully. Law will never achieve justice, but nor can it be satisfied to be a set of simple and fixed regulations. No law will ever be sufficient. The law will always require reform, because it will never be just enough, but justice will always elude law. No law could ever fully capture and stabilize justice. In short, law is the crystallization of a justice that cannot rest and will never actually be captured. Law cannot fix justice in place once and for all, and justice will always exceed law. Law has no other purpose than justice, and justice has no other ontology than law. Justice is nothing other than the will to justice within the law. Here, we have an adaptation of Bataille's schema: law attempts to fix and embody justice in the same way that the restricted economy attempts to hold the general economy in place. Law is the only possible instance of justice in the same way that the restricted economy is the only way in which the general economy can appear in the world. Bataillean economics is the parent of Derridean doubleness.

Things in the general economy do not only reach toward what lies beyond them. They identify themselves with it, even as they try to contain or refuse it. In the general economy, things are and are not their own excess. This doubleness challenges any logic either of transcendence or of immanence. Excess intensifies within it and cannot simply be seen as the thing beyond it to which it refers or aspires. Yet, nor can things ever rest within themselves. Even as they make themselves, they reach beyond themselves into their own excess. There is no simple separation in Bataille that distinguishes a self-identical thing from the context in which it arises or the antecedents that produce it nor from the excess to which every aspect of its being is inevitably directed. Thus, there is no simple separation between the thing and what is and remains intensely other to it.

In this way, the otherness from which the thing separates and which it installs within itself as its single double reality is not something else. It is the impossible, that which cannot be measured or known and which ultimately cannot be. To Bataille, "being is the excess of being, the upwards surge toward the impossible."[2] As we have seen, the general economy defies logic and representation because it cannot be limited and defined. It cannot enter into the world other than as the impulse toward self-overcoming and self-remaking in the self-identical thing. In Derridean terms, it exists only as the trace offering possibility but which is not itself possible. The general economy is the opening within the restricted economy on the possibility of otherness, but this possibility is indefinitely open and unformable. In itself, it is impossible and represents the absolute smashing of the thing that seeks to enter into the open field of possibility.

Sovereignty in Bataille goes well beyond the mere organization of human government, therefore. It is the drive toward excess and exaltation in the possibility of living an absolutely rampant freedom. It is fundamental to the very logic of human being and its relationship to excess. Sovereignty represents the aspiration in the human to live totally, to live excess, and thus to be the actualization and incarnation of the general economy. Sovereignty opens up human possibility, disrupting self-identity and meaningful order. In this way, it is irreducibly violent in its action. By necessity, it includes violence within ipseity, as the opening that both makes the self-identical thing possible and orients it toward its own excess. Yet, at the same time, the self-identical thing cannot transpose itself totally into the impossible. It cannot *live* the general economy. It cannot live a life of uninterrupted possibility, because this would mean living in a domain of absolute violence, a prerogative that belongs only to God, to whom infinite love and final judgement are one and the same thing. Attempts to live absolute sovereignty lead inevitably to horror. Any attempt to include them in daily social life destroys the self. Over and above this, however, it brings an unconscionable violence into the world, and thus societies anathematize and ban it. They could not be societies if they didn't. The definitive example of this for Bataille, as we will see, is Gilles de Rais: in his absolute cruelty and violence, and his light-headed, even hysterical, indulgence in incoherent necromancies, Gilles attempts to live the life of the pure sovereign. It unhinges him, and his society destroys him, even allowing for the political contingencies that actually undid him. He remains, even if not known, the archetype of what society cannot allow and that the law exists to smash. In sum, sovereignty arises as the necessary orientation of human being but is in itself impossible and cannot be lived.

The sovereign therefore lies always and everywhere beyond the livable, even though it remains the ever-receding horizon toward which human being must direct itself. It is by definition impossible, and the impossible opens on an abyss that must resist capture by the name, the theory, and the pronouncement. The impossible offers no satisfaction or insight. It does not end. It is horror itself as the possibility that there is no end at all, ever. This is what makes Bataille neither a philosopher nor an anthropologist. The impossible always exceeds these domains, and they expire in the face of the motility, unclarity, and inconsistency of the impossible. The impossible cannot be resolved in any way. There is no point of livable clarity and definition at which discourse may ever rest. The most intelligible way of discussing the impossible for Bataille is by way of the language of the sacred, understood here in terms not of its possible object but of the practices of reaching after the abyss of the impossible beyond.

Sacred practices revolve around sex and death and, thus, violence. They don't offer access to some transcendental or exceptional moment, from which we may gain sustenance or glimpse a beyond that should be our destiny. The truth of all being for Bataille is in continuity, the unrepresentable indistinction from which all self-identity must be deduced. The practical logic of means and ends through which we must structure the operations of our daily lives requires that we separate ourselves from the continuous and construct a world of strict demarcations and achievable acts. This stabilization of being defies the excessiveness that overshadows it, that precedes and exceeds it forever. Each act is a traitorous gesture of the specific being toward the excess of being that allows it, from which it draws its being, and which inhabits, explains, and threatens it. Such separation is in turn defied by the drive to find some outlet toward what lies beyond in the continuous. This drive is ultimately toward the impossible and thus can never know or even denote its object. The channels for this drive for Bataille are in the erotic, the unstable imbrication of sex and death: "For us, discontinuous beings that we are, death means continuity of being. Reproduction leads to the discontinuity of beings, but brings into play their continuity; that is to say, it is intimately linked with death. I shall endeavor to show by discussing reproduction and death, that death is to be identified with continuity, and both of these concepts are equally fascinating. This fascination is the dominant element in eroticism."[3] For Bataille, the drive toward reproduction responds to an impulse toward continuity and thus is consistent with the drive toward death. The sex drive and the death drive are effectively indistinguishable. They both seek the outlet of the discontinuous onto the continuous or, rather, the constant pull toward the continuous that must remain insistent in the domain of discontinuity. Bataille writes: "Continuity is what we are after but generally only if that continuity which the death of discontinuous beings can alone establish is not the victor in the long run. What we desire is to bring into a world founded on discontinuity all the continuity such a world can sustain."[4] The state of continuity is not a resting place. Our discontinuity cannot be shrugged off. Christianity to Bataille is the least religious of religions because it consistently pretends that this escape into the impossible can be reconciled with mundane life and that the two are not hostile to one another, even as they combine. As we will see, this is why we must acknowledge that, despite everything, Gilles de Rais must be seen as a Christian figure. To Christianity, continuity can be achieved in union with the absolute indefinition of the godhead, thus making the impossible an achievable goal. This is a betrayal or a weakening of the broader role of religious thinking, which is to incite an interminable self-casting into the abyss that offers nothing in return. The name of God is offered in Christianity as the possibility that even if the absolute is indefinable and in its final definition unknowable, it is still possible to have a relationship with it, one that can be even analogous to a personal relationship, between two types of being that are even said to have been made in each other's image. To Bataille, this is an abandonment of the true mission of the sacred: to expose the discontinuous world to a logic that can only destroy it. Salvation is the ultimate betrayal of the sacred, because the sacred is not a resting place, a redemption, or a gathering into glory but rather an endless and irredeemable loss, a loss without end, an absolute violence toward being and beings: "In essence the domain of eroticism is the domain of violence, of violation . . . there is most violence in the abrupt wrench out of discontinuity. The most violent thing of all for us is death that jerks us out of a tenacious obsession with the lastingness of our discontinuous being."[5] The drive toward continuity made possible in eroticism is implicitly and endlessly violent. "I am saying that the domain of violence is that of religion,"[6] Bataille writes. "God" is the attempt to disguise or hinder this violence, to conceal its abyssal nature: "Is not God an expression of violence offered as a solution?"[7] Derrida reprises: "God is the name of this pure violence."[8]

The continuous does not simply lie outside of the less charmed and mundane world of the discontinuous. It presses at it constantly, and this pressure must be dealt with somehow. We cannot live in the world of continuity, as this is, by definition, the domain of the impossible. It would involve us reaching endlessly toward ever more transitory and intense enactments of rapture, danger, and bliss, each one more indifferent to the practicalities that sustain us, and violently destructive of them. The continuous is implicitly unlivable. Yet, it cannot be simply ignored. Its enchantment and horror must have some access to the world of work and practice. Ipseity is open to what lies beyond it, as we have seen, and this beyond is in turn in thrall to what lies beyond that as well, and so on, indefinitely. There is no end to this supplementation. In this way, excess always presses on identity, opening it on the indefinite, bringing the abyssal within the self-same.

How can this ineluctable openness appear in human life, enriching it yet not sucking it into nothingness? The answer lies in the dynamic that is perhaps Bataille's most famous and well-known contribution to thought: the pairing of taboo and transgression. Since its celebration in Michel Foucault's essay "A Preface to Transgression," Bataillean transgression has become a byword for a type of cultural–political activism that challenges the normative and uncritical, unsettling identities and limits by way of usually aestheticized practices that mock tradition and promise a future that is more free and expansive. The risk with investing a dynamic like taboo and transgression with historical meaning, of course, is that it easily settles back into older patterns of political agency, especially those of priority and progress. The battle between tradition and innovation is restaged, this time in the form of norms and alternatives, rather than oppression and liberation, or progress and reaction. Dominant sexual identities are teased and tested to make space for repressed identities to be free. The taboo that had previously repressed and spurned any alternative becomes an object of ridicule. We present it as hollow, artificial, callous, and stifling—a mere construct. Beyond the taboo, freedom emerges first in other identities and eventually beyond identity altogether. The taboo seems vacuous and, above all, contingent and unnecessary.

Throwing off constraint in the name of something disruptive and other is part of the logic of transgression but so too is the disappointment that inevitably this complete openness, even local forms of it, does not endure. At most, we get a glimpse of the world beyond constraint, the world of the continuous interrupts the discontinuous but does not stay. It cannot reign without it settling into another pattern of restriction, as Foucault well knew. To challenge the taboo and believe in the future beyond it is merely to play the game of the taboo. But one crucial element is missing, and this is the one most important to Bataille: the taboo is only taboo if we believe in it. The drive to transgression is not opposed to the taboo, even though it violates it. Transgression is the ultimate tribute to the taboo. To violate sexual norms that you know are arbitrary and hollow is not to transgress them at all. It is merely to challenge a hegemony you don't believe in and that should be fought because of its oppressiveness. To believe that transgression is an alternative to the taboo and that it opposes it is to take what is a deconstructive logic and distort it, flattening it out into a kind of dialectic. This destroys or obscures the problematic and troubling doubles that make the taboo–transgression pair so important and so enduringly and productively problematic. As we have seen, the significance of the pairings of continuity and discontinuity and the general and restricted economies is not that they are opposites or alternatives to one another but that they are part of one and the same double operation. The restricted economy can only come into being as part of the flow of energy of the general economy, even though the general economy will always overwhelm and swamp it with more and more energy. On the other hand, the general economy cannot appear in the world except by way of the formation and overcoming of restricted economies. The restricted economy does the work of the general economy, even at the cost of its own stability and unity, and the general economy is only the drive toward self-overcoming in restricted economies. They are two and the same.

The relationship between taboo and transgression is analogous. Taboo is the attempt to set up limits and rules that withstand the drive to excess and chaos that lures the human in sex and death and that will always threaten every type of human structure and order. Transgression is the opportunity to experience the excess necessary to human society but impossible within it, if it is to stand. As such, it marks out the necessary limit of the social. It defines it. Transgression is therefore absolutely necessary to social order. It is a confirmation of the taboo and part of the taboo's operation. Taboo places limits on the flow toward annihilation in sex and death, a flow that is made visible in the festivals that constitute the transgressive. These festivals must occur, but they must also be ephemeral. A door opens in the wall of the taboo, and we project ourselves into the great undefined beyond. Yet, we cannot live outside, and the door closes on us again, leaving us safely inside, with only memories and dreams of what we have seen. In this way, by identifying the points where continuity can break through into ordinary life, the taboo itself is not hostile to the continuous but is a marker of it. It does not oppress continuity. It is the necessary pretext for its celebration. In sum, then, as with the general and restricted economies, and the continuous and discontinuous, taboo and transgression are part of a single double nature, requiring one another and arising only in relation to one another, both defying and celebrating one another.

Taboos make society what it is by marking out the limit to the drive toward death and unregulated sexuality. The fascination of eroticism must put pressure on the social, and it must find expression and release, but this release must be controlled because human society could not operate—human beings could not even feed themselves—without it. Taboos must be violated, but we must also believe in them, which is why crime is the ultimate denomination of transgression for Bataille. And crime here does not refer to the indulgence of romantic passion or liberating gesture. It is not the crime of a charismatic bandit outlaw or of a freedom fighter resisting oppression. It is the crime of degradation and not even the degradation of a liberating abjection but a petty even foolish crime, the despicable crime of a Gilles de Rais or a de Sade, to cite perhaps the most famous examples in a Bataillean context.[9] We despise Gilles de Rais for the horror he perpetrated, his mad cruelty, and the easy way in which he could torture and murder hundreds of children. And we are right to despise him, not only for his cruelty but for his pathetic gullibility and his treachery and cowardice. De Sade's heroes, too, are not simply violent but cowardly, consistently loathsome and unheroic. But this is what makes them such convincing exempla of transgression. We despise their crimes. We detest their cruelty because their transgressions reinforce our belief in the taboo against cruelty and violence. Everything Gilles de Rais does confirms our belief in the law against murder. Nothing can reconcile us to his acts. In a telling moment in *Erotism*, Bataille writes of de Sade's thought: "Such a strange doctrine could obviously not be generally accepted, nor even generally propounded, unless it were glossed over, deprived of significance and reduced to a trivial piece of pyrotechnics. Obviously, if it were taken seriously, no society could accept it for a single instant. Indeed, those people who used to rate de Sade as a scoundrel responded better to his intentions than his admirers do in our own day."[10] Those who admire de Sade as a model of heroic transgression betray him. They turn transgression into a model. They rob de Sade's fantasies of the only thing that motivated and explained them: their irredeemability. To turn them into a doctrine is to defeat them more resolutely than to police them by way of the taboo they serve.

Taboo thus requires transgression, and transgression is only possible as the ultimate form of service to the taboo. To transgress, you must sincerely and passionately believe in the taboo and see the transgression as part of the way of honoring the taboo. Transgression thus cannot be preferred to taboo. They are necessarily a pair. Yet, taboo is not the governing logic here. It controls and restricts the thing that is always striving to overwhelm it. The will to disrupt is inevitable, and it is this drive to the limitless and to horror that Bataille sees as the essentially human. Violence represents something definitive to the human: "Men have never definitively said *no* to violence,"[11] Bataille writes. The limitless drive that inspires transgression is a drive toward a potentially limitless violence. This drive is the most essentially human quality. To Bataille, it is the will to sovereignty.

"Sovereignty comes first,"[12] Bataille writes. In Bataille's account, sovereignty is the primordial, fundamental human quality. It is the insatiable and open-ended will to continuous and limitless overcoming. The drive toward sovereignty exceeds the ordinary workaday world of simple objectivity and practical logic. In its drive to overcome and continue overcoming, it scorns even the most fundamental goals of survival and purpose on which it might seem to depend. It risks everything, seeking an absolute freedom, though so far is it beyond the logic of daily life, it cannot understand this absolute as any kind of point of arrival. The idea of a destination for sovereignty is meaningless. Any imagined point of arrival is merely the starting place for yet more overcoming, even beyond the point of exhaustion and death. The drive to sovereignty knows no rest, reaches no point of satisfaction and order, and makes no meaning. If it touches on these things, it does so simply as a way to smash them, too, and pass beyond them into impossibility and the infinite. And this infinity is truly an open-ended trajectory. It is not some indefinite and mystical point of spiritually renewing contemplation. The annihilation it promises is a smashing of persons and bodies in an ugly and horrible meaningless entropy beyond triumph and defeat, even beyond liberation itself.

Yet, we should never think it merely spins out away from the world in which we live. As we have seen previously in the relationship between continuity and discontinuity, on the one hand, and the general and restricted economies, on the other, it always leaves a trace in the mundane world of daily life. In even the most impoverished and limited human act, there is the trace of the possibility of something larger, better, or different, something other and beyond, the possibility of an openness on an elsewhere or a future that always violates the here and now. Each mundane act also implicitly opens onto sovereignty, even in its most hypothetical or imaginary form. Nothing we do is completely without the trace of the sovereign.

Sovereignty, then, is not a shapeless or transcendental beyond reserved for the most extreme moments of our lives. It is not the most indulgent, passionate, or painful excursion we might undertake in a few brief excitable moments, nor is it the domain of the most wild, original, or transgressive individuals among us. It is embedded even in the most basic and fundamental acts of our daily lives. In this will to endless overcoming, sovereignty can be seen even in the simplest practical acts we undertake, even in our most general relationship with the world of objectivity and practicality, for example, our relationship with the animal world. Bataille writes: "It is man in general, whose existence partakes necessarily of the subject, who sets himself in general against things, and for example against animals, which he kills and eats. Affirming himself, in spite of everything, as a subject, he is sovereign with respect to the thing an animal is."[13] Here, the human constructs itself by dominating the animal world, which remains locked in thingness. In this way, the human frees itself from being a thing, ceasing to be an object and becoming a subject. Subjectivity is not simply identified with humanity, nor is it something humanity simply expresses. It is not simply some latent dimension of human nature that must come out at a certain time. Nor is it a socially or historically constructed fiction serving specific political formations or discursive mandates. It is something that humanity can partake of by way of its objectification of the world of things, the world to which it itself could so easily be relegated. In Bataille, the human always inhabits a world where things are made of the very energy that overwhelms them. Objects form as part of the drive that exceeds them, swamping them with the excess of energy that they need for their operation but that will inevitably thwart them. In other words, objects form on the way to their own explosion and indefinite expansion. As objects, they are conditioned by something that itself always exceeds conditionality.

The human occupies this world, simultaneously forming in it as an objectifiable thing and as reaching beyond that thing. It could simply settle into being an object, in the same way as the animal that the human kills and eats. However, a certain irreducible self-awareness on the part of the human blows open the process of its objectification by giving it insight into the larger world in which any object is situated. It becomes aware that the object forms as an interruption of something larger, toward which it is oriented. In short, it becomes aware that objectification is not the end. Something positions the object, something larger, unconditioned, and potentially infinite. This something larger is interpreted as the possibility of a perspective, turned back on the object. The human then *sees* its own objectivity. The imaginary position from which it sees itself is subjectivity. Subjectivity is the cardinal achievement of human self-awareness of its own objectivity. Subjectivity arises then as the beyond of objectivity, yet as with other Bataille005an doublenesses, it arises within objectivity as the possibility of going beyond it. This beyond is, of course, potentially infinite, and by necessity, there emerges an imaginary figure who can be thought to embody the final possible totalization of subjectivity, an absolute subject—God—known in the human world in the form of its avatar, the human sovereign. We will see later in Heidegger, in a discussion of Walten in the context of ontological difference, how Dasein is capable of grasping the world as such, while the animal is poor in world. This discussion will deepen our understanding of sovereign violence by rooting it in the very emergence of beings in relation to Being. It will provide a fuller account of what Bataille is starting to uncover here: subjectivity arises as the separation of the thing from its own possible objectification, manifest in its awareness of objectivity as such.

Sovereignty in Bataille then is the self-awareness of the object imagined on a potentially infinite scale. Sovereignty looks back at the human who feels locked in the world of objectivity, but it also represents the human's possibility of overcoming itself and being oriented toward something larger than itself. It is the goal of any impulse toward self-overcoming in the opening up of the object. Subjectivity opens as the doubleness of the human object in excess of itself, reaching toward the absolute of its own double nature. Sovereignty beckons as the ultimate human possibility, something toward which human subjectivity must always be oriented, but which it can never actually reach. In this way, it must be imagined as a model of an ultimate thing that we can imitate but never be.

This logic makes the idea of God necessary, especially a God who may walk among us, either as his own self-made flesh or as his lieutenant, the sovereign figure, what Bataille calls the traditional sovereign. The human then comes to see itself as the object of this ultimate subject, aspiring to sovereignty but not able to fully enter into it, partaking of subjectivity but never as fully as its most complete imaginary figures. The king as the most conventional image of sovereignty is the mere figuration of Bataillean sovereignty. We stumble on our journey toward absolute sovereignty, but before us, gazing back at us, are these figures that seem to represent sovereignty, the traditional figure of the human sovereign, and beyond that, God. We are oriented toward God but can never be him. He pins us with his gaze, the gaze we can imagine as hypothetically our own. Look: we can be God because there is one human like us who is God's representative. The human sovereign is not the totality of sovereignty but inflames our belief that the impossible is possible, that the possible within which we live is a version of the impossible, and that the impossible is always opening within the possibility with which we are so familiar.

Yet, this process of subjectification divides the human from itself as much as it divides the human from the animal. The social world forms around this divide, dividing one caste of humans from another just as readily as the human is divided from the animal. The traditional sovereign may exemplify what is most authentically human, but it also institutes a social hierarchy that separates the aristocratic from the plebeian: "In traditional sovereignty, one man in principle has the benefit of the subject, but this doesn't just mean that the masses labor while he consumes a large share of the products of their labor: it also presupposes that the masses see the sovereign as the subject of whom they are the object."[14] The ascendancy of the figure who is traditionally denoted as the sovereign—the king or feudal lord, for example—is to be explained by something far more significant and profound than is usually covered in more conventional materialist or political models. This ascendancy does not simply rest on an unequal distribution of labor and property, or even simply of prerogative. It is not simply the result of physical domination. In its most fundamental form, the sovereign is established in its social ascendancy by taking on full subjectivity and turning the socially inferior into its objects.

Yet here again, we see the same complex double dynamic we have already encountered previously. Those at the bottom of the social scale do not become like animals. They recognize subjectivity as the thing that orders their lives, even when they do not "partake" of it in the same way as the traditional sovereign. Subjectivity is both what they serve and the thing to which they aspire. In recognizing the sovereign, the "individual of the multitude" does not simply abase himself; he "recognizes himself in the sovereign."[15] The sovereign becomes not only the apex of social aspiration but the very identity of "inner experience."[16] Here, we can see the trace of an Hegelian logic. We recall that at the outset of his paper on Bataille, "From Restricted to General Economy: An Hegelianism Without Reserve," Derrida starts with the hypothesis that the account of sovereignty in Bataille is a direct transposition of the master–slave dialectic. In becoming the object of a subject, the subordinate class is offered the possibility of becoming subjects themselves.

The dynamic of sovereign subjectivity is crucial to the very possibility of the social itself. It structures social relationships by establishing the hierarchy between dominant and subordinate social classes. More importantly and more fundamentally, however, it instills the openness on which human sociality depends. The openness of the human on the sovereign, on the very thing that represents the infinite aspiration of openness, creates the possibility of full subjectivity. In being identified with sovereignty, subjectivity also reaches beyond any delimited or defined notion of individual self-identity toward the thing that aims to exceed limits and definitions. If the possibility of subjectivity is opened by sovereignty, the very inexhaustibly excessive nature of sovereignty will always threaten to smash subjectivity. Subjectivity becomes itself, therefore, in its reaching toward that thing that will always put it at risk, indeed destroy it. It is in this breach in the wall of subjectivity implicit in its reliance on the sovereign that the openness in the human we know as the social becomes possible. In this way, the sovereign as the thing that makes individual subjects possible on similar terms to and in the context of one another becomes the thing that binds humans together in communication and thus community.

The sovereign then governs the social by exemplifying individuality, but individuality is not a self-creating or self-sustaining thing. In its aspiration to sovereignty, subjectivity takes on an image of autonomy, but this apparent autonomy is only available to it by way of something outside of it. The individual thus becomes a highly complicated thing, along the lines of what we've seen for the human sovereign in chapter 1: autonomous but only by way of that which is outside of it; self-contained but only by way of its openness on the thing that is its model, which will always exceed, defy, and threaten it. In turn, this thing—sovereignty—on which it opens is the thing on which all other possible subjectivities are also open. This shared openness creates the possibility of the communion between individualities and, thus, social life. We will return to the political meaning of such universal openness later in a discussion of the way sovereignty necessarily suggests (but does not guarantee) justice.

Here, we must remember that this universal openness is always in tension with an unattainable supersubjectivity that divides the social by creating violent hierarchies. Individuality contests this inequality but cannot refuse it altogether because it is part of the complex that makes individuality itself possible. Individuality is a lived impossibility. It can only be provisional or fictional, an orientation toward a point or mode of being at which it can never arrive. Sovereignty seems to offer this mode of being as a version of itself, but as we saw with the traditional sovereign's relationship with God, individuality is trying to live a version of the thing it cannot be. If it were unified, self-identical, and the thing over which there is no greater power, it could have no relationship to the sovereignty that is its model and the thing that offers its very lifeblood: possibility itself. We have already seen this kind of dynamic in the relationship between traditional sovereignty and God, as outlined by Bodin, Hobbes, and others. We recall that there the traditional sovereign was a representative and image of God, but by having God over it, it could not be like God. Similarly, by taking its authority and identity from God, it could not be the self-contained and unified thing that God is. It therefore both was and was not in God's image. God was the thing that both gave it life and provided the model of which it was to be the image. But, in this way, it became both unsurpassed and subordinate; both unified and centered outside of itself, both autonomous and dependent. It was even more complex than that. Its being unsurpassed was only available to it by way of being subordinate. Its unity only came to it by way of that which was outside of it. Its autonomy is only available to it because it is dependent on something else for its structure and meaning.

Individuality is the same: it relies on the sovereignty that both makes and unmakes it. It thus relies on something larger than the human of which the human both partakes and which it fails. Individuality and subjectivity are thus impossible in themselves, because the sovereign is always in excess. Traditional political theory thus makes the mistake of vesting sovereignty in the human individuals who merely figure it. Sovereignty, thus, is not a person but the idea of itself that the human derives from its overcoming of the object world and which it then institutes as the logic of the social, even as it fails it.

Sovereignty offers the possibility of a limitless freedom. Nothing restricts it. It represents the possibility of the indefinite excess of energy, a kind of absolute extravagance, subject to nothing. This absolute liberty seems to be incarnated in a figure who becomes identified as himself sovereign. This traditional sovereign figure seems to channel the possibility of human openness altogether: the sovereign seems to be the point where absolute and unconditional, unrestrained freedom is actually livable. It is this possibility of absolute human openness that makes humans capable of being open on one another, hence, the fact that sovereignty is indispensable to human societies. Yet, the sovereign also represents a threat to human community and human life more generally. The social is organized around the idea of the sovereign, an idea it sees actually literally incarnated in the dominant social individual, whom the multitude use as an emblem of their aspiration and the engine of interrelationship. Yet, this figure of the sovereign is antisocial. It guarantees its own social ascendancy by savaging the social. Sovereignty is the "negation of prohibition,"[17] the confirmation of the social by way of the rupture of all limits and thus all rules. The sovereign is the lodestone of the social, but it transcends it as well. It may profit from the world of labor and utility, which indeed makes its extravagances possible but which it spurns in its radical commitment to the now, regardless of expense and consequences. It is the possibility of a life opening up "beyond utility" and "without limit." This denial of all limits reaches, of course, to violence. It is first and foremost a bringing of the possibility of absolute violence into the social order. Bataille writes: "This relative alienation, and not slavery, defines from the first the sovereign man who, insofar as his sovereignty is genuine, alone enjoys a nonalienated condition. He alone has a condition comparable to that of the wild animal, and he is sacred, being above things, which he possesses and makes use of. But what is within him has, relative to things, a destructive violence, for example the violence of death."[18] The sovereign represents to regular human beings stuck in their life of limitations and obligations the possibility of a life without limit. For the individual who realizes his individuality is conditioned by something outside of it, something greater, and itself not subject to limits and conditions, the sovereign seems to represent the possibility of being a self-contained and self-sustaining, self-identical thing. The sovereign figure seems to be autonomous and unanswerable. Death, for Bataille, is the true point of access to the absolutely limitless, and the sovereign becomes sacred by having jurisdiction over the point at which human life opens on the limitlessness of death. This openness on death brings an uncontrollable violence into human life, in fact, right into the heart of human community. Sovereignty makes human sociality possible and gives to human beings the image of the autonomous individual they use as their model. But at the same time, it also brings the possibility of absolute violence. It is in its intimacy with death that the sovereign's absolute contempt for limits and inhibition most clearly manifests itself. Death cannot be assimilated into the utilitarian logic of the workaday world. It defies the triumph of individuality that the sovereign would have seemed to ensure. The sovereign thus animates the complex, contradictory, and volatile, even impossible logic at the heart of human life and society. The sovereign is the archetype of human individuality in its freedom from constraint. It is because this individuality embodies openness paradoxically that human communities can form among these individuals. Yet by way of its openness on death, this archetype of individuality and source of social togetherness also threatens the individual with its absolute extinction and the social with an absolute violence that it can never quite forget. This freedom manifests itself not simply in risk and courage but in violence and killing. The sovereign may underwrite the social but only by exposing the social to that which transcends and defies its most fundamental rule, the prohibition against killing: "Sovereignty is essentially the refusal to accept the limits that the fear of death would have us respect in order to ensure, in a general way, the laboriously peaceful life of individuals. Killing is not the only way to regain sovereign life, but sovereignty is always linked to a denial of the sentiments that death controls. Sovereignty requires the strength to violate the prohibition against killing, although it's true this will be under the conditions that customs define."[19] The human is thus exemplified in the sovereign, which is a figure of the murderous violence that transcends and threatens the human, a violence in turn not answerable to the human. The multitude's hope of human individuality is grounded then in a murderous violence directed against it and which does not belong to it.

The openness on death is an openness on absolute extinction, and therefore, on nothingness. Sovereignty's investment in death brings nothingness to the heart of the social and the political. In spurning the real world of utility and teleology by way of freedom, sovereignty represents the human exposure to the nothingness that exceeds all purpose and meaning. Bataille writes of the exercise of sovereignty as "the miraculous moment anticipation dissolves into NOTHING, detaching us from the ground on which we were groveling, in the concatenation of useful activity."[20] Indeed, sovereignty itself becomes nothing: "The thought that comes to a halt in the face of what is sovereign rightfully pursues its operation to the point where its object dissolves into NOTHING, because, ceasing to be useful, or subordinate, it becomes sovereign in ceasing to be."[21] In exceeding the world of utility and purpose, the sovereign extinguishes itself as a real thing. This opening onto the abyss of nothingness is the miracle of the sacred to Bataille. As we have seen, the sovereign is routinely explained by way of its link to the divine. In Bataille, sovereignty's link to God comes by way of the category of the sacred. The divine power of which the sovereign partakes is the extra-ontological prerogative of ultimate subjectivity. The individuality or subjectivity that is available to the human by way of sovereignty is a trace of the sacred nothingness that makes individuality possible but that is always larger than it and defies it by revealing an otherness to which it aspires but with which it can never be simply identified: "What is sacred . . . is for example myself, or something that, presenting itself from the outside, partakes of me, something that, being me, is nevertheless not me (it is not me in the sense in which I take myself for an individual, a thing): it may be a god or a dead person, because, where it is concerned, to be or not to be is never a question that can be seriously (or logically) raised."[22] The sacred is not an other-worldly domain to which we look for some kind of transcendence of everyday drudgery. The sacred intervenes in the world, and I am part of it. It produces me at the limit of my individuality as coming from a zone where even the most basic ontological questions do not arise. It is the thing that is both me and not me, because such a distinction is meaningless in the domain of the sacred. The logic of sacredness and sovereignty defies reality, and we span not two separate worlds but a contradiction that can never be resolved. This defiance of the real world can be seen most readily in extravagance, waste, and ultimately death, which is "the appearance that the whole natural given assumes insofar as it cannot be assimilated, cannot be incorporated into the coherent and clear world."[23] Death is the ultimate luxury for Bataille, the thing to which individuality aspires as its apotheosis, but it appears in our world in terms of the absolute libertinage of excess, vanity, luxury, pointless waste, and mere displays like beauty and honor: "This miracle to which the whole of humanity aspires is manifested among us in the form of beauty, of wealth—in the form, moreover, of violence, of funereal and sacred sadness, in the form of glory."[24]

We have seen in earlier accounts how sovereignty opens on an unsignifiable abyss. This is most clearly articulated in Schmitt, where the sovereign decision brings into politics a moment of complete blankness. The sovereign decision cannot be explained by reference to any morality, program, or purpose. It is unaccountable to any institution, but it is also unaccountable to any logic. This vacuity, its unaccountability, and its unconditionality are what makes it sovereign. If it could be explained and justified, or even clearly represented, it would not be exceptional, and therefore, it would not be sovereign. Schmitt connects this abyss to the divine by way of the miracle, but in doing so, he is merely repeating the strategy of earlier thinkers, or following their thought to its logical conclusion. The divine in Bodin and Hobbes represents an identical reliance on the unaccountable, unsignifiable, and unconditional. Similarly, the law giver in Rousseau represents the intrusion into the state of something irredeemably outlaw, which cannot be answerable to the laws that it helps institute. Bataille's generalization of sovereignty as the presence within human life of a sacred nothingness merely intensifies this argument, by embracing its logical conclusions, in all their wildness, violence, danger, and above all, ambivalence.

As we have seen, according to Bataille, human beings have no choice but to live in a domain of distinctions and rational calculations that separate them from the continuous stream of being. Yet, the energy out of which they form and that is the only material of their physical reality is also itself part of that great continuity. Discontinuity shapes, warps, and inflects continuity but is not alien to it. In this way, the formation of discontinuous beings is both part of the flow of continuity and a resistance to it. Discontinuity segments the world into objects, each distinguished from one another and subject to control and use. This use reinforces the human immersion in the discontinuous by giving priority to the means-and-ends logic of a narrowly defined purpose. Human beings may be part of this world of objectivity, but they rise above it as well. Their awareness that they can define and control objects distinguishes them from the world of mere objectivity, even as it immerses them in it. In isolating and using the object, the human learns of its own separation from the world of objectivity, that it is not an object but a user of objects. It both belongs to the world of objectivity and elsewhere. It is engaged with the world of the object, but it is not locked in that world. It knows that the object world is both eternally transferable and interminably transforming. Within the very nature of the world of objects, there is always and unstoppably the drive to become something else. In belonging to the world, in manipulating it, the human reaches into the beyond that lies within it, the beyond-objectivity from which objectivity arises.

Because it is unstoppable and interminable, this world opens on the infinite that Bataille understands as nothingness. This beyond-within, to which the human reaches, is a zone of pure violence because it always opens the possibility of a rampant disruption and violation that cannot be contained by any code or purpose. In a world of no limits, there can be no higher priority to which excess can be subject or against which it can be measured. It automatically ruptures any identity, meaning, or purpose, on and on indefinitely and inexhaustibly. To Bataille, we perceive this excess, this abyss of nothingness, through the radical disruptions offered by death and sexuality. It is the domain in which human calculations of safety, purpose, and meaning are extinguished, where our concern for the future is overcome by an intense commitment to the present moment, a passionate disregard for consequences and any future. In this domain, there is no limit to what is possible, no definition to what is known, and no constraint on what is felt and done. It is a domain of absolute liberty: "Sovereignty is essentially the refusal to accept the limits that the fear of death would have us respect in order to ensure, in a general way, the laboriously peaceful life of individuals."[25]

The domain of the sovereign is not merely a liberation or ecstasy felt subjectively by individuals reaching beyond themselves in mysticism or art, however. Its unrestraint carries the human over into the inhuman and thus ruins any morality. It finds human expression in what is most unacceptable or taboo, what no human society can accept. In a social world whose priorities are stability, survival, and order, the most forbidden behavior is killing another human. It is in killing that the sovereign is manifest most emphatically: "Killing is not the only way to regain sovereign life, but sovereignty is always linked to a denial of the sentiments that death controls. Sovereignty requires the strength to violate the prohibition against killing, although it's true this will be under the conditions that customs define."[26] Killing another human is an act of sovereignty, which no society can tolerate, unless channeled into some putatively necessary purpose, as in religious sacrifice, legal process, or war. The drive to excess that makes us what we are directs us toward an inevitable violence, of which we routinely, even if vicariously, partake. The human is thus locked in contradiction with itself and needs to find ways of dealing with its own violence. The violence of murder, especially sadistic murder, may exemplify sovereign liberation, but it can only be meaningful when ruthlessly condemned. Such violence may most realize the human drive to break the constraints that demean us, yet cruelty can only fulfill sovereignty by being excoriated. If it were not crime, if it were not savagely repressed by the social, it would no longer be sovereign. If it were somehow acceptable or normal, it would no longer be taboo or a violation of law, accountability, and sociality. This would degrade it by making it defensible. Sovereignty "must be expiated."[27]

In its expansion into absolute possibility, sovereignty must be impossible. These feverish criminal acts that aspire toward sovereignty are not only to be condemned. They are also pale versions of what gives them their inspiration. Sovereignty is simply not livable. It is something that orients or draws our passion, something we experiment with, dream of, or reach for. It is even part of our self-definition, our understanding of what our glory is, but at the same time, it is not something we can have or be: "The sovereignty to which man constantly aspires has never even been accessible and we have no reason to think it ever will be. All we can hope for is a momentary grace which allows us to reach for this sovereignty, although the kind of rational effort we make to survive will get us nowhere. Never can we *be* sovereign."[28] Sovereignty can only flourish in our endless failed attempts to excise it. It confirms the taboo by transgressing it. By transgressing the taboo, it invites attention, even admiration, but it must be condemned, excoriated, crushed, and abominated, even as through it, the human reaches toward God. This ruthless repression of transgression provides a glimpse of liberation, but in the end, it only strengthens the taboo. Sovereignty's violence must be violently suppressed. It does not ever arrive at a point beyond the human. It does not transcend the human. The sovereign act defies the human by reaching into that most essential part of the human that the human cannot accept but from which all our aspiration comes. It should be unnecessary, because it can only lead to pointless savagery and destruction. The policing of our subjectivities in turn aspires to its complete erasure. It has to; yet at the same time, our social regimes will always fail to control the sovereign, even as sovereignty itself always and everywhere also fails. It cannot be reduced to zero, even as it savages itself. Indeed, Bataille draws attention to its self-destructive quality. "True sovereignty . . . conscientiously effects a mortal destruction of itself,"[29] he writes.

We are used to seeing our politics as the contest between different understandings of what society should be; or we see it as a long culture war between patriarchal repression and liberal opennesses. But more than that, it is the complex play of sovereignty, our simultaneous attraction to the crushing murderousness of power—which we routinely dissemble by all kinds of pseudoliberal rationalizations—and our loathing and suspicion of it. What defines our political divisions is not this opposition between those who love sovereignty despite its violence and those who loathe it, despite its effectiveness. Instead, what we see is the face-off between different denominations of pretense: between, on the one hand, those who pretend that sovereignty belongs to them so that there is nothing for them to be afraid of, and on the other, those who pretend to be separate from it. Before they are anything, our political positions calibrate themselves with sovereignty, whether they know it or not, in complex, obscure, and shifting patterns of enthusiasm, pragmatism, refusal, betrayal, and denial. As we will see later, it automatically follows from sovereignty's primacy here that freedom and justice are always at stake in politics one way or another.

Sovereignty, then, both makes us what we are and threatens us. It is the thing toward which we reach. We form our societies under its sway and construct institutions in its name, ostensibly allowing it to rule over us. But we are also, almost always, horrified by it, frightened and suspicious of it. Given its opening on absolute violence, and our routine identification of it with casual and bureaucratic violence, we have reason to be suspicious. Yet, in many ways, we also adore its violence. We cling to national sovereignty, for example, as some guarantee of our freedom from modern oppression. It is also a source of pride in which we adore our nation, language, or culture while overlooking its racial and colonial crimes, and repressive governments use national sovereignty as a way of avoiding critique for human rights abuses. The sovereignty of the state legitimizes violent systems of law and order, often racially inflected, yet at the same time, popular sovereignty is used to argue for the transparency and accountability of these systems. These are just examples from the most conventional understanding of sovereignty. If we take Bataille's more generalized account, we see it as the opportunity for religious invention—through the exploration of possible constructions of the sacred that free us from reason and history—and the license for the most extravagant violence. To Bataille, of course, these last two were not alternatives: religion is the opening of violence. This insight that sacred truth and absolute violence are indistinguishable and form one and the same event—the fundamental idea of Christian apocalypse—is what perhaps lies behind the contemporary construction of heroism as vigilante violence, the idea everywhere in popular culture that legitimate institutions have failed, a problem that only rogue, sovereign, violence can solve. In short, we appeal to sovereignty to protect us, use its freedom to invent systems of meaning to transport ourselves beyond our present state, resort to its freedom as a solution to problems and as a heightened form of pleasure and entertainment while, at the same time, being highly suspicious of it and even contemptuous of it.

To contemporary-left political thinking, sovereignty is often a byword for an unaccountable and insidious power controlling, simplifying, and monitoring society and subjectivity. Yet, as we have seen in our reading of Bataille, the destructive side of sovereignty cannot be seen as rigorously separate from its productive side. The violence and nothingness of the sovereign abyss risk horror but also create opportunity by installing possibility at the very center of all human social action. This is not to say that sovereignty is a kind of evil or cathartic God, renewing by destroying or cleansing by purging. The relationship between violence and possibility in sovereignty is not that stable or simple. Sovereignty on Bataille's terms cannot be programmatic or progressive. If it were, it would be subordinate to something higher than itself, some goal or idea of future improvement. Sovereign violence must be understood on the model of taboo and transgression, as the thing that reinforces order, but that order must anathematize and exclude. Yet, this exclusion will never be complete or satisfactory, and violence will always return. Sovereignty, therefore, will always be a problem, necessary, ordering, and perhaps liberating, but always dangerous. So, we will always be ambivalent about it. It is both legitimacy and chaos. States and institutions form only in reference to it, and this is what gives them authority, sometimes incontestable authority. Yet, because sovereign bodies emerge as part of the trajectory that leads to absolute openness and violence, they will always incorporate within themselves something frightening and destructive. Absolute violence itself is unlivable, yet all living is open toward it. This is how sovereignty is an example of transgression. Sovereignty is itself forbidden, yet we always attempt to reach toward it, even at times to live it, though this is impossible. Our determination to transgress this limit and to make sovereignty real allows us to form authoritative institutions but exposes us and them to danger. It incorporates not only hope and possibility within our institutions and, in fact, all our social acts but also a forbidden but inevitable violence.

Sovereignty defies death by immersing itself in it. It is that part of the human that is most divine, and our names for God are mere attempts to give sovereignty some identity, content, and meaning, the very things it does not allow itself to have. "Man needs sovereignty more than bread," Bataille writes.[30] Yet, it is by definition a threat to itself. It cannot sustain itself or be sustained, because of its potentially infinite "divine" violence.

CHAPTER THREE

DIVINE VIOLENCE AND JUSTICE

Divine sovereignty is an abyss of absolute limitlessness and interminable violation on violation. It is a zone of boundless prerogative and unaccountable freedom. It does not have a fixed or knowable ontology but simply names the tendency of everything toward an indefinitely open end, with everything giving way to something else interminably, infinitely quickly, and without completion. It is the hypothetically interminable self-overcoming to which all self-forming must tend. It is not a mystical or metaphysical identity, but the asymptote to which all becoming is directed. Divine violence is not a separate category or an alien zone. The unalterable tendency of all things is to fulfill their own drive ever onward toward becoming what exceeds them. Ultimate authority lies in the being that is imagined to occupy the presumed absolute end of this tendency, that has a power beyond worldly power, and that is therefore an exception to any of the rules of social definition or historical limitation. This sovereignty is beyond accountability because it is beyond identity and meaning. This is why from our side of the horizon, it seems a blank, vacant space—in other words, an abyss.

The name Western political philosophy has given to this abyss is God. Held out before us in delight and power, in pleasure and license, in freedom and violence, in sex and death is the illusory and elusive possibility that this absolute freedom can be lived. God lives it and God is the image in which we are made, so why not? Freedom lures us on, and our own actions cite and imitate it—our kings purport to be a version of it—but we can never have it. If, as Bataille says, this absolute freedom to which we tend is the definition of sovereignty, then sovereignty is something that orients our lives, lures them on, and offers them apotheosis. Yet, it is something we cannot be.

This has been the logic of sovereignty throughout Western philosophy. In Bodin and (in an inverse fashion) Hobbes, divine sovereignty provides both a model for and a limit to human sovereignty. God is the ideal figure that the human sovereign attempts to imitate, but he also puts it in a contradictory state: the attributes of absolute superiority and unity that are necessary to the sovereignty of God cannot be replicated by the human sovereign outside of a specifically defined political domain. The human sovereign may imitate God but can never have the completeness of God's sovereignty simply because God remains over and above it. God therefore is the model for the human sovereign but also the thing that, in the end, it cannot be.

At the other end of the history of Western thinking of sovereignty in Schmitt and Agamben, we see a comparable thing. Here, sovereignty is an empty space outside of human systems of meaning-making and political constitution. It is the blank space of the inexplicable and unaccountable decision that only the sovereign can make. The sovereign looks deep into the vacancy that the rest of us cannot see, the space that lies beneath ideological, moral, or historical meaning. Only the sovereign can see this space, not the human; the human can only get a small taste of this in the brief moments when it assumes sovereignty. This empty space may no longer take the name of God, but Schmitt still uses the theological as its measure, when he compares it to the Christian miracle, the transformative act that is both inexplicable and unrepeatable and that lies beyond all human explanation. Sovereignty remains a citation of what traditionally we have always known as the divine. Here lies the essence of the political in the Western tradition, according to Agamben. In sum, the human brings to earth a (failed) version or (fleeting) instance of the sovereignty it cannot be or have, yet, to which it must always refer and toward which it always directs itself.

The focus of this chapter is on working out how sovereignty enacts divine violence, and what this might mean for the heavily politically inflected terms of Derridean thinking: justice, democracy, and hospitality—key issues in contemporary global politics. Law emerges in the world in relation to a Justice that is itself abyssal, vacant, and hypothetical, supposed only. Instances of law can only emerge in reference to the sovereign abyss that always exceeds them and gives them their meaning and license and that, in this particular context, takes the name of Justice. We will see in a later chapter how sovereignty operates through the Derridean doubleness of absolute and conditional hospitality.

The other goal of this chapter is to show how divine violence in drawing us on toward exaltation risks opening before us a limitless destructiveness and cruelty in which everything is risked. This destructiveness reveals the danger of an uninhibited identification with sovereignty. We will look at two instances where the drive to identify with divine violence risks becoming enthusiasm for murderous cruelty: Benjamin's characterization of revolution as divine violence and Gilles de Rais' hysterical sadism. The risks of loving sovereignty become clear. We have no choice but to pursue sovereignty, but only so far. We must also refuse its infinity, because it can turn to license. Then, everything will be smashed. To cross the threshold into this argument, we must go by way of the text on which discussions of sovereignty and violence in their relation to politics pivot, both for Agamben and for Derrida: Walter Benjamin's "Critique of Violence."

Benjamin on Divine Violence

"Critique of Violence" ends with the statement: "Divine violence . . . may be called sovereign violence."[1] In Bataille, we have already seen one version of the identification of sovereignty with the absolute violence of the sacred, and by extension, God. Benjamin arrives at an analogous conclusion by a different route. "Critique of Violence" is largely given over to a discussion of the relationship between violence and the law, specifically in two forms: law-making and law-preserving violence. What interests us here is the oblique outline of a violence that is over and above the distinction between these two: the "divine violence" to which Benjamin dedicates the last third of the essay. What is at stake here is the connection Benjamin makes between divine violence and politics, specifically revolution. As his discussion concludes, Benjamin writes: "If the existence of violence outside the law, as pure immediate violence, is assured, this furnishes the proof that revolutionary violence, the highest manifestation of unalloyed violence by man, is possible."[2] Revolutionary violence in its pure and spontaneous form is the highest version of human violence. The prime condition by which the existence of this violence is assured is that it arises without or beyond the law. As we will see, Derrida balks at this romanticization of spontaneous violence, which he finds too "messianico-Marxist."[3] Yet,

Benjamin's identification of revolutionary violence, which earlier he had seen as the unacknowledged, even secret, history of democracy,[4] with divine violence offers to show how divine violence orients the political.

Let us now turn to Benjamin's outline of what he means by divine violence. The discussion of legal violence that has dominated the greater part of the essay serves as a mere prelude to speculation about the possibility of a violence free of the entrapment and compromises forced on it by law: "Since . . . every conceivable solution to human problems, not to speak of deliverance from the confines of all the world-historical conditions of existence obtaining hitherto, remains impossible if violence is totally excluded in principle, the question necessarily arises as to other kinds of violence than all those envisaged by legal theory."[5] It is here that the paper becomes famously enigmatic. Benjamin is trying to imagine a violence that makes truly justified ends possible "but was not related to them as means at all but in some different way."[6] The definition of *just ends* is not an outcome of rational thought, according to Benjamin, but comes from God.[7] We are fooled into thinking that just ends are rational because we want to believe they can be achieved by way of laws that are universal and part of a system of law.

Having uncoupled means from ends, he returns to the issue of a violence that lacks a goal. This violence achieves nothing and has no end. It is simply a "manifestation."[8] In keeping with the idea that the logic of means is part of the domain of fate, he argues that examples of a violence that is a means without an end can be found in myth. This kind of violence is not primarily an expression of the power of the Gods but simply a display of the fact of their existence. The example he gives is that of Niobe, who boasted of having more children than Leto, the mother of Artemis and Apollo. For this hubris, Niobe's fourteen children are killed. To Benjamin, Niobe is not punished because she is wrong or because she transgresses some kind of law. She has simply challenged fate, and fate must crush her to remind the world that it exists and cannot be flouted. Benjamin goes on to argue that this demonstrates that the law is not simply a set of rules for the operation of a society. There is always some pure manifestation of power for its own sake within the law. The law is not just about order and reason. It is also fundamentally about the establishment of power: "Lawmaking is power making, and . . . an immediate manifestation of violence."[9]

What mythical violence demonstrates therefore is that the violence of law is not primarily intended to ensure justice or freedom but rather to manifest power in its pure form, uncomplicated by any other program or ideal than the manifestation of itself. This reveals to us what Benjamin calls "the perniciousness of its historical function"[10] and raises the question of a violence that might be an alternative to mythical violence and not only go beyond it but also erase it. The perniciousness of mythical violence provokes "the question of a pure immediate violence that might be able to call a halt to mythical violence."[11] This is divine violence, which opposes mythical violence "just as in all spheres God opposes myth."[12]

Much has been written about the nature of divine violence in Benjamin, yet it remains enigmatic. At first it seems simple, when Benjamin starts by defining it negatively. It is the antithesis of mythical violence "in all respects." It destroys the law that mythical violence makes. It destroys "boundlessly" the boundaries mythical violence sets up.[13] But soon the distinctions become finer: "If mythical violence brings at once guilt and retribution, divine power only expiates; if the former threatens, the latter strikes; if the former is bloody, the latter is lethal without spilling blood."[14] In the domain of mythical violence, on the one hand, we see a violence keen to manifest its own power legally through a system where guilt can be clearly defined and punishment meted out. This legal system of violence exists to demonstrate a power that cannot be challenged. Therefore, it looms over our heads, constantly threatening us with punishment if we cross the line from legality to illegality. When we do so, we meet with a literal, physical violence, one that displays its irresistibility by spilling blood.

Divine violence, on the other hand, is not interested in the simple exercise of law or of a crime that offends the written statute and thus invites punishment. It is interested in something beyond the law, the possibility of expiation, a purging of the very essence of crime by exposing it to the violence of God's truth. Divine violence does not want to keep the subject in suspense, conscious of a threatening, looming violence it should not challenge. It does not maintain its subjects in a perpetual state of fear and obedience. Its aim is to get beyond fear to the vision of higher being that the divine offers. Therefore, it does not hesitate to strike, and it does not do so in a petty physical way. It strikes in an apocalyptic form, where violence is greater than the merely physical: it is the opening of truth itself in an exposure of the human to what is beyond mere life, a violence that scorns to spill blood, because blood is simply the sign of the base physicality of mere human being.

Where the case of Niobe had been exemplary for the explanation of mythical violence, Benjamin offers the event of the Korah in Numbers

16 as his illustration of divine violence. Korah disputes Moses' authority, claiming that Moses has set himself up above the rest of the people. For that he, his family, and all his allies are struck down by God: "And the earth opened its mouth and swallowed them up, with their households and all the people who belonged to Korah and all their goods" (Num. 16:32). The violence enacted on Korah is bloodless violence, an opening up of the earth. God does not explain or justify his act. He does not formulate it into a general principle like a law that the people must obey. He strikes. The incense bearers that Korah and his kin have been told to bring with them are hammered out into altar covers. Korah, therefore, is not punished by a general unalterable principle. He is annihilated. Even his descendants are literally expunged from the surface of the earth, forever, not in a mere display of power, as in the case of Niobe, but in a cleansing enacted by an irresistible and bottomless violence that erases any sign of the transgressor and transforms what is left of him into a means of worship of itself.

In a case like this, the guilty are not purged of their guilt as individuals, according to Benjamin. Instead, humanity is exposed to a violence that is above and beyond the merely human, "mere life," and the system of law. Instead of instituting a law that we in our daily lives must understand, respect, and obey, here we see something greater than and incomprehensible to us, that wipes away whatever stands in its path. Korah is not given the opportunity to understand and repent what he has done wrong. The nature of his crime is never defined. It cannot be formulated because what judges him is beyond definition. It is a violence that destroys not only what stands before it but also the law itself. In this event, we are "purified" of law, in Benjamin's terms.[15] In a much-quoted formulation, Benjamin writes: "Mythical violence is bloody power over mere life for its own sake, divine violence is pure power over all life for the sake of the living."[16] It is lesser human life that is ruled by mythical violence, using the law to formulate the limits within which mere life is allowed to subsist. Divine violence is a pure unaccountable violence, but its scope is much greater than mythical violence. Instead of encompassing only the narrow, petty world of basic human survival, divine violence offers a higher and richer conception of life, what Benjamin calls here "all life." And this violence's goal is not to demonstrate its own authority but to reveal a higher way of being.

Benjamin then goes on to give two further examples of divine violence. The first is the educative power, which goes beyond any inherited limit. There then follows a richer discussion of the commandment "Thou shalt not kill." To Benjamin, this commandment is not an absolute. No society can respect it completely, and, according to Benjamin, this has been widely understood in Judaism. As with mythic violence, the formulated law belongs to the smaller world of mere life. The real question is, how are we to understand what it means to cross over beyond the law into the unmapped domain where killing occurs? No society can absolutely forbid killing, and none does. Benjamin describes the commandment: "It exists not as a criterion of judgement, but as a guideline for the actions of persons or communities who have to wrestle with it in solitude and, in exceptional cases, take on themselves the responsibility of ignoring it."[17]

This is the domain of divine violence. We may be tempted here to see God's violence as a model of sovereign violence in the sense of constituted authority. This is what Agamben does when he tries to shoehorn Benjamin's argument into Schmittian sovereign exceptionalism. Yet, this is to limit and reduce what Benjamin is trying to capture here. As we will see, Derrida ends his treatment of Benjamin—a struggle that required several iterations and which he still could not complete—by acknowledging the open-ended, credulous submissiveness Benjamin shows not just to a greater authority but also to something wild, abyssal, and infinitely, chaotically violent. This is not the violence of the Schmittian sovereign, which is supreme, calculating, and patriarchal, a model of stewardship that we should respect, even when it conceals the logic of its decisions from us. Divine violence for Benjamin is the unleashing of a cataclysmic force that knows no limits, purpose, or restraint. Benjamin's interest in it is not for the authority and rigor it offers as a kind of model of the authoritarian state but for what might become available after infinite violence has washed away whatever stands before it. To Benjamin, staying within the confines of the commandment, on the grounds that what God means is that life on any terms is sacrosanct and must be protected, is "ignoble,"[18] "false and ignominious,"[19] a view that guts God, reducing him to the patron of mere life, when what God really stands for is the possibility of something higher, a truer life, coming after divine violence has erased the static here and now. What is sacred in the human is not our mere existence. Our true sacredness is offered by what comes after the expiation of mere life. This mere life is what bears guilt in the domain of the law and mythical violence.[20] To open ourselves to our true sacredness, we must reach beyond into the unmapped zone made available by the ruthless open-ended violence of the divine.

Benjamin concludes by identifying how a conventional perspective on history is only able to detect the "dialectical rising and falling"[21] in the relationship between law-making and law-preserving violence, expressed in the change from one law-making era to another. This is the rhythm of mythical violence. The possible dawn of a new human epoch depends on a violence beyond law, one that breaks the cycle of law-making and law-preserving violence and finds a new order beyond myth. What this "divine" violence shows, according to Benjamin, is that revolutionary violence, "the highest manifestation of unalloyed violence by man,"[22] is indeed possible. The challenge is to see when this violence has actually taken place, because it is not strictly speaking "detectable" to the human eye and may have occurred without us knowing. We are only really able to see the different types of mythic violence. Divine revolutionary violence is beyond us. Yet, this violence, which has been twisted and distorted by being made into law, is everywhere still available, even if it is beyond our knowledge and understanding. It may appear in things as disparate as war, what Benjamin calls "true war," or it may appear as the orgiastic judgmentalism that the "multitude" directs at the criminal, a judgement that Benjamin, in a connection horrific to our post-Nazi consciousness, calls "divine." So, we return to the last enigmatic sentence of his essay, which reads: "Divine violence, which is the sign and seal but never the means of sacred execution, may be called sovereign violence."[23] Divine violence looms over our historical acts as their meaning, their "sign and seal," even though it does not literally intervene in history itself. God does not make history. We do, but only by referring our actions to God, not as a really existing deity but as the ultimate image of sovereignty. It is by referring what we do to divine violence that we glimpse the sovereign meaning of the pivotal historical event: revolution. We reach to a possible divinity in becoming the conduit of revolution. Sovereignty enters history through us, even as it remains beyond us, perhaps beyond our awareness. As in Bataille, sovereignty is more than us, even unlivable. It is the domain of the divine. Yet, we orient and direct ourselves toward it, and it works through us, as the meaning of what is possible for us, abolishing the pettiness of "mere life" and reaching toward something greater and undefined—true life. The distinction between mere life and true life in Benjamin is not the same as the distinction between *zoe* and *bios* that Agamben would like it to be. True life is the beyond of the human world toward which we orient ourselves. Divine violence may enter the world through our actions, but it does not settle into a standard political arrangement. The flash of revolution offers us the promise of a future free of limit, law, and authoritarian regimes, so it cannot become a regime itself. It is in the holes it opens in the conventional and repressive mythical arrangement that we can glimpse a freedom and a new world.

Derrida on Justice and Violence

As mentioned previously, Derrida's political thinking clusters around a set of doublenesses. One of the most important of these is law and justice. To show the importance of sovereignty to Derridean doubleness, it is important to start with Derrida's response to Benjamin's discussion of violence in his paper: "Force of Law: The Mystical Foundation of Authority." This reading will firstly allow us to demonstrate Derrida's cautious engagement with sovereignty, as revealed in his skeptical attitude toward Benjamin's enthusiasm for divine violence. Secondly, it will initiate a discussion about the political value of Derridean doubleness, one that will be investigated further in a later chapter's discussion of sovereignty and hospitality.

The accuracy of translating *Waltende* in the final words of the "Critique of Violence" as "sovereign" may be disputable. Derrida broaches this issue by generalizing the meaning of *Gewalt* in the title of Benjamin's essay. Usually translated as violence, Derrida reminds us that the meaning of the German word is not as simple as the English meaning, "violence," nor does it have its negative connotation. Gewalt "also signifies . . . legitimate power, authority, public force. . . . *Gewalt,* then is both violence and legitimate power."[24] The more general nature of the German word means that the meaning slips between chaotic destructiveness and formally instituted authority. It means that in Benjamin's and consequently Derrida's discussions, sovereignty is always at stake and always unstable. This is reinforced by the deconstruction Derrida later performs on the binary opposition between the violence that institutes the law and that which preserves it. Derrida argues that in every act of the enforcement of law, there is a re-iteration of the violence of law's founding moment. In other words, the meaning of the origin and logic of constituted authority, and thus sovereignty, is always at issue in the discussion.

Following from the title of his article "Force of Law," Derrida begins by arguing that the law is implicitly violent: "There is no law that does not imply *in itself, a priori, in the analytic structure of its concept,* the possibility of being 'enforced,' applied by force."[25] This violence can be traced to the very founding moment of the law, hence, Derrida's subtitle: the violence of the law as "the mystical foundation of authority." What does this mean? Derrida adapts a phrase from Pascal, derived in turn from Montaigne,[26] to capture the nonhistorical moment of the law's founding: "The operation that amounts to founding, inaugurating, justifying law, to *making law*, would consist of a *coup de force*, of a performative and therefore interpretative violence that in itself is neither just nor unjust and that no justice and no earlier and previously founding law, no preexisting foundation, could, by definition, guarantee or contradict or invalidate."[27] It is this abyssal groundlessness that Derrida chooses to call "mystical"[28] because of a "silence walled up in the founding act."[29] Derrida goes on: "Since the origin of authority, the founding or grounding . . . the positing of the law . . . cannot by definition rest on anything but themselves, they are themselves a violence without ground."[30] The origin of law is itself violent, but the crucial thing about this violence is that it is without any basis. There is no prior discourse of legality to which it can refer to justify itself. Nothing precedes it. When Pascal tosses around a series of possible justifications for the law—"the authority of the legislator, . . . the interest of the sovereign . . . present custom"[31]—the apparent randomness of the selection indicates less rival constitutional theories than the arbitrariness and obscurity of whatever it is law rests on for its justification. As we will see later with the name of God in Derrida's reading of Benjamin, these explanations are merely labels used to cover over what is impenetrable, unknowable, and unsignifiable: the thing beyond the law to which the law owes its value. It is this "violence without ground"[32] that Derrida chooses to call "the mystical foundation of authority."

What can be said about this abyss that founds the law in violence? It is always to be known as that which exceeds the law and beckons to it. Law belongs to the world of knowable and measurable practice. In the domain of the law, it is possible to draw on real information to perform meaningful and transparent operations. "Law is the element of calculation," Derrida writes.[33] Law has been founded in a particular moment, and it exists in the rational world of knowable conclusion. Yet, what lies beyond and before it as the thing that founded it is not itself calculable. Derrida identifies this incalculable thing as justice, which is always in excess of the stabilities and identities of the practical world. "It demands that one calculate with the incalculable."[34] Although it gives the law its foundation, justice is itself without foundation. Derrida's way of describing it refers to its mystical quality: "Justice would be the experience of what we are unable to experience. . . . Justice is an experience of the impossible."[35] The law may seem to occupy a world of knowable logic, but its calculations must take place in relation to that which exceeds it and allowed it to arise and which is itself not calculable. It requires that the calculations that take place in law must always have one eye to their own excess, the domain that cannot be calculated.

However, we must not make the mistake of thinking that justice is merely a reference point for law, a mild reminder of some larger moral or social principle that it should not forget. Justice is hyperbolic. It remains always in excess of the law, and not just marginally, but potentially infinitely. Justice "hyperbolically raises the stakes" and inspires a "sensitivity to a kind of essential disproportion that must inscribe excess and inadequation in itself."[36] Justice never rests. It always keeps going even beyond itself—never settling, never resolving, never being satisfied—even by formulations of what is just, which always in the end fall back on a kind of timid piety and dogmatism. Derrida puts it like this: justice "compels to denounce not only theoretical limits but also concrete injustices . . . in the good conscience that dogmatically stops before any inherited determination of justice."[37] Any fixed or dogmatic formulation of justice merely mimics the calculability of the law, when in Derrida's account, justice's primary function is to constantly question, challenge, and trouble even the most liberal and acceptable formulation of law. Justice is never satisfied. It is always open. Some quality of otherness keeps justice unfinished, unstable, and oriented outward and onward. This uncloseable openness on the other and insatiable impetus to self-questioning and self-overcoming allows Derrida to identify justice with deconstruction.[38] We will see later that the inextricable bond between deconstruction and justice is what allows Derrida to finally refuse what he considers Benjamin's lack of restraint in relation to divine violence.

Derrida refuses this kind of absolutism because his focus remains on the negotiation between law and justice as the way of making sense of political practice. On the one hand, an abandonment of justice's connection with law, about which Benjamin and, later, Agamben fantasize, risks exposure to a kind of messianic violence without limit.[39] On the other hand, a liberal fantasy of a stable and knowable justice is also impossible, misunderstanding the fundamentally abyssal nature of justice by trying to reduce it to some precise formulation. Justice for Derrida remains potentially terrifying. An overinvestment in justice, like an overinvestment in sovereignty, can lead to cruelty and destruction. An underawareness or underexposure to the dangerous nature of an ever-excessive justice risks dogmatism and institutionalized injustice. In Derrida, therefore, there must be both law that remains exposed to justice in all its irregularity and extremity and a justice that remains aware of the need to somehow deal with the regular world of calculation and decision. In this light, deconstruction becomes a kind of high-level pragmatism, aware of the ever-expanding horizons of critique, but not abandoned to the romance of the pure idea.

We can see this pragmatism in evidence in Derrida's account of decisionism, an issue he will return to later when reading Benjamin. The practical conundrum presented by the complex relationship between law and justice comes alive in the moment of decision. Derrida writes: "For a decision to be just and responsible, it must, in its proper moment, if there is one, be both regulated and without regulation, it must preserve the law and also destroy or suspend it enough to have to reinvent it in each case."[40] The decision must know the law and correlate with it, but it must also expose itself to the ungrounded founding of the law in the disruptiveness of justice. It must occupy the aporia between law and justice and, in typical deconstructive doubleness, be both calculable and incalculable at once. Derrida's rhetoric captures the way the decision troubles any drive to stability or identity in legal processes: "The test and ordeal of the undecidable, of which I have just said it must be gone through by any decision worthy of this name, is never past or passed, it is not a surmounted or sublated moment in the decision. The undecidable remains caught, lodged, as a ghost at least, but an essential ghost, in every decision, in every event of decision. Its ghostliness deconstructs from within all assurance of presence, all certainty or all criteriology assuring us of the justice of a decision, in the truth of the very event of a decision."[41] There is no refuge in either an absolute, uncontrolled, and fanatical justice or any simple resting in established and sanctioned legal processes. Justice is not just an enlarged form of liberal generosity, reminding us to always consider the other. Despite, even because of, the radical disproportion and clash between law and justice in Derrida's account, each decision must be a difficult and dangerous confrontation with what is finally uncertain. We will return to these key issues—the relationship between justice and deconstruction as negotiation and the perils of the decision—as we navigate Derrida's reading of Benjamin, to which we now turn.

"Force of Law" proceeds cautiously. Derrida acknowledges the openness of Benjamin's argument to the challenge violence proposes to the law and the political, while he remains unwilling to be seduced by its extravagance. Before approaching his close reading of Benjamin on political violence, Derrida announces his position: "I believe this uneasy, enigmatic, terribly equivocal text is haunted in advance . . . by the theme of radical destruction, extermination, total annihilation, and first of all the annihilation of the law, if not of justice."[42] Benjamin's project is heroic and radical for Derrida: "the graft of the language of Marxist revolution on that of messianic revolution, both of them announcing not only a new historical epoch, but also the beginning of a true history void of myth."[43] In the end, however, he will pull back from Benjamin, too conscious of the consequences of extreme political violence. At the end of his reading, he says: "This text . . . is still too Heideggerian, too messianico-Marxist or archeo-eschatological for me . . . if there were a lesson to be drawn, a unique lesson among all the singular lessons of murder, from even a single murder, from all the collective exterminations of history . . . the lesson that we could draw today—and if we can do so then we must—is that we must think, know, represent for ourselves, formalize, judge the possible complicity among all these discourses and the worst (here the 'final solution')."[44] Given Benjamin's fate, it is a big call to suggest he was complicit with the logic of the final solution. Yet, for our purely theoretical purposes, it is crucial to see how clearly Derrida marks his separation from Benjamin's enthusiasm for "radical destruction." Here, we see the path of Derrida's negotiation: on the one hand, not oblivious to the violence of the abyss and never attempting to disguise, hide, or wish it away by some thundering liberal pronouncement on peace and progress, but on the other hand, unwilling to be simply seduced by the charisma of political violence or by the revolutionary will to blow up everything.

The question Derrida proposes as he embarks on his close reading of Benjamin seems at first an odd one. It sidesteps all the high serious issues and terms that would seem to be most at stake—power, law, justice, and politics—to ask instead: "Who signs violence?"[45] What authority not only explains this violence but also puts its name to it, not only its name but also its signature? "Will one ever know it?" He answers straight away: "Is it not God, the wholly other? Is it not 'divine violence' that will always have come first?"[46] Then, he quotes the final words of Benjamin's essay: "Divine violence which is the sign and seal, but not the means of sacred execution, may be called sovereign."[47] So, it is clear to Derrida that what underwrites sovereign divine violence is God, but not God in and of himself, but the name or signature of God. Sovereignty is *named* as God even if it finds other indirect, perhaps human and historical, means to enact itself.

A relatively simple formulation belies what remains an impenetrable idea. How does Derrida develop this complex argument? Derrida works the rich seam in Benjamin "between the divine justice that *destroys law* and the mythic violence that *founds* it."[48] Benjamin's goal, as we have seen, is to produce a conception of justice that is not constrained by the universalism of law. Universality might be inscribed in law's appeal to justice, but "this universality is in contradiction to God himself, that is, with the one who decides the legitimacy of means and the justice of ends *over and above reason and even above destinal violence*."[49] God is in excess of the justice that provides law with its horizon and meaning. In his "irreducible singularity" and unquantifiable excess, God defies even the justice that might seem to be the ultimate in law and politics.[50] This singularity announces that the meaning of justice is not just to be found in the way it defines and orients the law. As we have seen, justice is not a simple entity, a stable resting point or fixed and knowable idea. It represents the absolute horizon of law, and thus, more than anything, it is the name given to the self-overcoming of law itself. It is that within the law which explains and guides it. Yet, this is not the end of the matter. Justice in its openness has a wilder meaning, a more potentially terrifying one, and the only way of characterizing this absolute terror is to use the name of God.

So what is this justice that is "no longer tied to the possibility of law"?[51] In the Greek construction of law, according to Derrida's reading of Benjamin, the gods' violence does not enforce a law that is already established and that it inherits, but it takes on a mythic form that founds the law. This violence takes the form of an obscure and inexplicable fate[52] that is not transparent to the human beings to whom it is applied, because it does not exist prior to its application. Fate is not completely destructive in that in the retribution it unleashes on Niobe, it leaves her alive so she can feel the impact of its might. It remains obscure and esoteric, not readily understood, and therefore a "privilege of kings."[53]

The violence of Yahweh, however, is different, "feature for feature . . . from all points of view [mythic violence's] opposite."[54] It destroys the law, instead of founding it. "[I]nstead of threatening, it strikes."[55] As we have seen previously, its key defining attribute is that it kills bloodlessly, whereas mythic violence spills blood. The significance of this is that blood is the emblem of the most basic, physical human life. This is not the true life of the spirit, which is the focus of divine violence. "Blood is the symbol of life Benjamin says, of life pure and simple, life as such"[56]: "In making blood flow, the mythological violence of law is exercised for its own sake against mere life, which it causes to bleed, while remaining precisely within the order of life of the living as such. In contrast, purely divine (Judaic) violence is exercised on all life but to the profit or for the sake of the living."[57] Physical life itself and what goes with it—"goods, life, law, the foundation of law"—are attacked by divine violence, but it does not attack that thing in the living, which is higher than life, "the soul of the living."[58] Divine violence then is committed not to the banal, inane preservation of life for its own sake. Benjamin disdains those who value any and all life as if it has intrinsic value and as if its preservation must be assured no matter what. Benjamin's interest is thus in a violence that is committed not to simple life but to "the most living of life, of the value of the life that is worth more than life (pure and simple . . .) but that is worth more than life, because it is life itself, insofar as life prefers itself. It is life beyond life, life against life, but always in life and for life."[59]

Again, taking a slightly unexpected route, coming at the most confronting aspects of Benjamin's argument indirectly, Derrida asks himself, what is the most "provocative paradox" of the essay? His answer is its announcement that it provides the only possible philosophy of history. What is at stake for Derrida here is the decision. Benjamin's approach to critique in the "Critique of Violence" allows for one "to decide and to cut in history and on the subject of history."[60] To Benjamin, this is the only approach "that permits, in respect to present time, the taking of a position, of a discriminating, deciding and decisive position."[61] Only divine violence makes decision possible. He connects undecidability with mythic violence, the violence that founds and preserves the law. To Derrida, this has two key implications. Firstly, divine violence is on the side of the historical. It offers the possibility of moving into a period of history beyond the mythical era. By sundering the link between politics and the state, divine violence opens a new era and a new relationship with justice.

The second implication of Benjamin's argument is the way in which it characterizes the mythic era: as one of undecidability. The mythic-state era operates according to a dialectic where the founding of the law must repress any alternative moment of founding, any "hostile counterviolences."[62] Here, the need to preserve the law by rejecting any alternatives to the present regime must by definition reconfirm and thus restage the founding of the law. This preserving of the law is thus a constant representation of the law's moment of founding. The state is locked in an automatic cycle where decision is already foreclosed because of the automatic way in which the founding of the law is repeated without opposition.

We have reached a point where the opposition underpropping Benjamin's text seems clear: that between "the decidability of divine, revolutionary, historical, anti-state, anti-juridical violence on one side and on the other the undecidability of the mythic violence of state law."[63] But, this is not the end of the matter for Derrida. Two bombs remain to go off as we head toward Benjamin's final sentences. He first cites Benjamin's reference to "revolutionary violence": "if, beyond law, violence sees its status insured as pure and immediate violence, then this will prove that revolutionary violence is possible. Then one would know, but this is a conditional clause, what this revolutionary violence is whose name is the purest manifestation of violence among men."[64] Derrida wants to know why Benjamin poses this statement in the conditional tense. His explanation is not that Benjamin is being tentative or speculative. It is that the decision revolutionary divine violence proposes is "not accessible to man."[65] It is decision reserved for what lies beyond the human in history, figured as divine, a logic that Derrida sees as "messianico-Marxist"[66] or as "the graft of the language of Marxist revolution on that of messianic revolution, both of them announcing not only a new historical epoch, but also the beginning of a true history void of myth."[67] Amid this impersonal force of history understood as a destiny only a God could understand, we have a kind of decision inaccessible to human subjectivity. History will decide or God will decide, not us: "This has to do with the essence of divine violence, of its power and of its justice. Divine violence is the most just, the most historic, the most revolutionary, the most decidable or the most deciding. Yet, as such, it does not lend itself to any human determination, to any knowledge or decidable 'certainty' on our part."[68] Derrida then extends the opposition between divine and mythic violence into an opposition between two types of decision. In the divine domain, decision does not rely on any kind of knowledge we would understand. It is a decision "without decidable knowledge."[69] In the case of mythic violence, we have an irreducible undecidability but in a domain where there is at least some certain knowledge, albeit "the certainty of the undecidable."[70] In this way, in Benjamin's model, "knowledge and action are always dissociated."[71]

It is here where, quietly but insistently, Derrida makes clear what lies behind his departure from Benjamin, his refusal to commit to—and even his distaste for—its violent enthusiasms. We recall that to Derrida what distinguishes law from justice is that in attempting to apply the law justly, a leap into undecidability is necessary. If we pretend that the law can be applied without interpretation, and thus without confronting uncertainty and openness, then what we are doing is mere mindless calculation. To Derrida, such straightforwardness is chimerical. To be just, the application of the law must always involve some exposure to the otherness that exceeds it and challenges it in its very foundation. For Benjamin, this logic would remain locked in the domain of mythic violence. This is not the case for Derrida, who characterizes the action of divine violence as that which "destroys the law, we could even venture to say, that deconstructs the law."[72] The exposure to justice is not simply the law reflecting back on its founding moment, in the way mythical violence consistently does in its attempt to exclude the counterviolences that threaten it. It is also an enactment of the rigor and risk of deconstruction. The phrase that hangs over Derrida's article and looms in the memory of its many divergent commentators is the proposition that "deconstruction is justice."[73] The exposure of the law to justice is its exposure to divine violence. Deconstruction always involves this risk. It is not the risk in Benjamin that Derrida resiles from. It is its absolutism. It is not its recognition of violence that troubles Derrida but rather its almost careless disregard for what violence actually means for the merely living. Deconstruction is not afraid of justice. To Derrida, it is always in every way oriented toward it. What it fears is the absolutism that lies behind dogma and that, thus, risks a complicity with the worst kind of violence, which is identified here with the Holocaust.

Deconstruction has to be open to real danger, but it must also remain provisional, hybrid, mixed, ambiguous, unresolved, and never absolute or dogmatic. When posing himself the question of what side of Benjamin's divide deconstruction might be on, Derrida writes: "If I do not answer questions that take this form, it is not only because I am not sure that such a thing as deconstruction, in the singular, exists or is possible. It is also because I believe that deconstructive discourses, as they present themselves in their irreducible plurality, participate in an impure, contaminating, negotiated, bastard and violent fashion in all these filiations . . . of decision and the undecidable."[74] Benjamin's account is overly enthusiastic and careless, but it is also too simple. The political complex that emerges from Derrida's deconstructive approach to Benjamin's distinction between mythic and divine violence is one in which complex and uncertain negotiations between different modes of politics are required. There can be no simple preference for divine over mythic violence but a painful navigation in each instance of the obscure way in which the two overlap, compete, interpenetrate, and contradict one another. Derrida does not choose revolutionary abandonment to a superhuman unfolding of time greater than human decision—whether it be Marx's or God's time—nor does he withdraw from the risk of political violence into a kind of willingly blind liberal insistence on a nonviolent politics. The law must be founded and enacted, but it must also be aware of and risk divine violence. It must engage this violence, even include it, but it cannot commit to it or believe in it. By the same token, justice must somehow come to earth and find a logic in which it can be made historically real. Deconstruction, resistant to the ideological seduction of simple, clear, and enduring preferences, is the way in which this complex can be worked through, once and once again, in the unfolding of historical events on a human scale but never in a way that brings things to an ultimate conclusion. For Derrida, we need a bastard not a pure, "legitimate" politics.

Derrida now turns to the second bomb Benjamin sets off in the final words of his essay. We recall Benjamin's final words, as Derrida quotes them: "divine violence, which is the sign and seal but never the means of sacred execution, can be called sovereign violence."[75] We are already familiar with the link between sovereignty and the divine, even the divine's prerogative for absolute violence. This absolute violence is the abyss within sovereignty, and the name that is given to it—its sign and seal—is the name of God. As Derrida writes: "God is the name of this pure violence—and just in essence: there is no other, there is none prior to it and before that it has to justify itself."[76] Sovereignty, hidden under the name of God, is "the sovereign and not an other,"[77] the otherless other, the other beyond which there is nothing more. This is because it is endless and offers to subsume everything that comes after it, which is always forever directed toward it, in other words, everything: "absolute privilege, infinite prerogative."[78]

There can be no politics without the clash between divine and mythic violences. One of these violences cannot be preferred to another, nor can either be wished away, by dogmatism, on the one hand, or the refusal to face politics' irreducible complexity and its stark risk of horror, on the other. The most resolutely liberal regimes can exercise a limitless violence, even in the name of freedom or human rights. There is no correctness in politics. It remains the messy, dangerous, and interminable exercise, not of power play directly but of the different denominations of violence in their inextricable relationship with one another: the violence of the regimes of knowable truth and law and the violence of the abyss of sovereignty, which sets the human over and above itself in its aspiration. In politics, there is no shutting off either the duty to make society work or to bring into the social the awareness of that thing that is greater than it, that provides justice and justification, even as it remains dangerous. In every politics, therefore, there needs to be both an institution of law and an articulation of justice. The usual way that this articulation has been made in history has been to find a name to give to sovereignty. We know what these names have been historically, in a range that runs from a sacred divinity (God) to a secular humanity (the people) and, as we have seen with Benjamin, on into "the future." Yet, there can be no forgetting that this name, no matter how necessary it may be, can be the pretext for horror as well as for order or liberation.

The Indulgence of Sovereignty: The Case of Gilles de Rais

There is no being that is not prey to what is in excess of it, even if that excess is only its own further self. Excess seduces by presenting itself as livable. It is this possibility of the livability of excess that Bataille identifies as the apotheosis of sovereignty. In the drive to an unstoppable unfolding of the excessive, the human glimpses the possibility of the sovereignty that is the fulfillment of its truth. Since the logic of excess always involves an interruption, a crossing, a change, or a cutting, excess always means violence. It is in violence that excess and thus the absolute freedom of true human sovereignty would seem to reside. The conclusion would seem to be, therefore, that human truth and freedom, real human sovereignty in fact, would only be available in a life of absolute license and thus in acting out absolute violence, in Benjamin's terms, a divine violence. We have already seen a note of caution from Bataille about this, when he argued that any adoption of sovereignty as an ethic—in fact, the adoption of any ethic whatsoever—involves submission and slavishness, the setting up of an ideal that automatically places a limit on freedom. In other words, a commitment to freedom reduces freedom and thus fails to live an absolutely rampant sovereignty. The living of sovereignty is thus not even theoretically possible. A life of commitment to violence is a moralization and, thus, not freedom at all, for Bataille.

Our discussion of sovereignty as divine violence has taken us further, however. Benjamin sees the enactment of divine sovereign violence in revolution, the moment when the political agent reached beyond the mundane "mythic" opposition of law-establishing and law-preserving violence, beyond the limitations of mere life to the higher order where life can be lived in a true way that honors the living properly. Derrida hesitates before this absolutism, because it licenses an apocalyptic, even orgiastic, violence. Instead, he proposes another politics, a "bastard politics," in which the openness to violence is acknowledged and even allowed to contaminate both thinking and action, but is not embraced. Violence is necessary, but it is not to be an object of enthusiasm. How does this hesitation meld with our discussion of sovereignty and the human relationship to it? If sovereignty is the most human of things, according to Bataille, why should we hesitate before its full expression? What then should our relationship to this truth of ourselves be?

We will now try to approach these questions by way of the case of Gilles de Rais. Gilles is seen by Bataille as exemplary of the attempt to live sovereignty by way of absolute violence and extravagance. This extravagance took the form of the squandering of a great fortune on self-indulgence and theatrical spectacle. It also took the form of an incontinent aggressiveness as a warrior both on the battlefield and in petty local political rivalries. But above all, it took the form of the cruel and gratuitous, sexualized murder of perhaps hundreds of children. As a feudal lord, Gilles lived sovereignly, as we will see, but the murders he committed exhibit the attempt to cross from human to divine sovereignty, from enacted political prerogative to incontestable transcendent freedom and absolute license. But for Gilles, there was to be no triumph and no exaltation. Despite the intense religiosity with which he interlaced his sadistic violence, there is for Gilles no becoming divine and no living as God. This endless grasping of the opportunities of ever greater excess does not lead to becoming absolute or to freedom but rather to unforgivable cruelty, chaotic degradation, and miserable failure. Religion offers a oneness with God that seems to extinguish the self in a blaze of absolute glory, but at every point, we are reminded divine sovereignty may be something we can imitate weakly, but it is not something we can actually have.

How do you locate Gilles de Rais (1404–1440)—military figurehead, national hero, serial child killer, archetype of Bluebeard—in any cultural, historical, political imaginary, or in any religious inscape that can make sense of what he was: warrior, homicidal maniac, and despicable fool? This is precisely what Bataille attempts in his essay "The Tragedy of Gilles de Rais," where Gilles finds his place as a remnant of the collapsing world of the feudal seigneur, a world he had outlived, which was increasingly subject to military reforms and complex ecclesiastical politics that limited seigneurial prerogative. Gilles' behavior and fate are tied up in the reconfiguration of a wealth and prestige he had inherited and that he chose to squander recklessly. He could do what he did because of the liberties and resources available to the medieval lord: the property, the wealth, the disposability of the plebeian masses ("the little beggars whose throats he cut were worth no more than the horses"[79]), the stunning irresistibility of the spectacle of aristocratic indulgence ("he gave way without measure to his need to astonish through magnificent fairytale expenditures"[80]). To Bataille, Gilles was a savage child, an animal: "Joined to the god of sovereignty by initiatory rites, the young warriors willingly distinguished themselves in particular by a bestial ferocity; they knew neither rules nor limits. In their ecstatic rage, they were taken for wild animals, for furious bears, for wolves."[81] The career of Gilles de Rais is caught up then in the rampant libertinage of feudal sovereignty, which Gilles risks sovereignly, without regard for the future, his property, lives, his social and political place, or eternal afterlife. It is in the unfolding of Bataille's account of sovereignty that his story makes sense in its abandonment of sense, its extravagance, and its determined, cruel, unnecessary, and pointless waste. Yet, Gilles' fate is also wrapped up in the meaning of Christianity or, for Bataille, religion more generally, a religion Gilles embraced by toying with necromancy and that governed his decisions, even when he was at his most insolent, and to which, in the end, as he approached his execution, he submitted. We cannot separate Gilles' uninhibited violence from his religiosity, however unconventional, desperate, or idiosyncratic it was. About this religion, Bataille says in a telling aside: "It may be that Christianity would not want a world from which violence was excluded."[82] Gilles' Christianity was a religion in which facing God meant seeking exultation in the limitless violence of divine power.

Religion then emerges as an instantiation of the nexus of violence, excess, and subjectivation that we call sovereignty. Here, we will try to situate Gilles de Rais in relation to the account of sovereignty we have developed previously to clarify the relationship between human sovereignty and violence and to show how the aspiration to divinity in sovereignty both triggers and limits the freedom to enact violence in a politics that takes sovereignty seriously. Sovereignty exposes us to the abyss as authority, an authority that offers us a violent and thus meaningful, commanding subjectivity that lures us on but that will never fully become ours. Then, through Gilles, I want to read Derrida's account of Abraham's near sacrifice of Isaac to see God as a figure of this violence that we cannot have. This provides the second instance, after his reading of Benjamin, of Derrida's recognition of sovereignty as a fundamental political impulse open on violence, but his insistence on the real and extreme danger we court by romanticizing it.

Gilles de Rais is a figure of both violent triumph and vile degradation: a warrior-general-hero who fought beside Joan of Arc, yet the most disgusting child killer. During his trial, the following is said to be the material of his confession:

> He took and had others take so many children that he could not determine with certitude the number whom he'd killed and caused to be killed, with whom he committed the vice and sin of sodomy; ... on which children sometimes he and sometimes some of his accomplices ... inflicted various types and manners of torment; sometimes they severed the head from the body with dirks, daggers, and knives, sometimes they struck them violently on the head with a cudgel or other blunt instruments, sometimes they suspended them with cords from a peg or small hook in his room, and strangled them; and when they were languishing, he committed the sodomitic vice on them in the aforesaid manner. Which children dead, he embraced them, and he gave way to contemplating those who had the most beautiful heads and members, and he had their bodies cruelly opened up and delighted at the sight of their internal organs; and very often, when the said children were dying, he sat on their bellies and delighted in watching them die thus and ... he laughed at them, after which he had the children burned and their cadavers turned to ashes.[83]

How many children did he kill in this way? Hundreds perhaps. So many "such that the exact number cannot be certified."[84] The Western fear of the monstrous lord in the forbidding castle into which little children disappear never to return is said to spring from the story of Gilles de Rais.

Gilles is a figure of "sovereign monstrosity"[85] to Bataille. Why? As we have seen in the outline of Bataille's account in chapter 2, traditional sovereignty is first identified as a phenomenon of social ascendancy: "He is not just any man in the world, but a noble ... the nobility of Gilles de Rais is the distinguishing mark of the monster."⁸⁶ The fact that Gilles did not act alone but enlisted a network of servants and lackeys to lure children into his hands showed that his crimes did not automatically repulse people, because they were, after all, simply "to do with a great lord and miserable children."⁸⁷ Nobles had, according to Bataille, "every chance to take almost unmerciful advantage of young serfs."⁸⁸

This social ascendancy not only allowed the spectacular self-indulgence of the nobility but also required it and was defined by it. The point of the feudal economy was to license the wasteful splendor of the aristocracy: "Men, on the whole, produce; they produce every kind of good. But in 15th-century society, these goods were destined for the privileged class, for those who among themselves can devour each other, but to whom the masses are subordinate. For the mass of men it is necessary to work so the privileged class can play, even if they also sometimes play at devouring themselves to their ruin."⁸⁹ That hundreds of children would be at the disposal of a noble lord, who chose to destroy them simply for his own pleasure, is not in contradiction with such a noble system in which unproductive squandering of food, goods, and lives makes sense. It is true that Gilles was tried and executed for these crimes, but he only came to the critical attention of authorities because of some ill-judged threatening political behavior in which he stormed a church to hold hostage the brother of a political rival. These offenses against political enemies in an act committed in a church building and therefore taken as blasphemy were what exposed him first to trial. That he could no longer get away with this style of political intimidation may perhaps also signify that his way of being was coming to an end. Even in the way some of his crimes are reported in the official documents of his case, it seems that the sadistic murder of hundreds of unprotected little peasant children is taken to be less outrageous than offenses committed against aristocratic political enemies and the church. Bataille wonders if he would have got away with the murders if he had not blundered so badly politically.

The social reality that allowed Gilles de Rais to commit his crimes exemplifies the ascendancy that Bataille identifies with "traditional sovereignty." Yet, it also conforms to the fuller account of sovereignty as the exposure of the human to violence, chaos, and meaninglessness and thus religiosity. Of Gilles' "nobility of an ardor respecting nothing," Bataille writes: "[i]n Gilles' eyes, mankind was no more than an element of voluptuous turmoil; this element was entirely at his sovereign disposal, having no other meaning than a possibility for more violent pleasure, and he did not stop losing himself in that pleasure."⁹⁰ This sovereign exposure to that which exceeds sense and meaning in a violent pleasure in killing makes Gilles' monstrosity sacred to Bataille, not because he sees it as in any way elevated or something to worship but because it is in the violent bringing of death into the world that the sacred becomes visible. Gilles is a religious figure to Bataille, and indeed he found religious ceremonies "intoxicating."⁹¹ Even his murders were wrapped up in a comical religious experimentation, a pathetic and gullible necromancy in which he was fooled by retainers into a hopeless conjuring of evil spirits. Bataille writes of Gilles: "He doubtless developed a superstitious image of himself, as if he were of another nature, a kind of supernatural being attended by God and by the Devil . . . he had a feeling of belonging to the sacred world."⁹² To Bataille, Gilles' career belongs then to Christianity, a religion that cannot live without sacred violence, a religion that "is even fundamentally the pressing demand for crime,"⁹³ because it only makes sense in providing the strength to endure violence: "Gilles de Rais' contradictions ultimately summarize the Christian situation, and we should not be astonished at the comedy of being devoted to the Devil, wanting to cut the throats of as many children as he could, yet expecting the salvation of his eternal soul."⁹⁴ Gilles is an archetypal figure of Bataillean sovereignty, therefore, of its social ascendancy; its exposure to violence, chaos, and meaninglessness; and its immersion in the cruelty of a limitless death as a way of encountering the sacred. Yet, even in his sovereignty, Gilles is not only despicable and repulsive but also gullible, foolish, and laughable. We should not be seduced by the charisma of sovereignty or by the enthusiasms of transgression more generally. These are not things simply to admire or to advocate in Bataille. To advocate the shattering of values is impossible without turning shattering into a value and thus repeating the servility it is supposed to overcome. Advocacy would also reduce sovereignty to a realizable historical project, something Bataille explicitly excludes in *The Accursed Share*, where he writes: "Sovereignty cannot be understood as a form history would realize."⁹⁵ Gilles may be sovereign in his abject freedom, yet he is not a hero. He is, even in his cruelty, a ridiculous figure, a warrior superannuated by the military reforms of Charles VIII, which made his kind useless. His arrest shows that his style of behavior was becoming anachronistic. He represents no ideal or hope. Even as sovereign in his orgiastic and sacred violence, he is a fool and a failure.

God is a killer, too, of course, and God's battles with evil cause many deaths. Gilles de Rais was not the one to first introduce death as the meaning of religious subjectivity, whether that subjectivity be the eternal life available to the redeemed fraction of humanity passing to the right hand of God or our impertinent indulgence in luxurious necromancies. Yet, killing is God's right, a right that doesn't belong to humanity, and that Gilles usurps. I now want to compare the case of Gilles de Rais with that of the patriarch Abraham, especially as read by Derrida in *The Gift of Death*. The case of Gilles de Rais exemplifies the ambiguities of the human in relation to the sovereignty that defines it and to which it aspires. As we have seen, the sovereign is an elusive and illusory figure who seems to incarnate human possibility. In transcending the practical obligations of the diurnal world of purpose and work, the sovereign is the asymptote of human aspiration, the license and measure of human subjectivity, the lodestone of human sociality in its very defiance of the obligations of the social, the hero of human life and freedom in its embrace of death and oppression. It is in his determination to act out this sovereignty that Gilles de Rais becomes so monstrous. Yet, the riddle of Gilles is that what makes him so effectively to incarnate the heroism of sovereignty also makes him a ridiculous failure. His assumption of sovereignty diminishes him, and so we do not exempt him from his culpability for despicable crimes. Why does his smashing of the limits of logic, accountability, and practical social survival, his self-elevation to sovereignty, and his human attempt to make sovereignty livable still make him so contemptible? It is these questions that the comparison with Abraham helps elucidate.

God directs Abraham to kill his son Isaac. Abraham sets out on the journey as instructed, without questioning God's will, even though it seems to contradict God's own pronouncement that it would be through Isaac that Abraham would bless all the generations of the world. There is more at stake here than mere obedience or even faith. God is a figure of Bataillean sovereignty, the superhuman figuration that models, causes, and guarantees subjectivity from a position outside of conventional reason and meaning. In obeying God's will, Abraham is plunged into an aporia. He must maintain his paternal love for Isaac while also submitting to the absoluteness of God's decision. For his obedience to God to matter, he must love Isaac as intensely as ever, while at the same time honor God by killing him. His commitment to the domestic, economic logic of familial obligation must persist even at the same time as he commits most strongly to God's requirement that this familial duty be sacrificed. The sacrifice would be trivial or meaningless otherwise. To conform to the ethical requirement to obey God, he must fully feel his ethical obligation to protect his son while being determined to kill him. Derrida writes: "The two duties must contradict one another, one must subordinate . . . the other. Abraham must assume absolute responsibility for sacrificing his son by sacrificing ethics, but for there to be a sacrifice, the ethical must retain all its value; the love for his son must remain intact, and the order of human duty must continue to insist on its rights."[96] Abraham must thus fully respect the ethics God requires he destroy to serve another ethic. Abraham must be completely treacherous to be completely faithful. This obligation requires of him a conformity to rule and a precarious decisionism, a rule that marks him out as typical, yet unique. His is a decision that must be taken not by anyone anywhere, but by him, and now. This contradiction installs in him a unique interiority that can be neither shared nor even readily articulated, in Kierkegaard's terms, a secrecy.

This secrecy is his conformity to God's insane, unmotivated alogic of the gift—in this case, the gift of death. The domestic logic of known and reciprocal responsibility is sundered by God's asymmetrical, unaccountable command to sacrifice Isaac, against all ethics, even against God's own previous pronouncements. Isaac is to be killed now before he can be the father of generations God has said he will be. In God's logic, he will become the father of peoples yet be killed as a child. The mundane logic of duty and order, or fatherly care and responsibility, is shattered by the very father, God, who would have seemed to command it. He takes away from Abraham the reward for his piety, virtue, loyalty, and patience: the son born to him late in life as a recompense for all he has witnessed and endured. Abraham must conform to the chaotic, aporetic logic of God's gift, by making in turn a gift to God that he cannot hope to understand or explain. Yet, the absolute irony is that God restores Isaac to him, ordering him at the very last moment to hold back from killing his son and offering a substitute in his stead. This is the double insanity of God's logic: not only must the obscure law of the gift overcome the economic logic of obligation and return that Abraham had been living in his piety but even by way of the aporia of the gift, Abraham will still be rewarded. Another economy emerges, an even more insane Godly economy in which not only must Abraham give up everything he holds most dear but one in which, in the end, he will be allowed to keep it. He both sacrifices and does not lose, in what Derrida calls "the sacrifice of sacrifice."[97] Yet, what has been at stake is not only ethics but also subjectivity. Abraham's commitment to God's self-contradictory will, his immersion in secrecy, invents his subjectivity by installing a version of Godness within him. Derrida writes of this process of folding inward that installs the secret world of conscience: "God is in me, he is the absolute 'me' or 'self,' he is that structure of invisible interiority that is called . . . subjectivity."[98] Abraham commits to this subjectivity, even though it is built on what Kierkegaard identified as absurdity. Derrida sees it as an aporia, "the chaos of the undecidable."

Human subjectivity only arises then as a version of God's subjectivity installed within. God is the absolute self, and by taking on his insane logic in the madness of the decision to sacrifice Isaac and thus sacrifice fatherly obligation, domestic love, to sacrifice everything, in fact, Abraham can act as a self acts, can become the aporia as event, the obscure secret thing in action. Yet, the relationship between God and Abraham is not symmetrical. Abraham may become like God but is not God. God commands then changes his command. Abraham obeys. He doesn't make the decision to kill or not to kill. Abraham's decision is whether to obey God or not, not whether to kill or not. God is the killer. It is God who scorns the logic of the domestic and familial; it is God who is indifferent to love. Abraham preserves his commitment to all these things. His only decision is whether to subordinate them to something higher. God inhabits the world of rupture and violation. It is God who exposes Abraham to absolute risk, by bringing into the world a violence that Abraham is incapable of understanding, a violence constructed not on Abraham's terms but on God's and that smashes all the limits of the law. Abraham can make sense of the logic of obedience, but God violates obedience to the law by calling for an act of obedience to his own authority, which he then disrupts. God's ever-renewing violence is not itself comprehensible. It is limitless, self-contradicting, and beyond meaning. It signifies the absolute alienation of divinity in its terror from the logic of the human. God may install subjectivity within the human as a version of what he may be himself, but he always exceeds and confutes this subjectivity, going beyond it into a dizzying limitlessness. There is no end to the violence he can do to the human. This reminds us of what Derrida has said in "Force of Law": "God is the name of . . . pure violence."[99]

Abraham's subjectivity forms in relation to a divine violence that is not his. He cannot do anything other than enact God's violence, but from his point of view, the violence itself is not the issue. Or rather, it is not *his* issue. It is not his role to evaluate the violence, and he does not. His enactment of God's violence does not become his own violence, because what motivates him is not violence but obedience. He is not God. He does not kill the child. This is what distinguishes him from

Gilles de Rais. The right to kill the child does not belong to Abraham. It is God's right. Abraham only has the right to obey. His exposure to Godness elevates and enriches him in that it constructs within him the dynamic of the secret that is his subjectivity, but he does not become the pure violence that is God. His subjectivity depends not only on his being a version of Godness but also on how much he is not God. Gilles takes on the absolute violence of sovereignty but, in so doing, acts like he is sovereignty, that his power and violence are limitless. The absolute violence of sovereignty enlarges human subjectivity, but subjectivity does not lose its difference from that violence.

Human subjectivity becomes possible only in its orientation to that which exceeds and transgresses it, that calls it on toward what is larger, more disruptive, that violates human meaning and destroys what makes us secure. It is only in exposure to this danger that the subject can live the dynamic of self-overcoming that we call sovereignty. If the human loses the difference between itself and that which exceeds it, then it becomes its own excess. Yet, something cannot become its own excess without canceling excess out. Gilles takes absolute violence on himself and thus loses his difference from what constitutes his subjectivity by exceeding him. In short, he ceases to be a subject and becomes ridiculous. He shows that the attempt to live sovereignly will always end in failure. The more he gives himself over to savagery and cruelty, the more he shows himself to be a joke. Society rightfully condemns the Sadeian villain for his cruelty, but the logic of libertinage claims a certain freedom not from this condemnation but in it. Gilles demonstrates that even this claim of sovereign exceptionality is a pretense, a mimicry of a freedom that can only be lived in illusion and play acting.

We can now make sense of Bataille's statement about Christian violence. For all their posturing about love and peace, the religions of the book require the violence of God as the thing from which the human must separate itself. This violence arises as the absolute possibility of human failure, specifically the human failure to distinguish itself from violence, by making the mistake of thinking itself God. The Christian condemnation of violence as evil is not the pronouncement of the absolute separation of God's ethics from violence but the arrogation of violence to God himself. The worst evil a human subject could do is to lose the sense of distance between itself and the sovereign violence that God is. Then, the subjectivity that this violence makes possible becomes anchorless, free floating, and unruled. Only God has this right. The mistake of Gilles de Rais was not to imitate sovereignty but to act as if he had become sovereign. Thus, he became nothing. Abraham lives out a subjectivity in which he both is God (in the instantiation of his subjectivity) and not God (in that Godness moves within him without him actually becoming God). It is this aporetic Godly non-Godness that allows him to live on as loving father by withholding his hand. Gilles loses the difference between himself and his sovereignty. He forgets that even in acting sovereignly, he has not become sovereignty itself. Subjectivity sunders.

We are talking about the killing of children, perpetrated either by God or by a vacuous nonself, so we are not simply making a theological point or using violence as a metaphor. Suspended timelessly in the twilight world between fairy tale and nightmare, the terror of the children Gilles de Rais killed inhabits Western culture as the epitome of the unthinkable still widely thought. This unthinkable cannot be erased from our broader philosophical consciousness either. To Bataille, "God" was simply an attempt to literalize or personalize that larger phenomenon of the unreachable, undefinable, unlivable thing that oriented human subjectivity. Sovereignty is not merely the rhetorical abstraction of a religious consciousness. For Bataille, it is clearly the other way round. God is the name we use to protect ourselves from the sovereignty that is forever our horizon. This definition of sovereignty echoes in Derrida's account of the story of Abraham but also in his discussions of more political concepts, especially justice, democracy, and hospitality.

To Derrida, law is instituted in relation to a justice that is always larger than it. Law attempts to institute justice in the world and gains whatever authority it has by its evocation of justice and its perpetual attempt to enact it. Yet, the law will never be just enough. It will always be subject to reform, improvement, refinement and to being more effective, more far-reaching, and a purer enunciation and instantiation of justice. In this way, justice always requires more of law than it is capable of giving. It can always challenge, harry, or deconstruct the law. It thus always threatens, undermines, and violates it. The law arises only in this perpetual violation of itself in the name of pursuing justice. Law then must act out justice, but if it became justice, it would become only the violence that it does to itself. For law to identify with the absoluteness of justice, it would thus become pure violence, unaccountable, unlicensed, and massacring.

The same risk arises with democracy. To Derrida, democracy as an instituted political system is always oriented toward what he calls democracy-to-come, the horizon of ever-extending equity, freedom, and openness that gives democratic institutions their orientation, justification, and meaning. Democracy-to-come is not an ideal against which we measure our present arrangements, nor is it a goal that we can one day expect to realize. It is the impulse to reform and improve always and forever our democratic values and practices. We are open to the ever-expanding possibilities of democracy-to-come because it is itself openness. Yet, in its will to convert all, to saturate the human world and to remodel all societies, the orientation of democratic actors toward an infinite democracy-to-come threatens to become another unaccountable violence. A loss of the constituting aporia that puts democracy in relation to the democracy-to-come that gives it meaning but that it must not become, and that it must not mistake for something realizable, risks a violence that would persist beyond the world of the knowable and measurable.

How many children did Gilles de Rais kill? A hundred? Two hundred? A thousand? Nobody knows. His violence knew no limit because he mistook the sovereignty that gives rise to subjectivity for something that he could actually be. In this way, his violence knew no limit but he also became nothing. How many people has God killed? Or justice? Or democracy? Terrifyingly, these deaths matter to us less than the murders perpetrated by an individual killer. They have less weight because they were done in the name of things we still believe give us life and enlarge us, what Benjamin saw as the life above mere life. These gods kill in us. That a person, a nation, a culture, a "West" might think of itself as democracy means it bears its God into the desert of a limitless possibility of ever-extending violence whose primary function is to enrich a subjectivity by going beyond it in a promise to others that is never kept. That God would be the name of this abuse reveals not simply the religious logic of political enthusiasm but also the sovereign abyss that these eminently deconstructible terms (*God, religion, politics*) attempt to simultaneously articulate and conceal. The sovereign will to enlarge, extend, enlighten, and free both governs and threatens. This is the aporia of the transgression that endlessly suggests a violence we can neither approve nor do without. A bastard politics requires violence while distrusting it, reaching for a sovereignty necessary and elevating, yet still dangerous, that it must handle, even enact, but cautiously and skeptically.

CHAPTER FOUR

DERRIDA ON SOVEREIGNTY

Sovereignty is perched astride an abyss. The most explicit formulation of this is in Schmitt, where the sovereign decision is defined by its nothingness. It cannot be justified by its correctness either in terms of morality or justice nor even its practicality as a wise political outcome. The sovereign decision is right, not because it is better or smarter, but because it is sovereign. It is by definition unaccountable, but this unaccountability is not merely the freedom a leader requires to act resolutely and effectively. The sovereign decision remains sovereign and keeps its prerogative even if it is foolish and fails. Unaccountability is the very essence of the sovereign. The sovereign must be unconditional. Nothing precedes or predetermines it. Nothing anticipates or explains it. This anterior nothingness is its very logic and essence, known to us traditionally as divine violence.

In Bataille, this same abyssal logic appears in a different form. Here, the regular practices of daily human life involve the segmentation of the rampant energy of the cosmos into defined instances of a cut-and-dried, means-and-ends logic. These ephemeral discontinuities hide the true nature of cosmic order, which is undefined and continuous. Our schemes and practices are mere minor deductions from the infinitely large drive of cosmic continuity, where our truth lies. The fascination of our religions with death and sexuality represents the drive to return to this greater continuity where we feel a release into our truth. Continuity always exceeds our petty discontinuities, which even in their smallness and blindness remain oriented toward extravagance and abandonment. This abandonment always threatens to overrun and destroy these small workaday practices. The excessiveness of energy always surges within them, eventually overtaking them, transforming them into something else. Continuity, therefore, is not the enemy of the discontinuous, nor is it merely its antecedent source. Discontinuity is merely a segment of what remains continuous, a snapshot in a defined moment of time of what remains in motion, ever expanding toward what is irreducibly larger and further. The discontinuous always emerges with and as the operation of continuity. Through sex and death, the continuous opens the discontinuous onto a potentially absolute violence. So, as the discontinuous does the work of the continuous, it always bears within it the possibility of the opening of violence. Indeed, the discontinuous is always about to awaken violence in the process by which it forms, which is also the process that will transform it beyond itself into something else, infinitely. The discontinuous-continuous thus unfurls toward and through a violence that is always also a violence to itself.

Sovereignty is the investment human subjectivity has in the possibility of projecting itself into the unresting excess of the nothingness made visible in sex and death, with the ultimate horizon of becoming one with this nothingness. As we have seen in Bataille's account of Gilles de Rais, becoming one with nothingness is impossible and futile and leads to the very worst. The nothingness that represents the absolute dream of the human subject involves the unleashing of, even our identification with, a limitless violence. The orthodox way this violence can come into the world is by way of the figure of the living sovereign, but one who only appears to incarnate violence. The absolute violence of excess looms behind this historical figure who appears as our point of access to the absolute but can never become one with it. The absolute violence of sovereignty is the horizon of possibility of human subjectivity. We aspire to imitate it, but it appears in the world only by way of its mere human trace. It doesn't actually exist other than in the form of the human subjectivity oriented toward it. In this way, the individual human subject and the sovereign are always versions of one another, failing to replicate one another, while they also fail to represent the absolute excess and violence they aspire to bring into the world. As Derrida has remarked, God is the name of this absolute violence, hence, God's role as the centerpiece of the logic of sovereignty.

In sum, in Bataille, as the discontinuous emerges from the continuous, it both separates from and enacts the larger operation of the continuous. It is the continuous that provides the energy that the discontinuous embodies, but at the same time, the drive of this energy remains ever onward to exceed, even smash, the limits of any definition. So, discontinuity forms in fulfillment of and fueled by the very thing that contradicts and defies it. The discontinuous-continuous being bears in and through itself an irreducible doubleness, driving onward to rejoin that from which it has parted and not parted. In this doubleness, it carries a recollection of the absolute violence from which it has separated and which it identifies as the horizon both of sovereign selfhood and the meaning of the political exercise of social power more generally. Selfhood always emerges as a failed version of the figure mistaken as the embodiment of sovereignty in politics.

In Bataille, there is always something brutally literal about this complex of sovereignty, energy, representation, and violence. In Derrida, we see the same logic of violence as part of the inevitable event of emergence. As we have just seen, to Bataille, sovereignty becomes available to the human because it has the capacity to distinguish different orders of being: subjectivity, of which it partakes, and objectivity, which becomes the focus of its dominance. This subjectivity is enacted by the human being objectifying animals, which we "kill and eat." This way of seeing the emergence of the subject in relation to sovereignty can be compared to Heidegger's argument about the different ways that Dasein and the animal relate to the world. To Heidegger, what distinguishes Dasein from the animal is that the animal lacks the self-consciousness available to Dasein through a grasping of the world as such. In Bataille, sovereign dominance is enacted through the relationship between living beings, specifically through the process of objectification. In Heidegger, it is traced back to something much more fundamental: the emergence of beings in relation to Being in the unfolding of ontological difference. This chapter will show how Derrida reads Heidegger to investigate the irreducibly violent nature of the sovereign emergence that makes both subjectivity and sociality possible. However, where Heidegger wants to stabilize this around the logic of ontological difference, Derrida opens it on the inexhaustible and abyssal logic of *différance*.

Derrida is not an enthusiast for sovereignty but always acknowledges its centrality for our understandings of ipseity, subjectivity, and politics. He does not offer a definition of sovereignty according to what could or should be its correct operation. Instead, he reads sovereignty to understand its priority in the differantial formation of any identity. In so doing, he provides a complex account of the abyssal nature of sovereignty and sovereign violence in particular, one that expands on, channels, and accounts for sovereignty as it has been thought out in political philosophy. Derrida has discussed sovereignty in a number of texts, but the account that deals most explicitly with sovereignty in relation to the complex issue of emergence is in *The Beast and the Sovereign,* especially its second volume, where sovereignty is considered in relation to Heidegger's discussion of Walten. It is to this discussion that we now turn.

One of the defining attributes of sovereignty is its identification with indivisibility and autonomy. Derrida writes:

> If the beasts are not alone, a sovereign is always alone (that is both his absolute power and his vulnerability, or his infinite inconsistency). The sovereign is alone in so far as he is unique, indivisible and exceptional, he is the being of exception who, as Schmitt says . . . decides on the exception and has the exceptional right to suspend right, thus standing, in his own way, like the beasts or the werewolf, outside the law, above the law. The sovereign is alone in exercising sovereignty. Sovereignty cannot be shared, it is indivisible. The sovereign is alone (sovereign) or is not.[1]

Schmittian exceptionalism can only work because of the separation of the sovereign from others. This separation means that the sovereign is not accountable to any law, which he stands outside of or even precedes. He is like a wild beast in this way. His unaccountability is rooted in his solitude and his alienation from systems of law and reason. The sovereign rules in his own domain where law and reason do not apply. Only he can open this domain by suspending law. The sovereign does not only enact the empty space of the exception. He is that space.

We have seen how Bataille generalizes this abyssal quality to the point where sovereignty becomes the idea of living the abyss itself. This is a sovereignty not only before constituted political structures; it is before politics altogether and even before the versions of subjectivity, like individuality, that might be seen to require politics. Derrida's discussion of *Robinson Crusoe* identifies individuality as a prepolitical sovereignty, one where autonomous subjectivity commands its own domain.[2] Yet, Derrida is also interested in a sovereignty deeper than this, something itself also abyssal and impossible. To this extent, he is consistent with the trajectory of Bataille's account of the sovereign. Bataille persists as the deep background of Derridean thought, whether in his career-long adaptation of the language of the economic to the deconstructive project, a deep interest in the impossible, or acceptance of sovereignty as violent infinity. Yet, Derrida's ambition is to consider the contemporary political in terms of a set of doubles. We have already identified some of these: law and justice, absolute and conditional hospitality, instituted democracy, and democracy-to-come. These doubles represent Derrida's contribution to political thinking. The issue of sovereignty remains insistent in all of them, as we will see when we discuss hospitality. They are also descendants of the deconstruction of Heidegger's account of ontological difference, without which they would not have been thinkable. In other words, if we want to fully understand the relationship between sovereignty and Derridean doubleness, we must proceed via Heidegger. It is to a detailed reading of the term *Walten* that Derrida turns to make the sovereign quality in doubleness fully clear.

What Derrida derives from Heidegger is the logic of Walten as emergence. Sovereignty always refers back to the larger, anterior ur-thing that both generates and explains it, the abyss that has been mostly given the name of God. In Bataille, the brutal abyssal nature of sovereignty is laid bare, stripped of the name used to redeem it, and proposed as the potentially infinite violence of continuity. The discontinuous in Bataille emerges from the continuous that accompanies it, as the thing that both energizes and threatens it forever. The Derridean logic of doubleness captures the fundamental logic of deconstruction, the way in which identities and values are made possible by the originary process that also makes their stable self-identity impossible. In Walten, we see the logic of emergence that Derrida will develop to map the complex doublenesses that define the way he sees politics operating. Derrida's reading of Walten goes well beyond the mapping of emergence Heidegger provides and makes it almost indistinguishable from earlier accounts of différance. Walten thus is made to open on the Bataillean abyss. Derrida's account comes even closer to Bataille when he allows the deconstructive abyss to be loaded with violence. As we will see, this is an example of Derrida's equivocation around the issue of violence. From the start, however, différance and violence are often coterminous in Derrida, in an uneasy yet insistent relationship, one that is widely recognized by Derrida scholars but only reluctantly pursued. This uneasiness in relation to violence is not a flaw in discussion as much as a reflection of the necessarily unsettling and unsettled nature of violence itself, when properly, soberly addressed. Part of this disquiet, of course, results from ambivalence about the relationship between the violence of différance and sovereignty. If sovereignty is an identity, even the essence of self-identity, then it remains eminently deconstructible. But if it is also and always the name given to the irrepressibility of excess—something Derrida argues—then it must be seen as the always extant will to live excess, inerasable from our politics. Sovereignty is thus both something différance exceeds while holding out at the same time the chimerical possibility of living this excess, of living différance, in fact. This possibility may not be realizable or desirable, but it remains an orienting marker of politics and part of the affective charge or attraction of the deconstructive impulse itself. What our account of Walten will thus show is that the Derridean doublenesses we identify as the political in deconstruction always bear with them the trace of sovereignty because they use it to deconstruct, including to deconstruct sovereignty itself. In sum, instantiated sovereignty is deconstructed by the differantial sovereignty (misnamed as God) from which it gains its authority and likeness. Yet, sovereignty is not just one of a series of Derridean doublenesses. As we have seen in our previous discussion of justice and as we will see with hospitality, it is sovereignty that generalizes Derridean doubleness.

The logic of φύσις as Walten, as prevailing, is dealt with in Heidegger's *The Fundamental Concept of Metaphysics: World, Finitude, Solitude*. Heidegger here offers Walten as the most effective translation of φύσις, arguing that "prevailing" is a more accurate translation than the conventional "nature." Prevailing is not a property or attribute of the human but the possibility into which and through which the human can achieve itself. Heidegger writes:

> Φύσις means this whole prevailing that prevails through man himself, a prevailing that he does not have power over, but which precisely prevails through and around him—him, man, who has always already spoken out about this. Whatever he understands—however enigmatic and obscure it may be to him in its details—he understands it; it nears him, sustains and overwhelms him as that which is: φύσις, that which prevails, beings, beings as a whole. I emphasize once more that φύσις as beings as a whole is not meant in the modern, late sense of nature, as the conceptual counterpart to history, for example. Rather it is intended more originally than both of these concepts, in an originary meaning which, prior to nature and history, encompasses both, and even in a certain way includes divine beings.[3]

"That which is" is already a triumph, the achievement of an emergence, something that is not easy or straightforward. Emergence is an arrival at a state that is not necessary and that cannot be attained automatically or without effort. Woven into it is always a logic of power. φύσις is a field in which the human is threatened by overwhelming. It has no choice about this matter. The field of φύσις will never be less than dangerous. For the placid and ordered system of nature, Heidegger substitutes a contending field of forces. Every being is itself preceded by and opens onto the future possibility of violence. Derrida comments: "Physis is better translated, translated more clearly and closer to its originary sense, as Walten . . . as prevailing violence rather than as increase, growing, growth. And this better translation, closer to its original or the originary . . . in both cases concerns physis as totality of what is, and not, no longer, nature."[4] Physis is violence but not random violence. It is a violence that is the process of ordering itself. This violence makes more than it wrecks. It opens the possibility of the self-reliance of beings because nothing is larger than physis. Physis as the prevailing emergence of beings is not an expression or fulfillment of anything other than itself. It refers to itself, and its emergence is only on its own terms as itself. This is how Derrida puts it: "Physis is the Walten of everything, which depends, as Walten, only on itself, which forms itself sovereignly, as power, receiving its form and its image, its figure of domination, from itself. Walten as physis, physis as Walten is everything; physis and Walten are synonyms of everything, of everything that is, and that is, then, as originarily sovereign power."[5] The logic of sovereignty, therefore—self-referential, unconditional, without precedence, abyssal—is an extension of the nature of physis itself. It is achieved, not as a departure from or abandonment of physis but rather as its instantiation.

The key to understanding sovereignty is by way of a clearer understanding of physis then, and physis is Walten, but what is Walten? It is through Heidegger's attempt to identify the essential nature of Dasein's relationship to the world that the logic of Walten becomes clear. This explanation of Dasein's prevailing relies on the insight that what distinguishes the human from the animal is its ability to perceive the world as world. As Heidegger's well-known formulation goes: "The stone (material object) is world-less; the animal is poor in world; man is world-forming."[6] What does it mean to be *world-forming*? The human capacity for world formation rests on the human appreciation of the fact that the world is manifested. The human, therefore, is able to relate to the world as world, a capacity "withheld . . . from the animal."[7] The human relationship to this manifestness involves a recognition and appreciation, therefore, of its wholeness. Heidegger writes: "World is not the totality of beings, is not the accessibility of beings as such, not the manifestness of beings as such that lies at the basis of this accessibility—world is rather the manifestness of beings as such as a whole. . . . in however obscure a manner, world always has a characteristic wholeness."[8] Dasein experiences beings not simply as manifest but manifest in relation to a whole of which they are necessarily a part. This perception of the world as world pivots on the Heideggerian distinction between Being and beings. It is this distinction that is dramatized so intensely in the relation between Dasein and world. But what is the exact nature of this relationship, and how does it relate to the logic of prevailing, or Walten? We will now read closely the very final section of *The Fundamental Concept of Metaphysics* (section no. 76) to reveal this connection.

Heidegger identifies the distinction between Being and beings, not as structural or laid out systematically before us. The distinction is not topographical or taxonomic. It is not "at hand among things that are at hand," even though that might be how it is apprehended by "our ordinary understanding."[9] The distinction is not a state but an occurrence. As an occurrence, its meaning is not to be found in its stable nature but in terms of how it confronts Dasein. It is through analyzing the moments of this occurrence that we will begin to understand how this most fundamental and primordial thing unfolds. There are three of these moments: "holding ourselves toward something binding, completion and unveiling the being of beings."[10] These moments are to be recognized not as constituting elements of a thing or properties of a state or a structured situation but as what Heidegger describes as "directives for being transposed into Da-sein in an originary manner,"[11] the disposition toward opening in Dasein the possibility of an engagement that must be preliminary to all experience.

Heidegger then analyzes each of the three moments of the occurrence. The first is "holding ourselves toward something binding." He writes: "The binding character of things always already prevails throughout our comportment, to the extent that we comport ourselves toward beings and in such comportment also . . . conform to beings, without any compulsion, yet nonetheless binding ourselves but also unbinding ourselves and failing to conform."[12] Preliminary to any possible structured, organized, or principled arrangement of any kind, Dasein is in some undefined relationship with beings. Even this overstates it: a disposition toward the possibility of relationship holds Dasein, prior to any connection developing. This is a binding so virtual that it has not yet formed within itself the distinction between binding and nonbinding, which are as one here. We are in a state of potential binding before binding. Similarly, this pre- or proto-binding comes well before the establishment of any form of regulated or mandated structure, before any compulsion, to use Heidegger's term. It is through this complex web—before prebinding has separated into binding and nonbinding—and before necessity has entered the domain of representation and becomes a definable compulsion, that we can see the role of prevailing, or Walten, start to emerge. Binding holds us prior to all things, predetermining the fundamental nature of all the relationships that will subsequently arise as possibility opens into actuality. We find ourselves always already disposed to binding, and binding or the possibility of binding is thus always prevalent as the precondition of anything like a subject-object distinction and relationship ever arising. Heidegger writes: "We orient ourselves toward beings, and yet are never able to say what it is about beings that binds us, or what the possibility of such binding is grounded in on our part."[13] This binding, which is preliminary to the emergence of ourselves as any type of self we could recognize or denote, lies beyond any possibility of self-reflection or insight. We are prebound, and it is this prebinding, beyond and before any arrangement or any sense of Dasein as subjectivity, that allows us to see the incontestable logic, prior even to compulsion, that determines not so much the nature of our relationships but the very fact that we will have relationships. We are among beings, whatever the way in which our relationship with them eventually forms. It is this being among beings, being with beings that prevails always and that we cannot exempt ourselves from. As Heidegger puts it: "A binding character prevails throughout all being related to . . . all comportment toward beings."[14]

The second moment of comportment is "completion." As we have seen previously, the relationship of Dasein toward the world as such requires some awareness that each being is a part of a whole that must be thought. The thinking of a specific being is a thinking of beings as a whole and, thus, the world in its hypothetical totality. Our awareness of the fact that the beings we encounter belong to world as a totality is also an awareness of our open belonging to that world. Heidegger writes that even in the most mundane experience, "we become aware of comporting ourselves in each case from out of the 'as a whole.'"[15] As we hold ourselves toward something binding, we are aware that we are also orienting ourselves toward what is complete. Indeed, the prevailing of that to which we bind ourselves is "unitary,"[16] no matter the complexity of its nature and structure or any difficulty we might encounter in describing or knowing it. Completion prevails in the prevailing of binding: "However concerned we are to comport ourselves with respect to various issues and to speak in terms of individual things, we already move directly and in advance within a tacit appeal to this 'as a whole.'"[17]

So far, we have clarified two of the three moments of Dasein's emergence. The third—the unveiling of the being of beings—is not so straightforward. Heidegger identifies this as the unity of binding and completion. It is the relationship between Being and beings that gives the three moments of the occurrence their originary unity. How are we to characterize this unity? Heidegger proposes that it is *projection* that provides this unity—what he calls "the anticipatory regulating of human comportment."[18] The intrinsic nature of projection is anticipation, an orientation toward the opening of possibility in a hypothetically complete situation in which beings reveal themselves as instances of Being. It is this outward and onward orientation of Dasein that Heidegger hopes to capture in the term *projection*. In projection, there is always already a trace of completeness and thus of world: "World prevails in and for a letting-prevail that has the character of projecting."[19] Projection has a double nature. It both carries Dasein out of itself and gives rise to a self-reflexivity, a turning toward itself of Dasein. In Heidegger's terms, it both "carries who is projecting out and away from themselves" and, at the same time, what occurs is precisely a "turning toward themselves on the part of whoever is projecting."[20] Dasein pours itself forth into the world but not in a way where it loses itself there or that allows it to become simply another object. It ends neither with the loss of the self in the material world nor in a solipsistic withdrawal into pure interiority because it has the "character of raising away into the possible . . . in its possibly being made possible, namely into something possibly actual."[21] The character of projection is not one of a fixed or preexisting subject entering into a world that is already formed in its actuality, nor is it one of stable, ideal self-regard from which some world or worlds can be "constructed." It is not about finding oneself already fully formed in the domain of actuality or holding back purely in the domain of possibility. It is about becoming bound to the "making-possible," even becoming the site of that making-possible.[22] In a dense formulation, Heidegger explains the making-possible as a binding to "that which the possibly actual in the projected possibility demands of the possibility for itself in order to actualize itself."[23] The essential thing that Dasein is bound to, the exact moment into which its essential intrinsic nature is hooked, is the very thing that allows the possible to become actual, the pivot within possibility that opens it on actuality, the possibility of actuality within possibility itself.

Crucially, this means that we are not dealing here with an ever-expanding horizon of possibilities multiplying themselves endlessly. The opening within possibility of the possible event of becoming-actual means some restriction must arise. This is what requires projection to undergo both a binding and a fall under the sway of the logic of completeness and thus of world. Projection necessarily involves the sense of the possible entering into a limitation in which some sense of a complete and self-contained world is necessarily implied. Projection, therefore, is not the act of entering into or receiving the world, nor is it one of creating or imagining world. The fundamental orientation of Dasein in projection is opening. As Heidegger puts it: "The object of the projection is neither the possibility nor the actuality—the projection has no object at all, but is an opening for making-possible. In making-possible, the originary relatedness of possibility and actuality in general and as such, is revealed."[24] In revealing the point where the turn from possibility to actuality is possible, projection as the making-possible represents, then, the key point where the distinction between Being and beings is most intensely in play. Heidegger says of projection that it is "the irruption into this 'between' of the distinction."[25] It "unveils the being of beings."[26] Projection then allows beings to emerge only in their relation to an anterior Being and their implicit belonging in the world. We do not piece together a world, aggregating its individual elements into a whole. Instead, we only ever encounter those elements as manifestations of the whole: "What we previously pointed out as individual characteristics have now been unveiled as originally interwoven into the unity of the primordial structure of projection in a unitary manner. In projection, there occurs the letting-prevail of the being of beings in the whole of their possible binding character in each case. In projection, world prevails."[27] The consequence is that Dasein's world formation is not a construction of world from out of Dasein's own resources. Nor is it a simple reception of the world as it already is. Dasein goes out from itself toward world while not abandoning itself. It forms in world forming. It itself irrupts in the process of the irruption of Being in beings: "In projecting, something irrupts and erupts toward possibilities, thereby irrupting into what is actual as such, so as to experience itself as having irrupted as an actual being in the midst of what can now be manifest as beings."[28] This is what makes Dasein an historical creature to Heidegger. It is always in relation to what is present in terms of what is possible, to the present that will be the past of what is to come. It is in this way, in its historicity, a site of possibility and thus prone to astonishment at the world, even a feeling of being in awe or a state of terror.

Derrida's reading of Heidegger pivots on the meaning of Walten. In Heidegger, what distinguishes the human from the animal is Dasein's ability to appreciate the difference between Being and beings. The emergence of beings in relation to Being occurs as Walten or prevailing. Derrida says of the meaning of the term: "We were asking what this Walten (verb and noun) means, naming as it does at once the event, the origin, the power, the force, the potency, the source, the movement, the process, the meaning etc.—whatever one likes—of the ontological difference, the becoming-ontological-difference of the ontological difference, of the supervening of Being and the arrival of beings."[29] Walten is the name for the process by which emergence happens as the opening of the difference between Being and beings, which separate together in a paradoxical double event. Being makes the derivation of specific beings possible but is not a being itself; beings emerge only because Being has made them possible. They represent the only possible instantiation of Being but are not simply fractions of Being. Being enables beings because it is the very opening of possibility. Beings enact Being and are the only way it can possibly come into the world. In Derrida, Being itself is subject to différance, so Walten cannot be reduced to any kind of model. Derrida reads Walten differantially thus reinforcing earlier accounts that link différance with violence. Derrida sees the process of emergence in Heidegger as an event of force. Force is a necessary part of the emergence of ontological difference, because it always bears with it the anterior excessiveness of différance. This is what Walten means. Everything emerges as Walten, and Walten is violence, a violence Derrida goes on to resolutely identify with sovereignty. He writes: "The vocabulary of violence often imposes itself as an appropriate vocabulary to translate the same family of words in Walten, and these words ('domination' and 'potency' 'power') indeed seem to signify what is understood in general by sovereignty (superanus: that which is above, hierarchically transcendent; and which dominates by force, violence, power)."[30]

As we have seen, Derrida starts with Heidegger's recharacterization of physis as Walten. Beings emerge through a "prevailing violence," he writes.[31] The word *Walten* itself can never imply anything less than violence. "Walten," Derrida writes, "always the force of this same word, that bespeaks a force, a power, a dominance, even a sovereignty unlike any other."[32] In short, there is an irreducible sovereignty in Walten and thus in the emergence of beings in their difference from Being. Emergence always involves some assertion, a contestation if even just of the thing by itself. A hint of this logic is captured in the notion of prevailing. What prevails does not only emerge to pass on and disappear but also establishes itself, makes space for itself, and endures. In emerging in a field of beings, themselves emergent, it opens space for itself, as well as a trajectory forward in time, contesting what it is itself and what else it is with. It triumphs, both as itself and in its context.

Prevailing, therefore, is the process by which something becomes itself. Selfhood has to be achieved. It is not inevitable, but it is not simply the result of the thing's own work. It does not draw the resources of self-identity from itself in any simple way. Nor does it simply culminate in some fully constituted stable self-identical thing. In the end, what emerges has become itself. What is achieved is something that seems to refer only to itself and relies only on itself, "receiving its form and its image, its figure of domination, from itself."[33] But Walten is not simply the clearing of a space in which beings can fulfill their own nature. Beings do not simply become what they have always been destined to be, because of some preexisting, predetermined essence that is waiting to be expressed. Even though it may seem to end as a self-reliant thing, the emergence of the being itself is not an act of its own power but an event in and through the power of Walten, where the being emerges out of a force that precedes thingness itself, a nothing that forces. As Derrida puts it:

> Walten produces, bears, brings about, opens . . . the ontico-ontological difference and thus does not yet belong to either Being or beings. Not yet is not a chronological question about time or a logical question about order, but it designates a sort of predifference, or even an indifference to ontological difference, a preindifference that is nonetheless interested in difference and which prepares or precedes, outside the order of time and logical causality, the difference that is not yet—or that it is without yet being. If it were a force or a violence, it

would be nothing, but a nothing that is not nothing, a nothing that is not a thing, nor a being, nor Being, but which forces or efforces or enforces . . . the difference between Being and beings. The Walten resembles this neuter which is neither this nor that, neither positive nor negative, nor the dialectic, which neither is nor is not Being nor a being, but beyond or this side of Being and beings.[34]

Here, Derrida provides a strong reading of Heideggerean Walten in which it not only explains the unfolding of ontological difference but also denotes that which everywhere and forever precedes any difference. Walten is the possibility of difference before difference. Derrida here restages the deconstruction of ontological difference, but this time the thing that is a not-yet because there is not yet difference—what across the Derridean canon is called différance—is understood in terms of the language of force, not as violence itself but as always efforcing even enforcing. What this transposition, this move from the language of différance to the language of force, achieves is to insist on what is latent in Derrida, an acknowledgment of the recklessness of différance, and its necessary openness on a violence not just of disruption, but of overcoming.

Différance is in a complex relationship with sovereignty. It is that which "instigates the subversion of every kingdom."[35] It is also "the name we might give to the 'active,' moving discord of different forces, and of differences of forces, that Nietzsche sets up against the entire system of metaphysical grammar."[36] It is endlessly unsettling of structures and orthodoxies, but now this is to be understood as a form of prevailing, not simply as an endlessly productive dismantling of identities. By recasting différance in the language of Walten, Derrida corrects any drift that might want to see deconstruction as simply a messing with or mockery of self-identity. In the earlier article "Différance," the nondifference of identity and difference is described in Bataillean terms: "the *investiture* of a presence that is pure and without loss being confused with absolute loss, with death."[37] This investiture of beings by *différance* loads them irreducibly with a possibility that is never not open on violence: "a différance so violent that it can be interpellated neither as the epochality of Being nor as ontological difference."[38] The violence of différance can never be fully erased. It must be made to "appear/disappear."[39] Beings are both subject to and subjects of prevailing, because their bearing within them the trace of différance—the trace tout court—means they always both challenge and enact a violence that is so plural a difference of forces that it cannot be without the excess that must be lived sovereignly.

This is the most primordial possible characterization of sovereignty, not yet worldly sovereignty, but the sovereignty that makes that sovereignty possible, what opens it in the world. Sovereignty, according to Derrida's reading of Heidegger, is always latent in the very point where Being discloses itself in beings, because before difference, in the possibility of difference itself, is the forever and everywhere openness on an infinite and indefinite disruption, which can never not leave a trace in every being and from which every being receives its will to self-insistence. There is a vacant moment in which everything is latent and possible, what Heidegger understood as the opening of the possibility of the possible, as we have seen. In this moment, everything is possible, yet nothing has happened. Now, everything is ready and able to emerge as itself, in its own right. This sovereignty of emerging self-identity is what makes all other sovereignties possible. It is prior to all other forms of sovereignty—the sovereignty of states for example, even the sovereignty of God. Derrida writes: "This all-powerful sovereignty of Walten is neither solely political nor solely theological. It therefore exceeds and precedes the theologico-political."[40] He goes on: "This is not the sovereignty of God, it is not the sovereignty of a king or head of state, but a sovereignty more sovereign than all sovereignty."[41]

Sovereignty, then, is always already open, from before the beginning, even as the beginning. It is prior to the power of the state or the monarch, which can thus only mimic the absolute. Traditionally, in Bodin, for example, in a formulation that casts its light across the whole history of Western politics and philosophy, this power was seen to be the power of God, but Derrida here identifies a sovereign power prior to even the sovereignty of God, a sovereignty that emerges as the very possibility of thingness emerges. Only Bataille before him can produce as ambitious an understanding of sovereignty. In Bataille, sovereignty is the ultimate and essential meaning of the human, and its highest aspiration is the human longing to be most essentially itself, something impossible to achieve, and disastrous to aim for, as we have seen in our discussion of Gilles de Rais. In Bataille, this always means allowing the rampant energies of continuity their full freedom. Derrida extends the logic of Bataillean sovereignty by linking it with the emergence of ontological difference. Bataille had already treated sovereignty in relation to ontology via a discussion of possibility and impossibility, as we have seen in chapter 2. In Derrida, this logic is explained in relation to emergence. In Derrida's account, emergence, following Heidegger, is the opening of the possibility that something—everything in fact—might happen. This possibility of everything is the possibility of the possible and a "recourse to power, [a] discourse on possibility as power, on the becoming-power of a possibility."[42]

The pairing of law and justice is the classic example of Derridean doubleness. In their twin emergence in relation to the unsignifiable and abyssal, we can see how sovereignty is always at stake in the process of the formation of identities and values. It is this activation of sovereignty that makes Derridean doubleness always everywhere political. Indeed, the doublenesses that are most characteristic of Derridean discourse are all loaded with political meaning, increasingly explicitly, in doubles like absolute and conditional hospitality. Yet, even in the most apparently abstract doublenesses—essence and absence, inside and outside, for example—that were the main focus of early Derridean deconstruction, this trace of sovereignty was insistent. There is no more political discussion in Derrida than that around violence and writing in *Of Grammatology*. The consistent anxiety in the Derrida literature about the political meaning of deconstruction—is it or is it not political, and if so how, and if not, should we feel it is a failing?—is not the result of liberal neurosis but a sensitivity to the irreducible but always almost obscure political pressure in Derrida's work, itself an expression of the insistence of sovereignty, demanding, dangerous, potentially reactionary but also the potential horizon of new freedoms.

What comes before the sovereignty of the monarch? The sovereignty of God. What comes before the sovereignty of God? In Bodin's account, nothing can, and this notion survives right through to Schmitt, where the sovereign decision is seen as analogous to the divine miracle and cannot be explained or even represented. In Derrida's reading of Heidegger, as in Bataille, sovereignty comes even before God. It emerges in the most fundamental pre-event of all, when beings and Being emerge as the possibility of the possible. The emergence of ontological difference has a trace of sovereignty within it. God is a creature of this sovereignty not its origin or horizon. Everything emerges as power. Sovereignty precedes all things then as dominance. In Derrida's words, Heidegger's Walten "appeal[s] to a sovereignty of the last instance, to a superpower that decides everything in the first or the last instance, and in particular when it comes to the as such, the difference between Being and beings. . . . But which appeals to a sovereignty so sovereign that it exceeds the theological and political—and especially onto-theological—figures or determinations of sovereignty. Walten seems to be so sovereign, ultra-sovereign, in sum, that it would further be stripped of all the anthropological, theological and political, and thus ontic and onto-theological dimensions of sovereignty."[43]

Sovereignty is violence. This leads to an important paradox. One of the essential attributes of sovereignty, as we have seen, is its self-identity. The sovereign is one, which is what gives it status as a fixed point in a moving world, an absolute certainty that transcends the conditionality of all things. Yet, in our account of worldly sovereignty in chapter 1, we have seen that the human sovereign, at least, is always exceeded by a divine sovereignty, to which it refers and on which it depends. The human sovereign is both a version and an instrument of this divine sovereignty in the orthodox Christian account. Therefore, its authority depends on its referring to something greater than itself, which also is itself, since it can only claim authority because of the trace of divinity that inhabits it. We have seen in Derrida's account the insistence on a sovereignty that is even before divine sovereignty, that precedes and therefore subtends even the sovereignty of God. This is a sovereignty that emerges not only at the same time but also *as* the disclosure of Being in beings. This sovereignty is prior to everything, in Derrida's language, différance. Everything, even the absolute sovereignty of God, must defer to it.

Sovereignty, therefore, has a principle of excess inscribed within it. It is there in the logic of sovereignty from Bodin on and can be detected again in an account like Schmitt's in which the sovereign decision has a transcendent, unrepresentable, unaccountable logic that defies any human sense of responsibility or meaning. The abyssal nature of sovereignty means that the sovereign is always exercising a power before or beyond any logic of representability, or any logic whatsoever. Derrida writes: "But what does 'excess of sovereignty' mean, if sovereignty, in essence and by vocation, by its structure, signals and signifies itself primarily as excess itself, as normal abuse, surplus and transcendence beyond or compared with any determinable measure? Is there any possible excess of sovereignty or else is this hypothesis absurd? Absurd like sovereignty itself, which exceeds all responsibility of meaning, before meaning, before the law of language and meaning. Meaning and law are summoned to appear before the sovereign rather than the other way around."[44] We are not surprised to see sovereignty connected with the irrational. As Schmitt pointed out, in a theocentric universe, we must expect to submit ourselves to an authority we cannot understand or question that remains forever beyond us and unaccountable to us. We should not expect to understand or even know this sovereignty that no human reason or institution can check or even properly test. Part of the irrational logic of sovereignty is its absurd, paradoxical, self-identity: both full to the brim of itself and beyond itself at one and the same time. This is true of the fundamental sovereignty of Walten as much as of any account of sovereignty. Derrida translates Heidegger to say "'the 'more' is the essential character of Walten.'"[45]

If excess is a necessary part of the sovereign, and sovereignty is first manifest as the emergence of beings in the world, then the prevailing that is the first instantiation of beings must take the form of overwhelming. Walten must take the general form of dominance. The sovereignty of the emerging thing is the prevailing of "what is superlatively more violent, predominant in violence, [which] is the constitutive essential character of the dominance that is itself predominant potency."[46] Derrida goes on: "It is as if to be beings and Walten were the same thing, with this overdetermination of the 'over' precisely, this overbidding of the Über, of the extra, the excess of trans-potency, the pre-potency in the sense of the prevailing that wins out in a combat. If there is no longer any limit and if the whole of beings is, as Walten, das Überwältigende, one will not be surprised to find this Walten and this Überwältigende everywhere."[47] Prevailing is an endless restlessness, an infinite and thus indefinite opening. It is both always already here and yet to come. The Heideggerian world Derrida describes is a world of endless contestation, whether that contestation be of something with itself or with what lies beyond it. It is a world of domination and thus always potentially violent. Indeed, everything that is potential within it emerges as a violence. Dominance is always woven into all its events. This is why sovereignty is part of every event and everything from the very emergence of what becomes beings. There is no rejecting sovereignty. Politics then is sewn into the very texture of beingness. There is no emergence without overwhelming. There is nothing without violence, and violence is the medium of sovereignty.

Yet, there is no being in awe of this violence. We should not be willing soldiers in service of violence. There can be no simple enthusiasm for it, nor can we simply concede its precedence over every other kind of value. What prevails can be prevailed on, both by itself and what comes next or stands next to it. Everything that is established by violence is also disestablished by it. This follows the logic we have already seen in Bataille, where the drive of continuity generated discontinuous identities only to suck them back into its own rampant flow, before yet again transmuting them into some other momentary fixity. In Bataille, the sovereign was the possibility of incarnating this infinity of energy as a kind of totality.

Yet, because of the rampancy of energy, such a dominance is impossible and, as in the case of Gilles de Rais, poisonous and leading to the worst. Here, sovereignty is not an attempt to dominate the whole of the world of beings. It is the potential for dominance in every emergence and thus every possibility. Before God, before the king, before the state, before the individual, before all of its possible denominations, sovereignty emerges through the ontological difference of the double relationship between Being and beings, perpetually latent within them, part of their own salience in the world, in relation both to everything they are with and to themselves. We cannot resign from it, yet we cannot simply endorse it. In the end, because sovereignty is so dramatic in its contestation of itself, there is nothing to endorse. Sovereignty is violence, and it is nothing. There is no sovereignty in itself. It is not a thing that exists and then takes on a variety of forms. It is thingness in its emergence. Things cannot emerge any other way but as sovereign, and sovereignty's being in the world is always as thingness.

Sovereignty, then, is not embodied in things nor is it a property of things that they can deploy. Sovereignty is things. Their unsettling, jarring, clashing emergence allows sovereignty to become enacted, not in its will or with any particular aim but always violently. But for Dasein, the situation is richer: Dasein is not only traversed by violence. It can harness violence or at least design it. Like all beings, Dasein is exposed to violence, but crucially, it can grasp the relationship between Being and beings and thus inhabits violence to the point of self-awareness: "The violence that grips man is indeed that of the as such of beings that Dasein is and that he must take upon himself, in its Walten, as such."[48] Dasein therefore arrives at an ownership of violence: "Well, man also is deinon (unheimlich) inasmuch as, belonging in his essence to Being, he remains exposed . . . to this Überwältigende. He is thus doubly deinon . . . he is violent inasmuch as he is exposed to the violence of Walten, of beings, and in as much as he is in a position to exercise this violence himself, to do violence."[49] The human may feel ownership of violence, but it is illusory. Dasein uses violence, as if it is its property, yet Dasein receives this violence from the way beings emerge. The violence is not simply its servant or tool. This is what makes Dasein historical. Dasein is created by that which it controls. This contradiction means that the human exercises the force that always precedes and exceeds it: "For all of this concerns the historicality reserved to Dasein and to Being, denied to the animal and to the other forms of life. There is historicality of man (and not of the animal) only where the Gewalt of this Walten irrupts to make beings as such appear, in the middle of which man is gripped by violence."[50] Dasein is gripped by the violence that makes it what it is, but it also can feel ownership of violence. It is plunged into the untidiness of events that have always already overwhelmed it even as it tries to tame and direct them. Dasein acts, but only as it has received its possibility from what precedes it and only as it finds its orientation in its own subservience to that which it makes from that which grips it. It is free but not on its own terms. The autonomy of ipseity is thus indistinguishable from its emergence as an instrument of the violence that attends emergence. Dasein appears as a self-identity but one simultaneously projected outside of itself into a world it did not make: "a structural configuration . . . in which everything that can happen in the autos is indissociable from what happens in the world, through the prosthetization of an ipseity which at once divides that ipseity, dislocates it, and inscribes it outside itself in the world."[51] What distinguishes Dasein, therefore, is its ability to grasp things as belonging to world. It is able to understand the things that emerge before it are fragments or traces of a grand, perpetually self-synthesizing totality. They emerge as tokens in and of a world. Dasein's ability to understand this emergence means it can understand things as such. Things to Dasein are not simply obstacles or tools. They are not merely the blunt face of limits against which we smash or away from which we swerve, without comprehending more about them than their obstructiveness. Nor are they simply devices subordinated to our mean purposes. We are capable of grasping things in themselves as what they are. Because we grasp things in themselves in relation to world, we appreciate things in terms of how they emerge. To Heidegger, this emergence is a prevailing, a Walten, the assertion of the thing, of everything, in fact, into and across the world. Derrida emphasizes the rough clash that is an implicit part of this process: "It is through this violence that breaks open ground or path, captures, tames, that beings are discovered or revealed or unveiled, and appear as sea, as earth, as animal. . . . The als, the als-Struktur that distinguishes man from the animal is thus indeed what the violence of Walten makes possible. And one will not be surprised to recognize this same violence . . . in the violence of poetic saying . . . the project of thinking, the thinking project . . . the edifying image . . . and finally . . . the action that creates states."[52] This violent emerging means that a violence is implicitly involved in the emergence of all things. Self-sameness, then, implicitly involves a logic of potential domination. Possibility of self is always the possibility of power. Sovereignty thus becomes available as part of the forming of putatively self-identical things in themselves, as part of the world. Sovereignty is inalienable from our being because it always already exists in potential as part of our necessary—contestable, deconstructible, contingent, yet real—emergence as beings: "The violence that grips man is indeed that of the as such of beings that Dasein is and that he must take upon himself, in its Walten, as such."[53] The ways in which our societies organize themselves can only be arranged subsequent to and thus subject to a logic of violent sovereignty. Yet, because it is forever tangled up with the structure of emergence, this sovereignty is forever subject to volatility. It represents no fixed and stable point, even when everything is by necessity deployed only in relation to it. We will now look at how the logic of sovereignty oversees the specifics of Derrida's political thought, using hospitality as an example.

CHAPTER FIVE

SOVEREIGNTY AND HOSPITALITY

Justice deconstructs law; law enacts justice. You can't have one without the other. Sometimes, you can't even tell them apart. They are part of a single double act in which they refer to one another and try to make each other work. But they remain asymmetrical, incommensurable, and a perpetual challenge to one another. Law overreaches itself toward justice, thus forever outraging itself, in its aspiration to be better than itself. Justice needs law as the only way in which it can come into the world. They do violence to one another. When law is open to justice, it has its limits torn away, as it plunges into what is larger and more virtuous, but in so doing, it opens itself onto an infinity that will never allow it to rest. Justice itself, as the asymptote of law's aspiration to do right, can only enter the world by being straitjacketed or mutilated. The temptation, of course, is to seek refuge in one or the other side of this double monster: to believe either in the liberalism that can encode the just and right in stable formulations that are knowable and regular or in the open-ended hope of acting out the rage that will automatically usher in another world. It is the romantic recourse to either of these absolutes that "Force of Law" wrecks. The liberal idea of a stable law is forever challenged by the open-ended violence of its relationship to justice. The revolutionary idea of a life better than the life of the living shows itself to be careless of violence, a version of the human dream of taking on the violence of God, of risking a bottomless and infinite violence understood as both the path to freedom and a kind of ecstatic, exultant freedom in itself. After studying Derrida's warning against Benjamin's "too messianico-Marxist"[1] account of violence, we saw the same idea emerging from our reading of Bataille on Gilles de Rais, and Derrida on Abraham: the human must aspire toward the sovereignty that conditions all politics and even defines the horizons of what our politics could and should be, but the attempt to fully occupy or live that violence ends only in indifference to suffering, cruelty, and uninhibited killing.

Both law and justice are violent, therefore. Their violence can never be reduced to zero. To formulate law is both to do violence to justice by capturing and reducing it and to open on justice's violence. This double violence is part of any and every act that calls itself legal, but the violence that this complex evokes is sovereign violence. Violence is not the mechanism of sovereignty or its tool. Sovereignty is simply the meaning of violence: the infinite violence that we name God is the infinity of the drive to absolute limitlessness that we attempt to harness in our political structures. The constituted power that we call human sovereignty is the violent institution of this infinity. The law-justice complex partakes of sovereignty's doubleness, and sovereignty drives this complex, but sovereignty remains the larger term. As Derrida argues, we must negotiate our way through this morass by making decisions that hope to partake of the "lesser violence" but that can never reduce violence to zero. But what remains unavoidable is that in negotiating the law-justice complex, we are dealing with something much larger and more volatile. The law-justice complex is not about law and justice. It is a path by which we open ourselves on sovereign violence.

This chapter will deal with the same issue in relation to another key term in later Derrida: *hospitality*. What looms behind Derrida's discussion of hospitality is sovereignty. As we will see in two key examples, that of Lot and the Levite of Ephraim, what is at stake in the doubleness of absolute and conditional hospitality is not hospitality, which has attracted most attention (perhaps because the modern age has been an age of migrants, exiles, and refugees), but sovereignty. We have proposed earlier that the key political issues of our time are those that Derrida has most focused on: the possibility of justice after the demise of the political grand narratives of both liberalism and Marxism, whether democracy still has a future, and the movement of world populations, especially now that climate change will put further pressure on resources like water and arable land. The aim here is to show that these issues are not moral, theoretical, or administrative ones to be solved by correct thinking or good planning but are fundamentally political issues, questions in which sovereignty is in play.

In these examples, we see the dynamic of Walten at work historically. It is this dynamic we must understand if we are to deal with the political problems of our age.

Let us begin with a quick trip across the well-trodden ground of Derrida's distinction between absolute and conditional hospitality, between the Law and laws of hospitality. The distinction Derrida makes here can be compared to the one between justice and law. Absolute hospitality is infinite, unconditional, and forever open. Conditional hospitality, on the other hand, is limited, defined by local and conventional traditions of practice. Yet, what is crucial in this apparent opposition is the complex interrelationship between the two forms of hospitality. Let us see how Derrida himself describes them. On the one hand, we have the call of the absolute Law of hospitality "to say yes *to who or what turns up*, before any determination, before any anticipation, before any *identification*, whether or not it has to do with a foreigner, an immigrant, an invited guest, or any unexpected visitor, whether or not the new arrival is a citizen of another country, a human, animal or divine creature, a living or dead thing, male or female."[2] This is "*the* law of unlimited hospitality (to give the new arrival all of one's home and oneself, to give him or her one's own, our own, without asking a name, or compensation, or the fulfillment of even the smallest condition)."[3] This Law is above and beyond all the conventional practices of hospitality that may govern custom in any particular historical or social context. It "transgresses"[4] such laws in demanding that anyone who arrives be shown an "unconditional welcome,"[5] one in which they are not even required to identify themselves.

Meeting the demand of the absolute Law of hospitality is impossible and makes all situated practices of hospitality a kind of failure.[6] In other words, the Law of absolute, unconditional hospitality transgresses conventional practices of welcoming, but in turn, they transgress it. We saw with the relationship between law and justice that the two may be incommensurable, yet they are locked in a relationship where they each require the other. The situation with absolute and conditional hospitality is comparable.

Derrida writes: "Even while keeping itself above the laws of hospitality, *the* unconditional law of hospitality needs the laws, it requires them. This demand is constitutive. It wouldn't be effectively unconditional, the law, if it didn't *have to become* effective, concrete, determined, if that were not its being as having-to-be. It would risk being abstract, utopian, illusory, and so turning over into its opposite. In order to be what it is, *the* law thus needs the laws, which, however, deny it, or at any rate threaten it, sometimes corrupt or pervert it. And must always be able to do this."[7] The Law of hospitality is nothing if it's not enacted through specific practices of hospitality as governed by the protocols of specific cultures and situations. It would have no reality, otherwise, even though this process of historicization means that the Law will be challenged, reduced, or perverted.

On the other hand, the conventions or laws of hospitality only make sense if they are responsive to the Law of hospitality:

> Conditional laws would cease to be laws of hospitality if they were not guided, given inspiration, given aspiration, required, even, by the law of unconditional hospitality. These two regimes of law, of *the* law and the laws, are thus both contradictory, antinomian *and* inseparable. They both imply and exclude each other, simultaneously. They incorporate one another at the moment of excluding one another, they are dissociated at the moment of enveloping one another, *at the moment* (simultaneity without simultaneity, instant of impossible synchrony, moment without moment) when, exhibiting themselves to each other, one to the others, the others to the other, they show they are both more and less hospitable, hospitable and inhospitable, hospitable *inasmuch as* inhospitable.[8]

The relationship between the Law and laws of hospitality is both impossible and necessary. The two may be detected in one and the same act, but that doesn't mean they can be reduced to one another or finally reconciled. We do not have here a mere paradox where two incompatible things share the same space, yoked together uncomfortably. Two incommensurate and contradictory things find themselves combined into one without losing or even reducing the clash between them. Derrida's language tries to capture the absurdity of the situation here, especially the final phrase in which the two become hospitable only in so far as they are inhospitable, and vice versa. In the very attempt to fulfill the Law of hospitality, the laws find themselves departing from it. The more they fulfill the Law, the more they betray it. The more the Law guides the laws, the more it makes their operation impossible.

The temptation here of course is to moralize and see the Law of hospitality as the guiding principle for the laws that will always fail it, on the one hand, or the laws as the pragmatic operation of a Law that is wonderful but absurdly utopian, on the other hand. In this way, Derrida's account would provide some insight or guide or even exhortation for a world in which multiple, increasing, and callously resisted movements of at-risk people have become a charged political issue. The Law then would be something to aspire to as we reconsider our practices of hospitality, acknowledging that the Law will exceed and elude us. Yet, this attributes to the absolute Law of hospitality an innocence that it does not deserve, and it fails to understand the inevitably contaminated and compromised logic of Walten by which Derridean doublenesses emerge.

Before we use Derrida's distinction as a pretext for judgement, we should look at its broader context. What we find is that the issue in hospitality is not the most meaningful and defensible way of offering welcome in the world, but sovereignty and especially sovereignty in its relationship to violence, the limitless violence of God, in fact. As we progress through Derrida's account, we should notice that we are being warned. He repeatedly connects both the absolute Law of hospitality and the conventional laws to patriarchal power, not only in its sanctimonious caring but also its blunt, brutal forms. On the one hand, "it's the familial despot, the father, the spouse, and the boss, the master of the house who lays down the laws of hospitality."[9] On the other hand, as we will see, the absolute Law is also the reference point for a patriarchal prerogative that sees itself as incontestable. This comes out most clearly in the two examples that Derrida uses to round off the lecture of January 17, 1996, published as "Pas d'hospitalité." These are the stories of Lot from Genesis and the Levite of Ephraim from the book of Judges. After a discussion that seems to have perhaps cautiously celebrated the higher calling of the absolute Law of hospitality, Derrida slaps us in the face with these two stories of a brutal masculine violence entangled in the complex aporia of hospitality, a violence not only watched and allowed by God but actually endorsed by him, or even more, much more than that, a conduit of God's own infinite violence. Derrida asks: "Are we the heirs to this tradition of hospitality? Up to what point? Where should we place the invariant, if it is one, across the logic of these narratives? They testify without end in our memory."[10] And that's it. The discussion ends with this terrifying question. Is this violence ours? Is our kindness that violent? When we try and derive some "invariant" principle or even dynamic from the aporia of hospitality, what exactly are we risking? What are we exposing ourselves to? What are we exposing our guests to, since we tend to always think that Derrida addresses us not as homeless refugees or humble guests but always as hosts? So, we also have to ask what violence are we exposing our hosts to, in their generosity and humility or perhaps in their reluctant even embittered sense of obligation? My answer is we are exposing ourselves and others, even the other more generally, to the risks as well as the opportunities made possible by sovereign violence.

To understand what I mean here, let us look closely at Derrida's two examples, firstly, the story of Lot. Derrida starts with Lot's welcoming of the angels as they arrive in Sodom. Lot is sitting at the gate of the city and asks the angels to come and rest in his home. They say they can spend the night in the street, but Lot insists they be his guests. He feeds them, and before they go to bed, there is a clamor at the door. The men of Sodom have come to rape Lot's visitors: "Send them out to us so that we may abuse them."[11] Lot begs the men of Sodom to spare his guests and offers them his two virgin daughters instead. This ends the section Derrida cites.

How does Derrida read this story? He writes: "This is the moment when Lot seems to put the laws of hospitality above all, in particular the ethical obligations that link him to his relatives and family, first of all his daughters."[12] According to this interpretation, Lot offers his daughters to be raped by the men of Sodom to fulfill his obligation to the guests who have come to his house. He overcomes his role as protector of his family and household because of a higher commitment to the laws of hospitality. This allows us to see the aspiration within practices of hospitality toward absolute and unconditional hospitality. This is how the doubleness of hospitality works in Derrida. On the one hand, enacted practices of hospitality can never completely fulfill what the absolute Law of hospitality requires. They can only gesture toward it, trying to capture its higher demands in some deed. On the other hand, these fleeting, flawed offerings of hospitality are the only way that the absolute Law of hospitality can appear in the world. We have already seen other aspects of Lot's behavior that are consistent with Derrida's definition of absolute hospitality. He has invited the angels into his home after meeting them in the marketplace. He doesn't even ask them to identify themselves before he insists, against their inclination, that they come and rest in his home. Indeed, he seems to be in the marketplace simply to offer this hospitality. Derrida's point, then, would be to warn against becoming too rosy-eyed about hospitality. It comes at a cost, in this instance, one paid by the most vulnerable and powerless members of the household: Lot's unmarried daughters.

Yet, nothing in the story indicates that Lot has or feels any obligation to protect his daughters. There is no sense that he either regrets that he has to offer them up or that he should be condemned for it. The idea that there is some other obligation to protect them has to be read into the story as some transhistorical norm. There is nothing in the Biblical text to indicate he cannot treat his daughters as his own property to dispose of as he wishes, regardless of their happiness or well-being. To insist Lot feels or has this obligation introduces a level of naturalism into the story that it simply does not have. We have to remember it is a story in which angels blind men, God casts sulfur and fire on a city to destroy it for its immorality, and a woman is turned into a pillar of salt inexplicably for simply looking back at the destroyed cities. And the story of Lot ends with what looks like a misogynistic primal foundation myth in which his daughters seduce him to found a race of sons. This latter story could simply be a completely different foundational myth that has been incorporated into the text from somewhere else altogether, as some commentators have proposed. The same could possibly be said of the fate of Lot's wife, which seems to belong to a wholly other order of narrative. In short, this story seems an amalgam of texts from different places, in different genres, with no stable trajectory. It has been perhaps overlaid with a moralistic narrative that provides it with some coherence and moral purpose.

This narrative is not one of hospitality, however. It is a narrative about God's judgement and punishment, in short, about God's power. What provides the story with any coherence it might have is the issue of God's sovereignty and its deep and staggering violence. The story of Lot's hospitality takes place within the broader context of the covenant God is announcing between himself and Abraham and his descendants. Lot is Abraham's brother Haran's son (Gen. 11:27), and the whole narrative of Lot is subordinate to the story of Abraham. What happens to Lot merely serves to dramatize the intimacy developing between God and Abraham or to exhibit Abraham's strength, wisdom, consideration, and virtue. For example, when Abraham and Lot return from exile in Egypt, Abraham divides up the bounteous lands God has made available to them, so their flocks will not compete for feed: "Then Abram said to Lot: 'Let there be no strife between you and me, between your herdsmen and my herdsmen, for we are kinsmen. Is not the whole land before you? Separate yourself from me. If you take the left hand, then I will go to the right, or if you take the right hand, I will go to the left'" (13:8–9). Later, Abraham rescues Lot when he is held captive by the enemies of the Kings of Sodom and

Gomorrah (14:13–16). It is after this that the covenant between God and Abraham is enacted. His name is changed from Abram, meaning "exalted father," to Abraham, meaning "father of a multitude." It is this covenant, of course, that sets Abraham at the head of the three-part religion of the Book, giving him his unrivaled place as the most exalted patriarch in Judaism, Christianity, and Islam. It is the core founding moment of these three intertwined creeds: "I will make you exceedingly fruitful, and I will make you into nations, and kings will come from you. And I will establish my covenant between me and you, and your offspring after you throughout their generations, for an everlasting covenant, to be God to you and your offspring after you" (17:6–7). Male circumcision is announced as the sign of this covenant between God and his chosen people, and the birth of Isaac is foretold. It is in this context and to advance this theme of the covenant between God and Abraham and his descendants that the set of visitations take place that culminate in Lot's hosting the angels who bring destruction to Sodom.

The immediate prelude to Lot's hospitality to the angels is the visit by three figures to Abraham in Genesis 18. At the start of the chapter, it is the Lord who visits Abraham, and the subjectivity driving the dialogue is identified as God's, though it is sometimes represented as three men. The three speak as one, and as God, yet they remain three. This may be that the consciousness of God has been added later to a narrative of three figures visiting Abraham, so that the motif of three figures remains as a residue of a former story, now transformed into a narrative of God's dialogue with the patriarch. The alternative reading—that the figure is three-in-one—is not explained. If it is a prefiguring of the trinity, then it is an inarticulate one as no sense is made in the story of this threesome, and it is not continuous with the story of the visit to Lot in Sodom, where the visitors to Abraham are turning their attention when they leave. There are only two visitors in the Lot story, and they are angels.

The dialogue Abraham has with the visitors understood as the Lord does not touch on the issue of hospitality. Again, it is about the covenant between God and Abraham and his descendants. The centerpiece is the announcement to Sarai that she will be a mother before the Lord returns in a year's time, something she does not believe. As the three leave, God wonders if he should tell Abraham that he is about to destroy Sodom:

> Then the men set out from there, and they looked down toward Sodom. And Abraham went with them to set them

on their way. The Lord said "Shall I hide from Abraham what I am about to do, seeing that Abraham shall surely become a great and mighty nation, and all the nations of the earth shall be blessed in him? For I have chosen him, that he may command his children and his household after him to keep the way of the Lord by doing righteousness and justice, so that the Lord may bring to Abraham what he has promised him." Then the Lord said "Because the outcry against Sodom and Gomorrah is great and their sin is very grave, I will go down to see whether they have done altogether according to the outcry that has come to me. And if not, I will know." (Gen. 18:16–21)

The Lord is both first and third person and speaks of his own Law impersonally. What is at stake is the lesson Abraham and his line could learn from the example of Sodom. Again, what counts is the trust and intimacy developing between God and Abraham. The goal of that intimacy is to bind Abraham and the tribes he will father to God's Law, which will be entrusted to Abraham, which is why he should know about the example to be made of Sodom and Gomorrah.

But Abraham is not just to bow down to God's Law. He receives some indulgence from God, who is willing to listen to his plea for mercy: "Then Abraham drew near and said, 'Will you indeed sweep away the righteous with the wicked? Suppose there are fifty righteous within the city. Will you then sweep away the place and not spare it for the fifty righteous who are in it? Far be it from you to do such a thing, to put the righteous to death with the wicked, so that the righteous fare as the wicked! Far be that from you! Shall not the Judge of all the earth do what is just?'" (Gen. 18: 23–25). God tolerates Abraham's argument, though the patriarch is not finished, and they bargain down till God agrees not to destroy Sodom for the sake of ten righteous men. And there the encounter between Abraham and the three-man God breaks off, and the story of Lot's welcoming of the now only two angels begins.

The discontinuity between the stories despite the similarity of their themes and narrative trajectory seems to indicate some intertextual jarring: perhaps different stories are being hobbled together. Later, as we have mentioned, the story of Lot being plied with drink and seduced by his daughters to father a great race seems to be a completely different story about different people from a different source and even a completely different genre, in this case, a misogynistic founding narrative in which women are deceitful and the father of the nation passive and tricked. Yet, these stories have been put together, even though they cannot be perfectly assimilated to one another. They have been identified at some stage as involving some continuity at least of meaning, enough for us to be able to say that the story of Lot's hospitality occurs within the broader context of the covenant of Abraham and his kind with the Lord, a covenant whose purpose is to enact God's Law, in the context of God's caring reciprocation, where the chosen are both tested as examples of obedience to God and as beneficiaries of his mercy and indulgence. In other words, what is at stake here is the submission of the chosen to God's authority and the opening of a channel of meaningful understanding between God and the human. The story is about how God's sovereignty is manifest in the world. God does not spare Sodom and Gomorrah, despite the bargain with Abraham. This could be either because God does not find ten righteous men in the two cities, which would make the bargaining more or less redundant, illustrating nothing as it is not carried through or mentioned again, or it could be a further example of the failure to completely homogenize different intertexts, like the way God is going to, but doesn't seem to be one of the party, now reduced to two, who actually arrive in Sodom.

In Genesis 19, there is to be no mercy, and the discussion between the Lord and Abraham about sparing the cities has been forgotten. When the angels reach Sodom, Lot is at the gates of the city. It is unclear whether he is awaiting them or just sitting there. He seems to recognize who they are intuitively, and his enthusiasm for them to come and stay in his house lends itself to the reading that he knows who they are and understands the significance of their arrival. But there is no evidence for this in the text, and that would undermine one of the interesting aspects to this part of the story: he invites them into his house without asking them to identify themselves. Either he recognizes them, and we're supposed to understand this, or he is enacting Derrida's unconditional hospitality.

Before they go to bed, the men of Sodom surround the house (Gen. 19: 4–5) and demand the men be produced. Certainly, to Lot, the reason he seeks to protect his visitors (and offer up his daughters) is not because they are angels, but because they are guests in his house. This reinforces the reading of his original welcome as an instance of unconditional hospitality not because he recognizes who they are. When he does not give them what they want, the men of Sodom attack Lot. Their violence is no longer because of their lust for the angels (the daughters have been forgotten, and the men never respond to that offer). Now, the issue is that Lot is a foreigner in the town, who has turned himself into an arbiter of correct practice: "This fellow came to sojourn," the men say, "and he has become the judge! Now we will deal worse with you than with them" (19:9). The men of the town press hard at Lot, standing at the doorway, but the angels reach out and pull him back inside. They also strike the men of Sodom blind: "And they struck with blindness the men who were at the entrance of the house, both small and great, so that they wore themselves out groping for the door" (19:11). Maddened by unsatisfied lust and anger at the foreigner who presumes to become judge, the wicked men of Sodom continue to lash out viciously, even when they are struck blind.

The blinding of the men is merely the beginning of the angels' unleashing of retribution on the city. They ask Lot who is in the house that he wants to save: "For we are about to destroy this place, because the outcry against its people has become great before the Lord, and the Lord has sent us to destroy it" (Gen. 19:13). Lot's sons-in-law don't take this threat seriously, so remain behind, when Lot, at first hesitating, leads his wife and two daughters from the city. Once Lot and his party are clear of Sodom, God wreaks his punishment on the city, in another oddly phrased sentence implying the multiplicity of God: "Then the Lord rained on Sodom and Gomorrah sulfur and fire from the Lord out of heaven" (19:24). It is unclear whether the God referred to here is not the single, unified, self-identical God we have understood him to be, or alternatively, this sentence combines two versions of the narrative or two separate narratives. The outcome of the story, though, reinforces that the core of the narrative, its logic, and frame focuses on the broad issue of the covenant between Abraham and his family and God. Indeed, if a variety of stories have been put together to produce the text we know, the theme that would justify this is not hospitality but submission to God's authority. The morning after the destruction of the cities of the plain, Abraham looks out over the valley and sees how "the smoke of the land went up like the smoke of a furnace" (19:28). It is Abraham who provides the story with its coherence: "So it was that, when God destroyed the cities of the valley, God remembered Abraham and sent Lot out of the midst of the overthrown when he overthrew the cities in which Lot had lived" (19:29).

We cannot conclude whether Lot knows who the strangers are whom he welcomes into his house. Certainly, he protects them because they are his guests not because they are angels. He never mentions this. But framing these as alternatives is misguided. Even though he offers his powerless daughters to be raped, we are expected to see Lot as a righteous man simply because of his connection with Abraham and the fact that when Abraham asks God about saving the righteous in Sodom, we assume he means Lot. Hospitality is not an alternative issue to that of acknowledging and submitting to the will of the angels. Hospitality is important and exemplary here, but its meaning is not restricted to the ethic of hospitality itself. Hospitality is important here because it facilitates the enactment of God's power and will, firstly, in punishing Sodom for its sinfulness but, over and above that, in enacting the covenant with Abraham's line. The story is about putting into place God's plan for the world, one in which his infinite and unquestionable power enters into human history by way of Abraham's family. Hospitality is subordinate to this larger meaning, which overwhelms it in significance. The story of Lot then is a story of God's sovereign rule, exhibited in acts that are simultaneously acts of love and acts of extreme violence. As we have seen in Benjamin, behind the complexity of law is the issue of sovereignty. Here, behind hospitality, sovereignty looms as the larger issue and more fundamental meaning.

This same idea also emerges in the second example Derrida offers of the possible "invariant" logic of hospitality that we may or may not have inherited. This second instance comes from the final chapters of the book of Judges and involves the violence perpetrated on the wife of the Levite of Ephraim. The Levite married a woman from Bethlehem in Judah (Judg. 19:1). Her status is mostly translated as "concubine," though the implication of this word that her role is subordinate and sexual is misleading. The Hebrew word is *pilegesh*, which means more accurately a wife of secondary rank, though no other wife is ever mentioned.[13] Her relationship with the Levite somehow breaks down. Whether this is because one of them has been adulterous is unclear. She and the Levite may simply have disagreed, and she returns home to her father.

The Levite travels to "speak kindly to her" (Judg. 19:3) and has her return. No mention is made of her objecting to returning, and there is a substantial passage devoted to her father's insistent hospitality, refusing to allow his son-in-law to depart. They finally do depart, after extending their stay by two days. As sunset approaches, the Levite is reluctant to break their journey in Jerusalem, because it is a city of foreigners (19:12), and they push on to Gibeah, the city of Benjamin. They wait in the town square but are offered no hospitality until an old man, himself also from Ephraim, returns from the fields and invites them to his home.

As they feast, the men of the city beat on the door of the house and demand the Levite be produced, so they can "know him" (Judg. 19:22). The host refuses, and like Lot, offers his virgin daughter to them, as well as the man's wife: "Violate them and do with them what seems good to you, but against this man do not do this outrageous thing" (19:24). This is the only mention of the daughter, and when the men refuse this offer, the Levite forces his wife to go out to the men, "and they knew her and abused her all night until the morning" (19:25). In the morning, as the Levite arises to depart, he finds his wife "lying at the door of the house with her hands on the threshold" (19:27). He tells her to get up, but she does not respond, so he puts her on the donkey and returns home. Horrifying as the story already is, its final phase is even more confronting: "And when he entered his house, he took a knife, and taking hold of his concubine he divided her limb by limb, into twelve pieces, and sent her throughout all the territory of Israel. And all who saw it said 'Such a thing has never happened or been seen from the day that the people of Israel came up out of the land of Egypt until this day; consider it, take counsel, and speak'" (19:29–30). Derrida cites this passage, but he does not interpret or read it in any detailed way. Riding the wave of the horror it inevitably produces, it is here that, as we have seen previously, he asks whether this is exemplary of the tradition of hospitality we have inherited.

Derrida's question assumes the full impact of a naturalistic reading of the story, its undiminished sexual violence, and brutal, casual misogyny. The wife has some degree of autonomy: she leaves her husband and is obviously reluctant to go out to the men of Gibeah. Yet, her subjectivity is consistently erased. She never speaks, for one thing, and even worse, it is unclear when she dies, whether it is at the hands of the Benjaminites or whether her husband takes her home alive and even dismembers her alive! None of this is made clear.

What is certain is that what has happened is an abomination, for which the Benjaminites need to be punished, but it is unclear from the narrative exactly what the abomination is. Is it the rape? It can't be since that was the idea of the Levite and his host, one suggesting it, the other enacting it. Is it that it was excessive and causing death, or was it simply the men's original lusting after the Levite himself? This is not made clear in the first rendition of the narrative, though the Levite himself who is also weirdly silent for the first iteration of the story, soon retells it:

> And the people of Israel said "Tell us, how did this evil happen?" And the Levite, the husband of the woman who was murdered, answered and said: "I came to Gibeah that belongs to Benjamin, I and my concubine to spend the night. And the leaders of Gibeah rose against me and surrounded the house against me by night. They meant to kill me, and they violated my concubine and she is dead. So I took hold of my concubine and cut her in pieces and sent her throughout all the country of the inheritance of Israel, for they have committed abomination and outrage in Israel." (Judg. 20:3–6)

The response of the tribes of Israel is to demand that the perpetrators of this evil be produced "that we may put them to death, and purge evil from Israel" (Judg. 20:13). Yet, it remains unclear exactly what the evil is. The Levite produces a list of grievances in which the rape and death of his wife is only one aspect of the attack that is presented as primarily an attack on him. It is unclear to us now exactly what the sequence of events is. What is the significance of the mention of the daughter? When does the Levite's wife die? What is the meaning of the Levite's shocking gesture of sending his wife's dismembered body parts around the country? If the Levite and his host offer the one's daughter and the other's wife to be raped, what exactly would appall them? Yet, there is no doubt about the scale of the offense that's been committed. All the tribes of Israel are shocked and go to war to punish the Benjaminites: "All the men of Israel gathered against the city, united as one man" (20:11). God is clearly on their side, and after some setbacks, he promises the tribes of Israel that "I will give them into your hand" (20:28). In the end, they are victorious, and the Benjaminites are defeated but now by God himself: "And the Lord defeated Benjamin before Israel, and the people of Israel destroyed 25,100 men of Benjamin that day. All these were men who drew the sword. So the people of Benjamin saw that they were defeated" (20:35–36).

It is clear that it is God whose law has been transgressed by the men of Gibeah. It is God who punishes them through the tribes of Israel. But the story is not yet over. The people of Israel lament that one of the tribes of Israel has been cut off from the fellowship of the others. This situation is complicated because it turns out the other tribes have sworn that none of their daughters shall marry into the tribe of Benjamin. What then can be done to somehow revive the Benjaminites by finding women for them to marry? The solution is found in another tribe of

Israel, those from the camp of Jabesh-gilead, who had not joined in the battle. Apparently, an agreement had been made that any tribe that did not join in the war against the Benjaminites would be punished by being put to death. All of the people of Jabesh-gilead are killed, including "the little ones" (Judg. 21:10), except for four hundred virgins who are then given in marriage to the Benjaminites.

Such marriage seems to be the plan, but then another story intervenes, where the men of Benjamin are advised to lie in wait for the daughters of Shiloh who are going up to the feasts of the Lord there: "And they commanded the people of Benjamin saying, 'Go and lie in ambush in the vineyards and watch. If the daughters of Shiloh come out to dance in the dances, then come out of the vineyards and snatch each man his wife from the daughters of Shiloh, and go to the land of Benjamin'" (Judg. 21:20–21). There are two reasons why I have given this full account of the unfolding of the narrative of the Book of Judges. Firstly, it indicates that the story of the wife of the Levite of Ephraim, and what happens to her, is situated in a larger narrative whose meaning is obedience to God's law as enforced by the complex relations between the tribes of Israel. It is not merely a parable about hospitality. To a contemporary reader, if any lesson is to be learned from it, it is one about the callous piety of patriarchy, the silencing of women, and sexual violence. Yet, whatever is chosen as the focus of this narrow episode, and whatever is seen to be the transgression committed by the Benjaminites, the larger narrative is explicitly one about the Jewish people's relationship to the law of God, again whatever that may be.

The second reason is the nature of the book itself. The Book of Judges is a compilation of narratives about the political history of the Jewish people in the period from about 1250 to 1000 BCE. Contemporary scholarship now is inclined to see it as not the work of an individual author but a set of disparate stories probably later edited together by a single author.[14] The stories may or may not be in chronological sequence, and some don't seem to be related to the overall theme of the book. The story of Samson, for example, which runs through four complete chapters in the twenty-one chapter book and which is its most famous story, doesn't seem a story of obeisance to God or of the Jewish people, other than in the way it connects with the antipathy between the latter and the Philistines. It is clear that the text has a range of intertextual connections that make it impossible to see it as the simple unfolding of a straightforward naturalistic narrative. We have already seen that the concluding narrative about how the people of Israel find new wives for the Benjaminites has two versions jammed together without being properly assimilated to one another. The inexplicable introduction into the story of the Levite's host's daughter, who is never mentioned before or again, may also be the attempt to combine two versions of the story of the attack by the men of Gibeah. It may also be an attempt to highlight the connection between this story and the one of Lot and his daughters in Genesis 19 that we have already looked at. And there is another intertextual connection with the story that appears in 1 Samuel:

> Now behold, Saul was coming from the field behind the oxen. And Saul said, "What is wrong with the people, that they are weeping?" So they told him the news of the men of Jabesh. And the spirit of God rushed upon Saul and his anger was greatly kindled. He took a yoke of oxen and cut them in pieces and sent them throughout all the territory of Israel by the hand of the messengers, saying, "Whoever does not come out after Saul and Samuel, so shall it be done to his oxen!" Then the dread of the Lord fell upon the people, and they came out as one man. (1 Sam. 11:5–7)

As with so many of the stories we have seen, this one remains obscure. Like the story of Lot sleeping with his daughters, of Samson, or the two inconsistent stories of how new wives are found for the Benjaminites, this may be an ancient or local tale assimilated here into the larger story of the Jewish experience. How this story is connected to the earlier one about the Levite dismembering his wife is unclear. What is important to recognize is that a simple telling of an historical narrative is not what is at stake. A complex integration of a range of stories into a meaningful form has been the primary focus of whoever put this story together. The tales themselves are inconsistent, uneven, and not rigorously connected, but there is an insistent pattern of meaning making binding them together.

That meaning appears in the book's last words, which represent a kind of refrain for the narratives: "In those days there was no king in Israel. Everyone did what was right in his own eyes" (Judg. 21:25). Following is a fuller explanation of the logic of Judges:

> And the people of Israel did what was evil in the sight of the Lord and served the Baals. And they abandoned the Lord, the

God of their fathers, who had brought them out of the land of Egypt. They went after other Gods, from among the gods of the peoples who were around them, and bowed down to them. And they provoked the Lord to anger. They abandoned the Lord and served the Baals and the Ashtaroth. So the anger of the Lord was kindled against Israel, and he gave them over to plunderers, who plundered them. And he sold them into the hand of their surrounding enemies, so that they could no longer withstand their enemies. Whenever they marched out, the hand of the Lord was against them for harm, as the Lord had warned, and as the Lord had sworn to them. And they were in terrible distress.

Then the Lord raised up judges who saved them. Yet they did not listen to their judges, for they whored after other gods and bowed down to them. They soon turned aside from the way in which their fathers had walked, who had obeyed the commandments of the Lord, and they did not do so. Whenever the Lord raised up judges for them, the Lord was with the judge, and he saved them from the hand of their enemies all the days of the judge. For the Lord was moved to pity by their groaning because of those who afflicted and oppressed them. But whenever the judge died, they turned back and were more corrupt than their fathers, going after other gods, serving them and bowing down to them. (Judg. 2:11–19)

Judges narrates a series of episodes that follow this pattern. The people of Israel forget their proper Lord and flirt with the other Gods of the surrounding region. This wandering provokes God's anger, and he punishes them by allowing them to be conquered and plundered by their enemies. To save them from their suffering, however, God appoints a judge over them, who protects them. But when the judge dies, the people again forget their duty and wander again. And so the cycle repeats itself. The greater part of the book tells various stories according to this pattern. The story of the Levite of Ephraim and the subsequent battles followed by the double narrative of how new wives are found for the Benjaminites are all seen as a kind of appendix to the cycle of Judges stories. But the same logic remains. What we see here is a crisis of sovereign power, one that takes two forms: first, the power of God is challenged by persistent and incorrigible disobedience, but there is a second power at stake: human sovereign power. The problem of licentious behavior is seen as a result of the fact that Israel was without a king, and although judges were set up to provide some corrective leadership, they were not kings and could not provide the continuity and authority required.

We have seen how in Genesis 19, the story of Lot's hospitality is one episode in a larger set of interconnecting and interchallenging narratives whose overall purpose is to lay out the development of the covenant between God and Abraham and his descendants. The story of Lot is really a story of the display and meaning of God's sovereign power. We see here something very similar. What is at issue in the story of the Levite is an example of how some of the people of Israel break God's law and the attempt that is made by others to redeem the people by enacting God's punishment on the transgressors. Hospitality finds its meaning here, but it is swept up in a much larger issue: God's sovereign power and the absence of its human image, the king.

Derrida's reading connects the story with hospitality. This would mean that the crime of the Benjaminites has been their violation of the rules of hospitality. In that case, the violence perpetrated on them would be punishment for their failure to be hospitable themselves as well as their violent intent toward someone else's guest. The question Derrida is therefore asking us is, how do we connect with such a tradition of hospitality in which the obligations of hospitality are not only generous but also lethally enforced? The traditional reading emphasizing hospitality as an issue sees the sexual violence as evil because it is a failure of hospitality. This would be one of the aspects of the culture of hospitality here that we would find impossible to identify with because it treats extreme misogynistic violence not as something to be outraged by in itself but as a symptom of some other crime, the failure to be hospitable to a man! In the same way, the reference to the host's daughter would simply be a manifestation of a hospitality that we cannot accept, and the dismemberment of the wife would be a noble gesture in which the ethic of hospitality is displayed graphically, again something we can only find abhorrent. Derrida's strategy here is to complicate the possible idealistic reading of unconditional hospitality by showing the violence and potential horror of such a tradition, particularly in its patriarchal forms, and Derrida has consistently reminded us of the close association between hospitality and patriarchy.

Derrida is throwing down a challenge to us, therefore, in appending his own commentary to the traditional emphasis readers have placed on hospitality as the issue. This very emphasis in the tradition exhibits clearly the point Derrida is trying to make about the patriarchal quality of this story and of hospitality in general, both in the way the story itself unfolds and the emphases of its interpreters. Derrida interrogates this double tradition by first luring us to think of absolute and unconditional hospitality as something to aspire to, as the thing encouraging not only all hospitality but also potentially all generosity and, beyond that, all relationships to the other and then ruining our investment in this excessive hospitality by showing the violence and horror thoroughly entwined in its history in its dominant patriarchal form. But I want to argue beyond Derrida, that again when we read this story in its context, we have to see that the issue here is not hospitality but sovereignty. This is a point that needs to be made about Derrida's work in general: that behind its repeated logic of doubleness—where law is doubled by justice, democracy by democracy to come, and conditional by absolute hospitality—what looms is the larger formation of sovereignty, a deconstructed but still insistent sovereignty, necessary to us but always loaded with the possibility of a limitless violence. And this is a point to be made not only to Derrida scholars but also more broadly: in our attempts to formulate law, politics, and morality in our debates over justice, democracy, and openness, what is always at stake is sovereignty, in its compelling necessity and potentially limitless violence, a sovereignty that we must have but in which we risk everything, not only everything we have, but more frighteningly, everything other people may have, especially the powerless.

When we make decisions, it is sovereignty that is at stake, not morality or correct management. Yet, sovereignty is not the solution or goal but rather the problem of the political. It is what is at stake, rightly *and* wrongly. Following Bataille, we are not talking here of the sovereignty of nations, governments, and borders, but the sovereignty that is the emergence of being. What is understood as the sovereignty of nations and governments is a derived and artificial form. It is an attempt to distill from the wildness and aspiration of infinite sovereignty, an identity and system that can fix authority as a knowable thing. But this fixity is a fantasy. It claims the name of sovereignty because it is enacted by the decision, which is always perched astride the abyss of an infinity that is potentially infinitely violent. It is the deed undertaken in this uncertainty that makes the sovereign. Hospitality, therefore, is not driven by morality, and decisions about hospitality are not moral decisions. Before they are moral, they are acts of sovereignty. This means that their moral inflection can be either positive or negative or both, even when they may seem to be most generous. By extension, before it can fulfill any program or any ideology, the political is the enactment of the sovereign. This does not mean that it is contentless. We will see in the following section that this prior sovereignty means it is human will, freedom, and justice that will always be at stake in the sovereign decision but not necessarily as good things. Sovereignty is the problem that always predefines our political living, in all its promise and danger, and it is—and must always be recognized to be—implicit in all our political acts.

CHAPTER SIX

BASTARD POLITICS
Sovereignty and Violence

We can now bring together several strands of our argument to provide an integrated account of the relationship between sovereignty and violence. From a survey of canonical accounts of sovereignty, we identified how sovereignty in its specific, worldly, and historical versions always refers to a prior sovereignty and that this prior sovereignty is abyssal, in that it is a zone of instability and excess. This excess of sovereignty is open-ended and self-violating and therefore potentially infinitely violent. Our impulse traditionally is to try to give this abyss a name, and the most common way in which it has been named is as God. This means that in most traditional accounts, sovereignty is understood first and foremost as the authority of God, and all human instantiations of sovereignty are understood as versions of God's authority. However, God is merely the name we use to seal the abyss. We strive to pursue sovereignty, yet a radical commitment to sovereign violence, whether it be Benjamin's "messianico-Marxism" or that of a Gilles de Rais, risks, what Derrida calls "the worst," providing a new way of characterizing the nature of evil. From Derrida's reading of Heidegger, the self-violation of the sovereign is part of the logic of a differantial Walten by which beings emerge in relation to the deconstruction of Being. What makes sovereignty the specific and necessary way to understand excess, therefore, is that this trace of abyssal infinity emerges through the very logic of self-identity by which things form, albeit transitorily, thus making sovereignty inerasable.

In each of its instantiations, sovereignty draws on and repudiates violence. This violence is the extravagance of the wild excess that sovereignty understands as its own unaccountability and exceptionality. This extremism is the highest risk for sovereignty, as we have seen. More conventional real-world sovereignty represents a straitening and regimentation that are a constriction and violence as well. Sovereignty does not oscillate between these two as alternatives. They are not alternatives but rather a complex doubleness where one only arises in relation to the other. The sovereignty of wild excess and that of organized authority are not opposites or alternatives. They institute each other while also challenging each other. We have characterized this mesh of mutually reliant and internally clashing impulses "bastard" to capture their nature: their disproportion, provisionality, and necessary combination of legitimacy and illegitimacy. Sovereignty is a functioning yet writhing tangle of correct yet dangerous vectors, each enacting rightness, authority, and violence, sometimes despite themselves.

The best way to understand this dynamic of sovereignty is as "an economy of violence." This phrase comes from Derrida's early critique of the work of Emmanuel Levinas in the paper "Violence and Metaphysics." This paper canvasses many of the issues we've been discussing. Its focus is on Levinas's account of otherness, so issues of self-identity, otherness, and violence are all comprehensively dealt with. The goal of my reading of this paper will be to make sense of the term *economy of violence* as a way of understanding sovereignty. There is no sovereignty without violence, but we cannot approach violence willingly or enthusiastically. By the same token, we need to either embrace sovereignty or abandon the idea of critical democratic government altogether. How do we embrace sovereignty without succumbing to its potentially orgiastic and limitless violence? The answer lies in Derrida's account of a lesser violence in an economy of violence. What does that mean?

The outline of the economy of violence needs to be approached by way of Derrida's deconstruction of Levinas's philosophy of the other. Levinas attempts to develop an ethics that is prior to metaphysics and thus uncontaminated by the latter's drive to unity and totality. It is this totalizing impulse in metaphysics that suppresses difference and is thus inevitably violent, according to Levinas. An ethics that does not end in totalization but always allows for an otherness prior to it and beyond it would frustrate this drive to the total and thus resist violence. The problems with this argument from Derrida's point of view are firstly that it is not possible for Levinas's other to elude the logic of sameness that governs totalization, because the very terms on which otherness is defined—by language, primarily—mean always that otherness is understood on the same terms as the same. The other is, in short, the same as the same. The second problem is that it is not possible to be completely sure that the domain of the infinite—Levinas's alternative to the totality of the metaphysical—is not itself violent, or at least the condition by which violence becomes possible. In the end, ethics has to be seen to emerge in a domain where sameness and otherness cannot be disentangled from one another, or even clearly understood as separable identities, and their dual operation must take place in a complex domain of differential values, admittedly, but one from which violence can never be completely excluded, an economy of violence, in fact.

The situation with sovereignty, I will argue, is not merely analogous. The philosophy of sovereignty is a philosophy of otherness. Both sovereignty and otherness are grounded in a construction of God. Derrida quotes Levinas to say: "the Other resembles God."[1] Levinas's philosophy of otherness is an attempt to understand sovereignty without the sovereign. It tries to preserve the elevated meaningfulness of sovereignty, not only without naming it but also without the will-to-power, the authority, and thus, ostensibly, the violence that have so compromised it historically. Derrida respects this attempt on Levinas's part, and his later arguments about the inevitable openness of deconstructive justice on otherness both learn from its logic and are a tribute to its aspirations. Yet, as with Benjamin, Derrida is not seduced by the dream and recognizes both the inevitably compromised nature of otherness and the ubiquity of violence.

How does Derrida's argument unfold? Levinas argues that traditional philosophy—specifically in the form of phenomenology and ontology—are inhospitable to what is other. They control the other by constructing relationships of mediation that end by reducing the other to the logic of the same. The binary oppositions that this logic sets up—Does the relationship with the other end in identity or require some stable knowable bonding? Is it immediate or mediated?—trap the other in a way of thinking that will always subordinate and reduce it. The other is a threat to systematic thinking because it always surprises and challenges the ego, dislocating it by coming forward, in Levinas's phrase, as Derrida cites it, in a manner that is "'face to face without intermediary' and without 'communion.'"[2] This way of styling the relationship to the other frustrates and questions the traditional logos, which thrives on a logic of unification, systematization, and totalization. To Levinas, this makes phenomenology and ontology "philosophies of violence": "Through them, the entire philosophical tradition, in its meaning and at bottom, would make common cause with oppression and with the totalitarianism of the same."[3] The drive to situate and know the other by providing it with a place within the framework of systematic thought is implicitly violent to Levinas because it must abolish the other, destroy it in its otherness in fact, by fixing it as part of a larger formation or system. As Derrida puts it: "If the other could be possessed, seized and known, it would not be the other."[4]

Derrida summarizes it like this:

> What, then, is this encounter with the absolutely-other? Neither representation, nor limitation, nor conceptual relation to the same. The ego and the other do not permit themselves to be dominated or made into totalities by a concept of relationship. And first of all because the concept (material of language), which is always *given to the other*, cannot encompass the other, cannot include the other. The dative or vocative dimension which opens the original direction of language, cannot lend itself to inclusion in and modification by the accusative or attributive dimension of the object without violence.[5]

Language opens the address to the other, but it cannot shift from vocative to accusative or attributive without doing violence to the other. This shift from address to situating or defining the other always involves some mutilation or transformation of otherness, accomplished with such irreducible violence that the other loses its otherness, by having a relationship foisted on it that undermines the categories of the ego and the other.

If the system of metaphysical systematization is a totalizing one, the locus of otherness is the infinite, which defies the limits and parameters of the total. Derrida writes: "The absolute overflowing of ontology—as the totality and unity of the same: Being—by the other occurs as infinity because no totality can constrain it. The infinity irreducible to the representation of infinity, the infinity exceeding the ideation in which it is thought, thought of as more than I can think, as that which cannot be an object or a simple 'objective reality' of the idea—such is the pole of metaphysical transcendence."[6] It is important not to understate the outrage Levinas's thinking of the other seeks to visit on the philosophies of the same. It insists on the always excessive, outlandish, and illegal nature of the other, oriented always toward the "infinite" but that not even a thinking of infinity can accommodate. Any concept or representation of the infinite always risks falling back into the conceptualizing logic of metaphysics and thus of inflicting violence on the very otherness it is trying to theorize. It is toward this "pole," as Derrida calls it here, that Levinasian thought has to be oriented: "the entirety of Levinas's thought: the other is the other only if his alterity is absolutely irreducible, that is, infinitely irreducible; and the infinitely Other can only be Infinity."[7]

So, on the one hand for Levinas, we have the logic of totality, in which metaphysics deploys an ego that absorbs whatever is other to it into a rigid unity. The result is that the other's very otherness is abolished. In this way, the operation of totality is always violent. This system can be identified with the accusative and attributory, the positioning and denoting functions of language. On the other hand, we have the nondomain in which otherness persists, the domain of infinity, in which the other always eludes even the otherness we may try to ascribe to it. Infinity represents the perpetual disruption of totality, opening the always surprising and unassimilable face of the other in a way that will always shock and disrupt systematizing thought. Infinity emerges in language in the vocative case. Preserving its opening on the infinite, the other can be addressed but not positioned, known or described.

But what is the nature of this distinction between totality and infinity? Can these two be kept apart, and can the characterization of language here be sustained? I now want to look at how Derrida addresses these problems. It is here that the idea of the economy of violence emerges. To Derrida, the only way that it would be possible for Levinas to maintain such a strong conception of alterity, one where the other can fully resist any attempt at assimilation to the logic of the same, would be for him to disdain discourse itself. Even the terms *other* and *infinite* draw the other back into a domain of identification, a positioning that can never be reduced to zero. Indeed, disdaining discourse has been the traditional way that philosophy has coped with the alterity of God, by identifying for him a place, or nonplace, beyond language that is seen as human and limited: "The positive Infinity (God)—if these words are meaningful—cannot be infinitely Other. If one thinks, as Levinas does, that positive Infinity tolerates, or even requires, infinite alterity, then one must renounce all language, and first of all the words infinite and other. Infinity cannot be understood as Other except in the form of the in-finite. As soon as one attempts to think Infinity as a positive plenitude (one pole of Levinas's nonnegative transcendence), the other becomes unthinkable, impossible, unutterable."⁸ Even by ascribing it the name God, the infinitely other loses its otherness. Levinas is in a bind, therefore. The only way that he can really explain the other is by projecting it beyond discourse, though even then, it remains in discourse as the presence of an absence. Yet, the real problem for Levinas is that the primary significance of the other is the provocation it makes as it disrupts the world of the same. The Face is the primary instance of the other when it enters the world of the same and it must be addressed. Otherwise, it would have no ethical meaning. If the same was not disturbed or confronted by it, the other would be purely imaginary, orbiting outside of the possibility of meaning altogether. There must be a vocative case, therefore. The other must demand our address, and to at least that minimal extent, the other must have a place in discourse. It cannot be extradiscursive like the God of negative theology, a tendency Derrida has persistently presented as limited and nondeconstructive. As Derrida argues: "Levinas stands opposed to precisely this kind of philosophical discourse. But in this combat, he already has given up the best weapon: disdain of discourse. In effect, when confronted by the classical difficulties of language we are referring to, Levinas cannot provide himself with the classical resources against them."⁹

So, the question confronting Levinas is, how can we respect the alterity and infinity of the other while still finding a meaningful place within discourse to discuss it? This is the moment of the deconstruction of Levinas's logic: "If, as Levinas says, only discourse (and not intuitive contact) is righteous, and if, moreover, all discourse essentially retains within it space and the Same—does this not mean that discourse is originally violent?"¹⁰ If the other must remain within the domain of discourse, it must remain in thrall to the logic of the same. If the same can never be completely removed from discourse, then the implicit violence of the logic of the same, its drive to reduction and totality, must always at least touch the other. The other cannot be or be known outside of the purview of the same. It must always inhabit a field that is irreducibly violent, in this case the very field that gave it its possibility of opening the ethical. Thus "the philosophical logos, the only one in which peace may be declared, is inhabited by war. . . . The distinction between discourse and violence always will be an inaccessible horizon."¹¹ The domain that opens the possibility of otherness having any meaning is thus irreducibly violent. The only place where the other can announce peace is in the domain of war. Peace assumes and requires war. Ethics can only take place within a domain of violence it requires and assumes. Derrida writes: "Peace, like silence, is the strange vocation of a language called outside itself by itself. But since finite silence is also the medium of violence, language can only indefinitely tend toward justice by acknowledging and practicing the violence within it. Violence against violence. Economy of violence."[12] Silence, the withholding of language, is in itself an act of language and only makes sense in relation to it. If there was no pause in language, then there would be no silence. There would be no language either, since nothing could be distinguished from it. There would be no possibility of even conjecturing an outside to it. The situation with peace is entangled in the same logic. If language is an irreducibly violent domain, because it always appropriates the other, then it can only imagine what lies beyond it in a violent way. Peace can only be a version of violence, a counterviolence unquestionably, but a violence, nonetheless. We can only arrive at peace by a passage through violence. Peace is an enactment of violence.

Derrida characterizes this violence against itself as an "economy." He specifically distinguishes his use of the term *economy* from Levinas's. Levinas has discussed the economic in *Totality and Infinity* at some length. Derrida's is "an economy irreducible to what Levinas envisions in the word."[13] Later, in *Given Time*, the logic of economy will be elaborated to a point where it plays the role of the double to the gift in another canonical instance of Derridean doubleness. Here, however, it maintains its raw Bataillean inflection: the economy is the dynamic of fluid identities forming out of and against one another in an endless cycle of self-overcoming, clash, and interminable mutability. The counterviolence of war contradicts peace but forms only in relation to it and out of it, before itself transforming back into a remade war, that takes some other form somewhere else altogether. An economy in these terms thrives on its contradiction of what is both the same as it and the greatest threat and challenge to it, pressing ever onward to greater destruction, renewal, and expansion, both out of itself and in contradiction to itself. In this case, violence is ever shifting and creative, even as it remains dangerous and threatening.

An economy has no outside, so we have no choice but to enact violence, but we must find the *least* violence "in order to avoid the worst violence."[14] It is in this moment of discrimination that our unfolding of violence and self-unfolding in relation to violence become historical. Derrida goes on: "This vigilance is a violence chosen as the least violence by a philosophy which takes history, that is, finitude, seriously; a philosophy aware of itself as historical in each of its aspects (in a sense which tolerates neither finite totality, nor positive infinity), and aware of itself . . . as economy. But again, an economy which in being history, can be at home neither in the finite totality which Levinas calls the Same nor in the positive presence of the Infinite."[15] The choice between a ruthless philosophy of the same and an expansive openness to the other, between totality and infinity, is a false choice. Even to prioritize one over the other and thus construct an ethics—either a rigorously legalistic ethics built on metaphysical identity, on the one hand, or on the other, an open and self-questioning ethics alert to its own vulnerability to disruption by alterity—is to attempt to evade the complex historical situations within which we always find ourselves. The same and the other, totality and infinity, violence and nonviolence are always not only entangled with one another but also *loading, unloading, and re-loading* one another constantly with what both causes and threatens each and every possibility of identity. There is no space for clear-cut, resolute, or final choices. We always act out both sameness and otherness, the total and the infinite, violence and nonviolence, always both in contradiction to one another, in coordination with one another, and together. There is no purity. To revert to the phrasing from "Force of Law," our acts are always bastard acts, and we are always bastards. We have already seen this in relation to Derridean doublenesses, like the law-justice complex and the absolute and conditional laws of hospitality. Such doublenesses are also economies of violence.

The human world of discourse is only ever going to be a world contaminated with violence and with choices between violences, working with and against one another, whether these choices are made consciously or unconsciously in the automatism of historical or cultural predetermination. The only way for us to elude this complexity is to exempt ourselves from discourse altogether and enter the putatively prior and pure world outside of discourse. This world is not available to us except hypothetically or fantastically, but what is worse, the absolute commitment to an extradiscursive world would in its absolutism be a commitment to an absolute and limitless violence: "The philosopher (man) must speak and write within this war of light, a war in which he always already knows himself to be engaged; a war which he knows is inescapable, except by denying discourse, that is, by risking the worst violence."[16] We have seen in the case of Gilles de Rais that the attempt to make an absolute commitment—to inhabit, in fact—the limitless and absolute world of sovereign violence embraces "the worst violence," not only embraces it but invests in it, seduced by its orgiastic qualities, exulting in its sadism and charisma.

For Derrida, it is not a question of trying to transcend totality by projecting ourselves beyond the literalism and self-identity of the historical. The historical is always already this play of the interpenetrating—sometimes coordinated, sometimes identical, sometimes contradictory, usually some combination of all three—impulses toward both the total and the infinite. He writes:

> Within history which the philosopher cannot escape, because it is not history in the sense given to it by Levinas (totality), but is the history of the departures from totality, history as the very movement of transcendence, of the excess over the totality without which no totality would appear as such. History is not the totality transcended by eschatology, metaphysics, or speech. It is transcendence itself. If speech is a movement of metaphysical transcendence, it is history, and not beyond history. It is difficult to think the origin of history in a perfectly finite totality (the Same), as well as, moreover, in a perfectly positive infinity. If, in this sense, the movement of metaphysical transcendence is history, it is still violent, for—and this is the legitimate truism from which Levinas always draws inspiration—history is violence. Metaphysics is economy: violence against violence, light against light: philosophy (in general).[17]

The economy of violence is therefore the interplay of the combined impulses toward totality and infinity in their rich shared work. In every act, political or not, we negotiate this complex, willingly or not, consciously or not, never in any particular instance reducing either impulse to zero.

There is no simple outside or beyond to an economy, and whatever gets recognized as transcendence is within rather than beyond any arrangement. Thus, to Derrida, the other can never be outside of the logic of the same but must itself be an ego. It cannot be other if it is not at some level at least potentially a version of the same. Absolute otherness cannot subsist on its own terms outside of the logic of the same. It must tear at the logic of the same from within that logic. It is never pure and absolutely other in itself. In this way, it cannot transcend; nor can it ever leave the same untroubled. The two interpenetrate and challenge one another. They can never leave each other alone. Without such a tension, both sameness and otherness would be meaningless. Derrida writes:

The other as alter ego signifies the other as other, irreducible to my ego, precisely because it is an ego, because it has the form of the ego. The egoity of the other permits him to say "ego" as I do; and this is why he is Other, and not a stone, or a being without speech in my real economy. This is why, if you will, he is face, can speak to me, understand me, and eventually command me.

Dissymmetry itself would be impossible without this symmetry, which is not of the world, and which, having no real aspect, imposes no limit upon alterity and dissymmetry—makes them possible, on the contrary. This dissymmetry is an economy in a new sense; a sense which would probably be intolerable to Levinas. . . . The movement of transcendence toward the other, as invoked by Levinas, would have no meaning if it did not bear within it, as one of its essential meanings, that in my ipseity I know myself to be other for the other.[18]

The other can only be other because it is the same as the same, which is itself a version of otherness. By extension, the absolutely pure violence of the sovereign God can never exist on its own. It can thus never be purely, absolutely, or resolutely sovereign in the way imagined by the orthodox definition. It cannot leave the human world alone, either. Every human event is in a process of becoming-sovereign while alienating itself from absolute sovereignty, either by repudiating its violence or imagining its violence as the property of a superhuman beyond. Derrida writes of these alternatives: "The expression 'infinitely other' or 'absolutely other' cannot be stated and thought simultaneously; that the other cannot be absolutely exterior to the same without ceasing to be other; and that, consequently, the same is not a totality closed in upon itself, an identity playing with itself, having only the appearance of alterity, in what Levinas calls economy, work, and history. How could there be a 'play of the Same' if alterity itself was not already in the Same, with a meaning of inclusion doubtless betrayed by the word in?"[19] The other would not be other if it floated out on its own, separate from the language and logic in which the term, and thus the whole thinking, of the "other" becomes possible. Constructed as an outside, it cannot be completely outside. We have already questioned the idea of a world and a practice that sees itself as absolutely other. It is both impossible and doomed. It also exposes the world to a limitless violence. Yet, the converse is also true. There is no hither world from which the other in all its exaltation and danger would be absent. The same cannot be the same without the other. The opening of the other—the reaching toward sovereignty—can never be reduced to zero. If it could, the same would fold in on itself and disappear.

The economy of violence is not purely chaotic, however. Derrida now draws together the strands of his argument to outline exactly its prevailing tendencies. For Derrida, Levinas's other is impossible. Without bringing the other into relationship with the same, it could not be other. This ruins Levinas's original hyperbolic definition of the other as the Face that always disrupts the drive to normalization and totalization, which is the essence of the logic of the same. The other cannot be other without being a version of the same, and therefore it cannot be other. To be other, it cannot be other:

> In effect, *either* there is only the same, which can no longer even appear and be said, nor even exercise violence (pure infinity or finitude); *or* indeed there is the same *and* the other, and then the other cannot be the other—of the same—except by being the same (as itself: ego), and the same cannot be the same (as itself: ego) except by being the other's other: alter ego. That I am also essentially the other's other, and that I know I am, is the evidence of a strange symmetry whose trace appears nowhere in Levinas's descriptions.[20]

Derrida characterizes this as a "transcendental pre-ethical violence."[21] The other and the same emerge only in a tense double relationship of recognition and nonrecognition with one another but also in a dislocated relationship with themselves, in which any identity they produce for themselves is challenged and exceeded by something alien that it cannot quite assimilate or even dimly see. Any putative self-identity is dislocated, incomplete, and never completely discernible. Derrida writes:

> This transcendental violence, which does not spring from an ethical resolution or freedom, or from a certain way of encountering or exceeding the other, originally institutes the relationship between two finite ipseities. In effect, the necessity of gaining access to the meaning of the other (in its irreducible alterity) on the basis of its "face," that is, its nonphenomenal phenomenon, its nonthematic theme, in other words, on the

> basis of an intentional modification of my ego (in general), (an intentional modification upon which Levinas indeed must base the meaning of his discourse); and the necessity of speaking of the other as other, or to the other as other, on the basis of its appearing-for-me-as-what-it-is: the other (an appearing which dissimulates its essential dissimulation, takes it out of the light, stripping it, and hiding that which is hidden in the other), as the necessity from which no discourse can escape, from its earliest origin—these necessities are violence itself, or rather the transcendental origin of an irreducible violence, supposing, as we said above, that it is somehow meaningful to speak of pre-ethical violence.[22]

The other cannot be so other that it becomes completely disconnected from the same. The role of otherness is to challenge or disrupt the same. It can never have any less meaning than that, no matter how elliptically or paradoxically it is defined, as a "nonphenomenal phenomenon," for example. It must also be representable, even in as minimal a form as its simple nomination as "other." And discourse itself cannot reduce its own openness on otherness to zero. It must emerge in the same domain as the same, even if it emerges as obscure or unknowable, "hiding that which is hidden in it." As we have seen previously in discussing Walten, the process of emergence that allows us to talk of "same" and "other" bears with it the potential for clash, disproportion, and incompatibility that opens the possibility of violence. This violence precedes the violence of appropriation and domination that Levinas identifies as the work of totalizing systems. Levinasian ethics has been built on the idea of a transcendence of totality by infinity. The violence Derrida sees as conditioning the emergence of same and other must come before the distinction between totality and infinity. It is thus a pre-ethical violence.

This transcendental pre-ethical violence is an irreducible violence, out of which nonviolence must also come. Derrida writes: "For this transcendental origin, as the irreducible violence of the relation to the other, is at the same time nonviolence, since it opens the relation to the other. It is an *economy*. And it is this economy which, by this opening, will permit access to the other to be determined, in ethical freedom, as moral violence or nonviolence."[23] The economy of violence generates identities but only as they both determine and mutilate themselves and one another. It is an irreducible violence yet the only place in which nonviolence can arise. It both allows violence in all its purposefulness and subverts it. The choices we make, political or otherwise, can only emerge in this economy.

Derrida discusses the economy of violence as it emerges in discourse to elucidate the complex way in which this economy relates to itself. It is important to note that the violence here—necessary and irreducible as it is—is not purely chaotic and is not beyond moral choice or judgement. The choices we make must also take place within this economy, which Derrida sees as radically historical. Derrida maps it out: "Discourse, therefore, if it is originally violent, can only *do itself violence*, can only negate itself in order to affirm itself, make war upon the war which institutes it without ever *being able* to reappropriate this negativity, to the extent that it is discourse. *Necessarily* without reappropriating it, for if it did so, the horizon of peace would disappear into the night (worst violence as pre-violence)."[24] The assertion and self-validation of discourse can only take place in relation to the hypothetical pre-ethical violence out of which it emerges violently. This self-assertion does violence to this originary violence, yet the latter always exceeds and threatens it. If the secondary violence that discourse enacts to distinguish itself from originary violence lost its difference from this originary violence and became as one with it, it would succumb to the worst violence, the pre-ethical abyssal violence that we have already seen enacted in the orgiastic excesses of Gilles de Rais. Instead, it must choose a secondary violence, a "secondary war, as the avowal of violence, is the least possible violence, the only way to repress the worst violence, the violence of primitive and pre-logical silence, of an unimaginable night which would not even be the opposite of day, an absolute violence which would not even be the opposite of nonviolence: nothingness or pure non-sense."[25] Discourse must avow its own disproportion and agony as a lesser violence, the least possible, in Derrida's terms, to separate itself from the absolute violence that makes it possible, the rampant and dynamic indistinction from which all identities derive but which also always threatens to devour them. "Thus discourse chooses itself violently in opposition to nothingness or pure non-sense, and, in philosophy, against nihilism."[26] The only way that this would not be the case, according to Derrida, would be if history had come to an end already, if Levinasian eschatology had already been fulfilled. Only then could a world arise without the tension between violence and the other denomination of violence we call nonviolence, between war and peace, same and other. In fact, such a peace would only be possible if the distinction between same and other could no longer apply, by "suspending the difference (conjunction or opposition) between the same and the other, that is, by suspending the idea of peace,"[27] thus putting an end to history. But in what Derrida calls the "here and now,"[28] such an indistinction is not possible, except by another violence, the imaginary violent abandoning of this life. So, as Richard Beardsworth has pointed out definitively, there is a tripartite violence, yet what is important is to understand its dynamism, the way in which each of its components complicates itself and its others as they produce, inspire, edge, challenge, form, and unform one another in their rich competitive indistinction. In the definitive statement to cap this argument, Derrida simply writes: "This infinite passage through violence is what is called history."[29] If we choose to elude the economy of violence, we risk losing the possibility of enacting the lesser violences that protect us from the "worst violence."[30] In an economy of violence, what choice we have must be directed to choosing the least violence, but violence can never be reduced to zero.

The conclusion of this argument is shocking: "A Being without violence would be a Being which would occur outside the existent: nothing; nonhistory; nonoccurrence; nonphenomenality."[31] We may imagine a life without violence. It may even orient our politics or be the defining attribute of our moral philosophy. Yet, such an existence is purely hypothetical. It has a theoretical existence only. Here, the argument connects with what we have seen already in Derrida's reading of Heidegger's Walten. There, the conclusion was that prevailing or some at least notional domination emerged as beings emerge in relation to Being. This prevailing was not necessarily political in that it focused on the necessarily irruptive nature of emergence. However inevitable the process by which beings emerge from Being might be, the emergence of any particular being is not in itself absolutely necessary. It always adds one more than was hitherto required; it must always make room for itself, not only among others but also in the vast otherness of space itself; it must energize itself to make of itself a being. This is the necessarily irruptive nature of emergence. This petty violence is the opening of the possibility of sovereignty in which the ever-shifting horizon of ever-greater expansion, expression, and exaltation opens before the subject as its potentially limitless, infinitely energizing though potentially catastrophic promise.

In the discussion of Levinas, we see this complexity explained in the context of the relationship with the other. Here, because of the plural and self-contradictory nature of the multitude of impulses in the emergence of same and other, we see an economy of violence. Crucially, this economy is historical. Here, the dynamic of prevailing translates into the dynamic by which human societies are ordered. We learn that these societies are inevitably political: loci of domination and violence, necessarily and inevitably. This violence contradicts itself. It promises, extends, and makes, but it also threatens, represses, and kills. It is rich in the triumphs to which it can raise us but also mean, even cruel, in the way it can become partisan, discriminating, and racist. This is the challenge of sovereignty and violence: we cannot avoid this dynamic, we cannot refuse to be elevated and liberated by it, when we need elevation and liberation; yet, we cannot help but acknowledge its cruelty, which exists in the most daring but also the most petty forms. Any hope for the future—any politics in fact—must embrace the disruptive nature of the will-to-sovereignty, but it must also be cautious. It must also challenge sovereignty when it is evil, and we know from examples like Gilles de Rais, and much worse, such as the many sadistic and genocidal European imperialisms, from the conquest of the New World to Nazism. There is no way of making politics correct or pure in the way that the formulators of ideology once so naively and arrogantly imagined. Yet, the logic of sovereignty is always to go on. So, we go on.

But let us be careful: we have to remember that violence is a great seducer, a great urger of enthusiasms. History, science, even philosophy are replete with those who want to see violence as the key mechanism of human society, even the essence of what it is to be human. The very rhetoric of the original so easily becomes connected with violence, and all the implications of the term origin—primacy, source, predetermination—are hard to remove from any argument that sees violence as always already present, even as presence itself arises. There is nothing essential about violence, and nothing dutiful in our relationships with it. We do not follow it, nor do we arise with it as part of who or what we are. Violence may be inevitable, always possible and necessary, but it is not essential in any meaning of the word. We are fools if we want it. However, assertion, irruption, dislocation, disproportion, extension, excess, accident—all beckon to violence and cannot finally emerge without at least its possibility. Without violence, nothing moves. We cannot reduce it to zero or live in any place where it will not at some point happen. My argument here, then, is not enthusiastic for violence but simply acknowledges it will never not happen, because it is both the excess in relation to which all beings define themselves as they emerge and the spark that is always produced when beings contact one another, sometimes intensely and traumatically, but also often casually and trivially, even pleasurably, the haphazard politics of the petty incident. The place where there is no violence is unknown and unknowable, unmapped, and unreachable, and indeed, it's never been reached.

In our relationships with ourselves, we endlessly promote improvement, elaboration, and self-extension to fulfil both the demands we make on ourselves and on others, challenging and violating whatever we are to be different. In our relationship with others, clash leads to both improvement and clarification, on the one hand, and on the other, cruelty, distress, and disaster. In our relationship to worlds, both real and hypothetical, we are thrown beyond any status quo into the unknown, the fortuitous, and the crazy. How can these things happen without disruption, confrontation, disappointment, and pain but also excitement in the abandonment of what we no longer need, the destruction of what constrains or oppresses us and others, in the energized drive to what the world should be, whether we conceive this individually, in our intimate lives, or in our collective self-projection into the future?

Philosophies of violence or of counterviolence romanticize and reify violence, proposing it in its martial heroics, not in its casual generality. How can we imagine living without the many microtensions, clashes, confrontations, frustrations, changes, disruptions, evolutions, self-overcomings, brutal inequalities and coercive equalities, blatant injustices and straitening justices, disruptive diversity, and policed samenesses? All this loads our worlds with conflict and cataclysm. But we should never ignore the incidental nature of violence as well. There is no possible social or personal life without multiplying microcompetitions and conflicts. Nor is there any incident that is completely closed off from trivial disruptions, dislocations, disjunctions, mismatches, mistakes, and misrecognitions, all triggering or scattering microviolences or simply the possibility of violence. We don't have to court it to inhabit it. It is not ours, but it is both present and latent everywhere. When was the time without violence, and how can we imagine a world ever being without it? This is the destination of our argument: sovereignty is about the open-ended process of making the world what it should be, in other words, just, in its broadest meaning, "just as it should be." And there is nothing about this process that is not violent.

∽

Law and justice; the economy and the gift; democracy and the democracy-to-come; conditional and absolute hospitality—these are the doublenesses that recur in the so-called late Derrida. The first thing to remark about these doublenesses is their political nature. What is at stake here are the key terms on which political discussion in Derrida pivots. They do not provide a general politics, because under the Derridean dispensation, it would be impossible and undesirable. If a Derridean politics is to be sought—one relevant to the pressing political issues of the climate-change era—it is to these themes that it must look: how will law enact a justice that cannot be formulated, because we no longer inhabit a world where ideal social arrangements can be imagined, and where intergenerational inequities are unfolding obscurely and slowly along an unprecedented and unmappable trajectory in real historical time? What is the future of the democratic impulse in a world where freedoms are simultaneously enacted outrageously and threatened legally, while democratic states seem exhausted, corrupt, the focus of intense disenchantment, and vulnerable to the most pathetic forms of demagoguery? What is the logic of sociality itself: a routine of measurable and quantifiable exchanges, or an enlarging sense of inexhaustible mutual opennesses? And what finally is the logic by which human populations move globally, shifting between being, on the one hand, unjudging hosts or mean agents of judgmental exclusion and, on the other, unwanted trespassers (refugees, asylum seekers) or smugly entitled invaders (tourists, exploiters of primary resources, and the mobile economic and professional elite)?

These questions are all versions of the ways in which Derridean doubleness relates to our contemporary political situation. Recognizing that in these doublenesses sovereignty is always already at issue offers us a way of rethinking the political in relation to otherness and violence, without simply reducing the argument to a vague promise of justice to the other or seeing political injustice simply as when violence occurs. Alain Badiou has argued that deference to the other characterizes contemporary orthodoxy about the fundamental meaning of ethics.[32] To Badiou, this is a weak model of ethics and limits political action. Even allowing for Badiou's argument, it is not possible simply to erase the other from our political meaning, either conceptually or practically. However, because we see ourselves deprived of higher conceptions of political possibility outside of the aspirations of individuals, nations, and corporations, we do currently risk reducing political ambition simply to the eradication of violence. Injustice then simply becomes equated to suffering violence, including symbolic violence and microviolences. Human and climate crimes are not seen as the consequences of a fundamentally wrong social order but as petty tricks or excesses that can be corrected by the appropriate administrative fiat or correct economic planning. The failure of utopianisms should not be an excuse for not having a better political order as a goal. The reduction of violence is desirable, but it is not a complete politics.

Sovereignty is an implicitly violent concept. It is also necessarily open on otherness. We have seen this in relation to Derrida's account of the doubleness of hospitality, where openness to the other and violence engage with one another uneasily, risking confusion, not only conceptually but literally and physically. The play of sovereignty fuels Derridean doubleness because it understands the wildness of otherness, its economy of violence, in relation to decision, thus in relation to agency, however transitory, contingent, or fictional that agency may be, and the ambiguous possibilities of power. Derridean doublenesses describe the way key political terms emerge in the world as instances of ontological difference. Sovereignty is not another instance of this emergence. It is the language we must use to describe how any emergence—with its necessary disproportion and disruption—always takes place with violence entailed in it. Sovereignty is always already there and speaks through these doublenesses irrepressibly. In an aside in the second year of the lectures on the death penalty, Derrida was quite explicit about the importance of sovereignty as anterior: "[L]et me ask you this," he says:

> Is sovereignty in general, the position of absolute power, as power over life and death, of the "I can watch over, give or suspend, give or take" the life of the other just as "I can with the law, that is, just as I can give, make or suspend the law," is this form of exceptional sovereignty, which is a form of sovereignty, not an earlier form (older, as it were, more archaic, in fact, the archaic itself, the *arkhē*, commencement and commandment), absolute anteriority, absolute antiquity, the absolute archaicity that precedes both life and death, and law, and above all the oppositional distinctions between legal and illegal, nature and law, nature and right, *physis* and *nomos*, thus also between *poena naturalis* and *poena forensis*, but also like the Father himself, between God and man.[33]

Sovereignty here is not a simple identity. It is not the root or parent of all things. It is less an object of thought than the direction of a speculation. It enters discussion here, not as a metaphysically anchoring origin but as the only means of prior emergence. The emergence of the grand doubles Derrida mentions here (from legal–illegal to God–man) cannot take place other than after and thus through and as sovereignty, as subsovereignties or the enactment of a sovereign force that will never leave any emergence alone. What emerges emerges sovereignly, after sovereignty and in the form of projections of the sovereign. This is why it has to be mentioned here not as a constative statement but in the form of a question. Sovereignty brings whatever is into being. Everything that is entails the sovereign but in the form of a speculation, a projection, a possibility.

In this way, the Derridean construction of sovereignty is larger than the structural political meaning to which we usually connect it and of which we are understandably suspicious. This is because it is the language of sovereignty that encompasses any account of both the banality of the incipience of things and the insanity of the meaninglessness that always looms under and ahead of them. In the same way that each of these doublenesses is an account of coming into being, they are all also defined and menaced by an abyssal quality that always opens beneath and beyond them, before them in all senses of the word: an abyss of the absolute open-endedness, in-definition and impossibility of justice, the gift, democracy-to-come, absolute hospitality, and so on. It would of course be un-Derridean to simply say Derrida subscribes to this model of Walten, of violent emergence, as a general truth of the nature of beings and human being in particular. Derrida's work acknowledges a certain irreducible violence (from "Violence and Metaphysics" on), but it is also cautious of a generalized or romanticized violence. Yet, a certain irreducible drive to or enactment of sovereignty is allowed to stand in this account of the nature of beings. Behind the doublenesses mentioned, a logic of latent political violence is always at stake, and our discussion of these pairs is always charged with political meaning, opening the way necessarily to the possibility of political intent.

In Bataille, the abyss of sovereignty looms as the end of human will, the drive to excess, self-destruction through self-overcoming and the endless fatality of religion, of true religions, ones that admitted their drive to transgression by way of death and rampant sexuality. The abyss appears in Bataille then as a kind of limitless religious violence. We try to stabilize this violence by fixing it in a sacred meaning, most clearly in the figuration of God. God is a trope whereby we attempt to resist the limitlessness of sacred violence by personalizing it and claiming it to be meaningful. Benjamin in "Critique of Violence" is also attracted by a kind of supreme, "divine" violence, which he links to sovereignty and revolution. This is the messianico-Marxist violence Derrida finds a step too far, of course, because the romanticizing of violence as somehow bringing meaning into the world is not, or should not be, available to us, post-Holocaust. Only a few pages before expressing his reservations about Benjamin's interest in violence, Derrida does, however, repeat Bataille's gesture, when he says "the name of such absolute violence is God." In the doublenesses we have been discussing, the abyss looms in the very open-endedness, impossibility, and in-definition of the justice that can never be realized, the gift that can never be given—the gift, "if there is any," as Derrida's account so frequently puts it—the democracy-to-come whose first attribute is that it will not and cannot come, and the absolute hospitality that welcomes the guest beyond the logic of social identity and at the risk of absolute violence, in the cases in which Derrida is interested, against powerless women. These motifs open on the indefinite because they open on the other, and Derrida is quite clear that this openness is potentially cataclysmic and disastrous, even though that awareness is all too often lost in our latter day longing to do the political right thing and see openness to the other as uplifting and liberal in all meanings of the word. It is enlarging, definitely, but it does not have a necessary moral inflection. It can represent the risk of absolute evil, as Derrida often reminds us. Openness on otherness is abyssal because it is blank, undefined, and undefinable.

There is no Derridean politics if we think of politics as the discovery of a right thinking leading to a right acting, the politics on the model of ideology, for example. We all know this, so we have taken recourse in another model of correct agency, the ethical model of preference, to perpetrate as little violence as possible, or to withhold from participating in injustice. The mistake this makes of course is that it must choose and hierarchize, and it makes the cardinal error of thinking justice and law, or absolute and conditional hospitality, are in tune with one another. This is to misread them, to wish away their complexities, and to expect a model of thought to make political decisions for us. Decisions cannot by definition be made for us. Then they would not be decisions. Our politics will always be messy, incomplete, provisional, hybrid, and thus, a failure. It must be open on the blankness of otherness, but not settle for that, either as the lodestone of authority, or as the guarantee of benignity. It will always be a site of uncertainty and messiness, a politics that can never be resolved and that we can never actually get right, a *bastard* politics, in the sense Derrida means in "Force of Law," when he speaks of the "impure, contaminating, negotiated, bastard and violent fashion in all these filiations . . . of decision and the undecidable."[34] Politics cannot be gotten right because politics is sovereignty in action, both uplifting and dangerous, liberating and oppressive, enlightening and obscuring, all at the same time together in endlessly complicating and self-defying fractions of itself, vigorous partialities, both storming and releasing one another in ever compounding, ever open-ended, unique but serial events, and with the promise of violence everywhere. We would prefer it otherwise, but even to say that repeats the sovereign gesture. Sovereignty repels us even when we want it. Freedom and justice, like the nation, like God, are the names we give to it, but they are more than names. They are the fundamental characteristics of the will-to-sovereignty, as we will see below. Sovereignty, in sum, is not right in any resolvable sense, and it does not simply make right, but it is the only game in town. It empowers and energizes everything, bringing with it absolute possibility and absolute menace. It is the only thing that works.

But it's all very well to elaborate a complex account of a volatile dynamism and call it politics. Politics is nothing if it lacks content, if it doesn't do things and explain why we do things. If we make decisions, not in a vacuum, but somewhere, and not a fixed somewhere but at a point in movement, a somehow orientating point, what are the characteristics of sovereign politics? This will help us answer one of the questions we posed at the very beginning of this study. It is assumed without question that it is right and necessary for humans to survive climate change, but why? The answer lies in the unquestionable *insistence* of human sovereignty. It is because of sovereignty's insistence that the question of the worthiness of our survival is unraised and unraisable. Our drive is always toward a godliness that exceeds us and that remains an image of our possibility and aspiration; but at the same time, this excessive possibility of an outrageous and violent other horrifies us even as an image of what we might be. What is shared by these conflicting "heterogeneous but indissociable" impulses, to use Derrida's terms, is the energy of impulse itself, the success of emergence, the unstoppability of the opening of beings and of their irreducible engagement, in a word, the *sovereign insistence* of Dasein. Sovereign insistence is the drive to reach toward godliness but also to not ever settle for being ruled. It both admires godliness and refuses it; it believes in a sovereignty beyond the petrifying sovereign orders we have received. It both embraces sovereignty and resists it and, in resisting it, emulates it further.

The generalizability of sovereignty as insistence arises by way of the deconstruction of orthodox accounts of sovereignty in Bataille and Derrida. Orthodox sovereignty never fully separates itself from political theology, which spans from Bodin and Hobbes through to Schmitt. This is the predeconstructed sovereign whose role is to make the social order safe. This sovereign is the pinnacle of the political order and a single, unified point of power. As such, this sovereign is self-identical and single. Nothing precedes or conditions it. It is beholden to nothing. Not only does this sovereign make laws but also it decides when the law is not to operate. In this way, the conventional sovereign has access to a higher order of value and meaning, which other human beings are unable to comprehend and with which other human institutions cannot be trusted. The sovereign is the point where the human world reaches toward a logic that is beyond the human, the sovereignty of God, of which the human sovereign is not only a representative and agent but also a version or image. As the former, the sovereign operates according to a logic other subject humans cannot understand and have no access to. Schmitt identifies this super-human logic with the miracle, something incomprehensible that intervenes in the human world from elsewhere, turning death into life, and transforming one thing to another inexplicably. The sovereign is alien and otherworldly, the image of something that takes its meaning from itself. It is therefore a model of an autonomous and individual selfhood, which thus becomes available to the human as the most asserted representation of what it means to be a person. There is potentially no limit to the prerogative of the sovereign. It is free to exert its rule in ways that only need to make sense to it. This prerogative is also unrestricted. It is open on a potentially infinite violence. We have seen in Benjamin this special nature of divine violence, in its purity and absolutism, but above all, in its limitlessness. The human sovereign is free to enact this violence.

Because it is the sovereignty of a power that is not accessible to all and beyond ordinary human understanding, it is fundamentally undemocratic, even when it is seen as necessary for the protection of democracy. It presents human political order as something that derives its meaning from, and is guaranteed by, the otherworldly. It has a higher understanding of what human society and human life mean and a sense of a higher truth to which that society must be calibrated, even when it is not fully revealed or understood. This is a logic not only of unaccountability but also of obscurity. Human societies are ordered in a way that they cannot understand. However, if this unsignifiable thing is arrogated to some and not others, then it risks becoming license for obscurantism and abuse. Sovereignty is by its nature a form of abuse. It institutes inequality in the social order and unaccountability in political practice. Sovereignty is risk and danger.

This sovereignty is ripe for deconstruction. As we have seen from our account of the history of representations of sovereignty in Western discourse, there is always something in excess of any instance of the sovereign. The clearest example of this is the way in which the sovereign is an image of the unity and authority of God, when it is not God, who remains in excess of it. But even God in turn is a term used to cover over the potential infinity and open-endedness of the unsignifiable. Even the God on which the sovereign depends for its logic gives way to an endlessly open and chaotic, even entropic plurality, the fragments of which themselves are destined to shatter into even further unstable pluralities. The self-identity and stability of the sovereign are perpetually sundering. Sovereignty, by its nature, requires the drawing into itself of its own excess. In this way, the very unaccountability on which both the sovereign and God rely is a fiction unable to withstand the very mystery on which its authority depends. This mystery both guarantees sovereignty's esoteric authority and ruins it endlessly. So, the only way in which the authority of sovereignty can be enforced is by denying or obscuring its nature. For this reason, the double language of legitimacy and stability is the most fundamental and persistent language of sovereignty: illegitimacy and instability are part of the very nature of sovereignty, things that can only be dealt with from sovereignty's point of view, by denial, obscurantism, and the violence that silences.

So, in every instance, the sovereign is a fixed point of authority and gives way to another higher point beyond it. If this sovereignty is a model of self-identical individual subjectivity, this subjectivity in turn also gives way to that imaginary thing higher than itself, on which it is modeled, but which crucially, it fails to be. Like all instances of sovereignty, it cannot really be itself. This holds for all individual and corporate selves: they are both established and sundered by their relationship to sovereignty. It both oppresses and frees them, and they remain in thrall to it as part of their aspiration. It is understandable for human aspiration to be loaded by something unsignifiable, a meaning that cannot be simply quantified or calculated. The openness of human society on what is in excess of its own calculations represents a fundamental way to make values possible. It also makes values highly dangerous and always potentially violent. Too thorough an identification with the sovereign is a license for evil as the case of Gilles de Rais teaches us. But within the selfhoods we form, there remains an impulse toward self-enlargement that overcomes any static instance of sovereignty and threatens any attempt to petrify it into a fixed authority.

Conventional sovereignty attempts to incorporate openness on infinite possibility as a marker of the mystical quality of its authority. The deconstructibility of sovereignty means that this openness cannot be so simply foreclosed. It cannot even rest on the nameless name of God. The deconstruction of sovereignty shows that there is no fixed point of any nature where sovereignty can rest. Authority is always undermined and surpassed. This endless surpassing is the trajectory of sovereignty itself, the possibility of a self that is constantly in the process of self-overcoming toward something always and ever larger and further, something undefined—in short, the abyssal. This opening on infinite possibility is larger than any possible instantiation of God. The potential wildness and vertigo of the abyss, its horrible infinity into which we project our endless self-extension and aspiration, cannot be tamed. This is the logic of sovereign insistence: in projecting ourselves toward this abyss, there is a little godliness in all of us, at least as the measure of our hope and possibility. The deconstruction of conventional authority does not reduce the mystery or enigma of sovereignty but generalizes it into an account of emergence. Attempts like Schmitt's to keep sovereignty esoteric represent the contrived and enforced closure of an excess that cannot ever be closed. The very reliance on the anterior and superior that gives Schmittian sovereignty its exceptionality must shatter it as well, breaching specific sovereignties in the name of what gives them authority but that cannot itself ever be limited or named.

To Bataille, the will to absolute license in human beings was the trace of this potential godliness, horrifying in its dangers but uplifting in its opportunity for limitless ascendancy. As we have seen in chapter 2, Bataille's account of sovereignty is not simply a celebration of license or excess for its own sake. Excess is an inevitable part of the logic of sovereignty, but a radical commitment to excess can only reduce it to a value and thus betray it. Yet, there are several crucial things that sovereignty inevitably proposes. The first of these, as we have seen, is its unstoppable insistence. The second is that this insistence always entails freedom as a necessary part of its logic. Sovereignty in its drive always to overcome limits will always challenge constraint, even if it has to do so in the form of a countersovereignty, challenging a prior, more rigid and repressive sovereign gesture. The third and most easily forgotten sovereign motif in Bataille is his emphasis on human interconnectedness. Sovereignty in its inevitable openness keeps any sense of subjectivity open on the possibility of human community. It is this sovereign openness that Derrida will characterize as justice. Each of these three motifs—the sovereign insistence toward the excessiveness of godliness, the provocation of freedom, and the irrepressibility of justice—persists in the account of sovereignty we have developed.

So, there is more to the pursuit of sovereignty than simply a wild expansion into unknowable possibilities as adventure or orgy. In a reading of Derrida's reading of Heidegger, we have used the term *Walten* to help characterize the nature of Dasein's emergences. In even the most petty and regular of these, we both make and attain a space in which we can unfold ourselves toward a possible, if fictional or ephemeral, selfhood. Dasein begins as a drive into openness itself, an openness that Dasein both makes and occupies in one and the same movement. In this making space for ourselves, we are oriented toward *freedom* as a value, the second of Bataille's motifs. Indeed, freedom is the inevitable trajectory of the opening of Walten. It both makes and requires space. It pursues its own insistence. There is not space here to provide a full account of the relationship between sovereignty and freedom. Suffice it to say two things. Firstly, freedom relies on the very sense of separation that we have identified as emergence. Without the distinction a being grasps in Walten, freedom could not be imagined. Secondly, because it is always the embrace of possibility, freedom requires that we project ourselves toward being otherwise across time. Put together, these two factors show freedom as the pursuit of sovereignty toward a further and yet further self-identity, which deconstructs itself in the name of self-identity.

Freedom opens before us, but the space we enter is not nowhere. It is always already occupied. There is always something there, and someone. The making space of Walten is not a conquering, because Walten does not happen to an individual alone. There is no possibility of a blank space into which the liberal individual, that counterpart of absolute blankness, can be seen as somehow primary or even possible. Walten cannot take place alone, and there can be no first Walten. In other words, emergence cannot be without companion. It does not make a world. Its orientation is from a world already made by the other and toward a world extended by and toward otherness, a world not just of acknowledging or recognizing otherness, but of community, in Bataille's terms. As we have seen in the case of Gilles de Rais, any absolutism of the sovereign is at best chimerical, at worst and perhaps inevitably, the purest form of evil. This oppression of the other always fails, however. A world without community is inconceivable, because otherness has its own insistence that can never be reduced to zero. We do not allow the other a modicum of justice simply to be fair or correct. The other demands justice, because the domain of otherness requires it, and we cannot live anywhere else than in community, a domain already required by, owed to, and made by the other. The other has already demanded justice and not from us. Justice is not something we give or concede. Liberal individualism conceives of justice as something to be enacted. Yet, justice is always already gaping ahead of us. It requires us, rather than the other way around. In Derrida, as we have seen, justice is this infinite openness on the irreducible awareness that the other not only requires space but also has always already made space for itself and will go on to require it indefinitely and infinitely. The orientation of any instance of Walten, therefore, is into a domain in which emergence has already happened and to which we must be accommodated. It is a fantasy to think we can choose otherwise.

The orientation of sovereignty, therefore, is three part: through insistence toward the possibility of freedom and the priority of justice. Yet, what we are dealing with here is not a simple whole divided into three neat sections. Insistence, freedom, and justice overlap and clash with one another even as they feed one another. They are in a state of radical nondisjunction in which their collaboration with one another is potentially indistinguishable from the way they undermine or challenge one another. The drive to freedom can become the aspiration to godliness, yet the potential rigidity of that which aspires and what it aspires to can channel or restrict freedom. Similarly, the drive to justice expresses an empathetic will to shared freedom while potentially rigidifying it into institutions, which can both maximize and minimize freedom. The history of politics is the history of the unleashing and the clash between these three impulses.

I will not argue that sovereignty is always the driving force behind these three things. It does not simply promote or facilitate them. Yet, these issues will always be proposed—provoked—as a consequence of sovereignty. Some versions of sovereignty will advance them to the point of excess; others will repress them, yet they will always be suggested or unloosed wherever sovereignty is at stake. From our contemporary point of view, the most orthodox types of sovereignty, the sovereignty of unaccountable authority, for example, will always tend to crush freedom and justice. Yet, often this takes place in the name of another type of freedom—élite prerogative—and another type of justice—a conception of the rightful and balanced, even divinely sanctioned way of ordering the world as it should be ordered. And in turn, this sovereignty will be resisted by other sovereignties, the sovereignty of the corporate body of citizenry acting in revolution, for example. Sovereignty is not simply either a regime of repression or an avenue of liberation but a complex and unstable tension between stabilizing inhibition and radical possibility.

Yet, what is possible is also impossible: it beckons us but it cannot be achieved. The impossible here is what we activate and make but which is never finished. It is both undoable and never done with. To Derrida, there is an impossible "that would not be negative, . . . an im-possible that would escape the alternative between the possible and the actual."[35] This impossible is not a barrier against which our plans smash. It is not the site of limits or frustrations. It does not defeat us. Nor is it a romantic dream of a sublime absolute too good for us, but against which we throw ourselves to achieve some level of moral heroism. It is the fact that we are in a movement that ends before it can ever be completed. It is the ineluctable fact that we occupy an opening.

What opens before us in sovereignty, therefore, is neither an ideal nor a choice, but something toward which we are inevitably oriented as we arise. We cannot choose its fundamental nature, which is its ambiguous orientation of insistence, freedom, and justice. Sovereignty is both a logic of unaccountable and potentially abusive authority but also of the open-ended impossible possible. In the former, a blankness occupies the space where understanding seeks to penetrate thus making of sovereignty a mystery to which we must be subject, but this blankness is also the locus of a possibility we cannot foresee, in the acting out of a freedom we always seek in party with a justice we cannot ignore. But there are not two forms of sovereignty, only one, even if it is a double one. The obscurantism of authority and the openness on infinite impossible possibility both rely on the same uncertainty and indefinability. The same thing makes them both available, and indeed they cannot ever be clearly separated from one another: on the one hand, people find their freedom by identifying with the extravagant prerogative of the violent lord—in our age, the callous plutocracy or buffoonish masculinized demagogue—even when they cannot share in it and even when they are its victims. On the other hand, the possibility opened by revolution dreams of the brutal power that will secure equality and progress. These are clichés, but we see in them at least the historico-fictional point in which our versions of sovereignty converge on one another and become entangled. In doing so, they always question one another: the authority figure sees the open-ended possibility on which it relies for its meaning as a threat, as the route to pluralism and thus dissent and chaos. The drive toward possibility sees authority as implicitly limiting its need for freedom and commitment to justice. Authority represses freedom, possibility subverts power, but all this is part of one inevitable double act in which the search for human possibility that is implicit in the emergence of beings from Being throws up in the sovereign figure something that is both a caricature of itself and a fundamental instrument of its ambition, as well as the greatest threat to it. And in turn, the sovereign figure needs this vital drive to enact and embody the force of its will while seeing in it the thing that most challenges and ridicules it.

But this tangled language of doubles and sides obscures the dynamic complexities at work here, in which neither "side" can be so simply identified or reified. There is no resolutely separating power from dream or aspiration from limitation. What we have is an uneasy deconstructed formation in which authority and the impossible, government and anarchy, legitimacy and illegitimacy converge on one another, inspiring a "bastard" politics. The aim of Derrida's use of this term was to capture the hybrid, self-contaminating, irreducibly unstable, and complex way in which identities undermine themselves, in short, the way in which they cannot ever settle into the purity of continuity, simplicity, and unity, even when they aspire or claim to. In "Khora," Derrida characterizes the predistinction out of which identities emerge as something that "does not proceed from the natural or legitimate *logos*, but from a hybrid, bastard or even corrupted reasoning."[36] He goes on: "It oscillates between two types of oscillation: the double exclusion (*neither/nor*) and the participation (*both this and that*)."[37] This language could be used to describe the sovereignty we have been discussing. It is neither the resolute purity of stable and meaningful authority nor the unrestricted joyousness of absolute openness, freedom, and justice, while at the same time, it is both of these things in their failed, blended, incomplete, and irresolute forms. In another less brutalized context, Derrida connects this with the logic of auto-immunity. It is what it cannot be, or what it must stop itself from being. Thus, both our systems of authority and our dreams of freedom fail, because they must make each other possible and thus always be in disharmony with one another, even as they need and make each other.

But there are other ways in which our politics is a bastard politics. Firstly, we have to recall that this tangle of sovereignties installs an irreducible violence at the heart of our politics, and secondly, it means both that our systems of authority must be constantly challenged and that our logics of freedom must themselves be programs of power. Our politics, therefore, remains a bastard politics because it will always be brutal. The violence that opens the human possibility of sovereign insistence, freedom, and justice is implicitly and necessarily disruptive in its endlessly elevating imaginaries and necessary dissatisfaction. It always risks exploding, even simply in orgiastic and symbolic gestures, vandalism, banditry, and the running street battle. In its most organized form, revolution, it opens—like the exclusive authority figure it most despises and often recreates—on divine violence, the most dangerous thing of all. For sovereignty, then, the choice is between the violence of state power in its rigor, secrecy, and narrowness and violence as the possibility of exultation and exaltation. These may be alternatives facing off against one another. They may be phases of the same history, but they will always be found together, even if simply in the latency of the risk posed to each of them by the other. Possibility risks becoming tyranny; authoritarianism inevitably ends in chaos. Sovereignty operates as and through such an economy of violence.

CONCLUSION

Politics is sovereignty in action. The orientation of human rising is always toward the insistence that is our trace of godliness, and to freedom and justice, but because they are enactments of sovereignty, they always risk hardening into ideology and thus dogmatism and ruthlessness, the contextless, unsocialized individual or the demagogue. These may also serve freedom and justice: the liberal ideology of human rights may collaborate with the worst derealizations of history and imperialism, but it also offers avenues of protection and liberation. Authoritarian regulation may police and normalize, but it can also smash privilege, redistribute the good, and cure the sick. The will to freedom and justice may itself become ruthless, silencing or crushing whatever stands in its way. This is the bastard game of politics. There are no simple ways forward, and no way of thinking like a clear-cut ideology that will solve this problem for us.

Yet, it is the game we are playing and must play. We find ourselves always already in the domain of freedom and justice that authority both makes possible and threatens. We cannot pretend that power is simply something to question or subvert but not to wield. We must exercise power while remaining suspicious of it to continue along the trajectory Walten requires of us. There is no enactment of freedom and justice that is not at the same time an act of power. And there is no occupation of power that does not awaken the possibility of freedom and justice. This entanglement is important because we are now living in an era, in Western democracies at least, in which these two types of sovereignty seem to have separated into opposing political positions, even though they still imagine themselves as a left and a right: we see, on the one hand, a contestation of power that sees violence itself as the most important sign of captivity and injustice, and thus sees power as always everywhere anathema, and on the other hand, a fetishization of power that validates freedom and justice only in the form of increased license for its own rampant, usually retrogressive, patriarchal prerogative. Yet, in my reading, these are both complexes of sovereignty, one articulating its drives without admitting its need for power and violence, the other enacting power without respecting the necessarily destabilizing and limitless expansiveness of freedom and justice. Sovereignty is the path of freedom and justice, and it must embrace power to energize them, without succumbing to power's own divine stupidity.

Above all, sovereignty is highly unstable. Its different meanings converge but do not settle. In fact, their identity with one another is clear, while at the same time, always failing. Let me give an example from Derrida's *Death Penalty* lectures, in a reading he provides of Benjamin's figure of "the great criminal." The great criminal is a fascinating figure for the general population, both attractive and repulsive. The attraction is because the people recognize in the great criminal someone who has contested the authority of the state, which has arrogated to itself the right to violence. The great criminal asserts against the state its own competing sovereignty by attempting him- or herself to also claim a freedom of violence. Derrida describes it like this: "Even when it demands a death sentence, the people recognizes in the criminal, in the 'great' criminal, in the one who has been condemned to death, an absolute, almost sovereign power. In the end, the 'great' criminal becomes in his person . . . something like the representative of the people in its latent protest against the law or against the sovereign state that has deprived the people of its violence, that has dispossessed the people of its violence, that has violated the public in order to have a monopoly on violence."[1] What is interesting here is the slippage in the term *sovereign*. On the one hand, we have the sovereignty of the sovereign state, which has consolidated itself as the single legitimate owner of violence and has incontestable rule over the law and the people. It is the state exercising its legitimate authority that punishes the great criminal. On the other hand, we have sovereignty as the freedom exercised by the great criminal and for which he or she is being punished. This sovereignty is hypothetically "absolute." There is something about it, therefore, that resists questioning and accountability. Even when it is wrong, and we acknowledge it to be wrong, and even when we condemn it and despise it, this sovereignty remains somehow superior to us and offers to us the possibility of ourselves being superior. This is what makes it not just a spasm or symbol of sovereignty, but sovereign *power*. It does not only mimic or parallel state sovereignty; it challenges it as something state sovereignty both excludes (sovereignty in its state form does not acknowledge any alternative sovereignties) and aims to annihilate. One of these sovereignties instantiates the law; the other contests it. One has a power not available to the other or to anyone else. The other, by its own daring, claims this power for itself while never being troubled whether or not it exercises it legitimately. Great criminals both refuse to accept the exclusivity of this power and choose to exercise it. In this way, they embrace the very unaccountability that will hold them to account. They are both accountable and unaccountable. And by claiming the sovereign state's power of violence, they also hold its unaccountability to account.

These two sovereignties are the same but different, and their sameness and difference are not complementary. Nor do they simply overlap. They are the same in their difference from one another: both absolute and contesting absoluteness; both unaccountable, though questioned and questioning in their unaccountability; both violent themselves and refusing but enacting their own and the other's violence. In other words, both violent and a judgement on violence. Derrida continues his reading of Benjamin: "Even if his crime does not appear to be political, even if it is a common law crime, the fact that he has, by his crime, defied the political violence of the law, the state monopoly on violence, any great crime is a political crime."[2] He goes on: "But we might also take the view that a Rousseauian-type logic of the 'public enemy,' which consists in justifying the death penalty by defining the criminal in general as a public enemy who denounces the contract and defies the law, consists in making every crime a political crime."[3]

Sovereignty is volatile and always at stake. Even routine and trivial crime is a test for sovereignty. It allows and exhibits the sovereign, both as the exercise of power and the resistance to that power that is itself a form of power. Instituted sovereignty manifests itself in the exercising of sanction, but a countersovereignty challenges this sanction and applies a sanction of its own in the form of an anticipatory unlicensed violence and in the threat, implicit in any act of resistance, to become itself an alternative state. We are always somewhere at every moment in this dynamic and unstable field of sovereignties, microsovereignties, faux sovereignties, and countersovereignties. In the end, sovereignty is both the authoritarianism that needs to be checked and the possibility that needs to be pursued.

NOTES

Introduction

1. Walter Benjamin, "Critique of Violence," in *Reflections*, trans. E. Jephcott (New York: Schocken Books, 1978), 300.
2. Jacques Derrida, *Learning to Live Finally: An Interview with Jean Birnbaum*, trans. Pascale-Anne Brault and Michael Naas (New York: Palgrave Macmillan, 2020), 51.

Chapter One

1. Jean Bodin, *On Sovereignty*, ed. and trans. Julian H. Franklin (Cambridge: Cambridge University Press, 2015), 23.
2. Bodin, 11.
3. Bodin, 8.
4. Bodin, 31.
5. Bodin, 31.
6. Bodin, 4.
7. Bodin, 8.
8. Bodin, 46.
9. Bodin, 92.
10. Bodin, 13.
11. Bodin, 38.
12. Bodin, 45.
13. Bodin, 76–77.
14. Ernst H. Kantorowicz, *The King's Two Bodies: A Study in Medieval Political Theology* (Princeton: Princeton University Press, 1957), 164.
15. Thomas Hobbes, *Leviathan* (Oxford: Oxford University Press, 1996), 78.
16. Hobbes, 66.
17. Hobbes, 100.

18. Hobbes, 84.
19. Hobbes, 100.
20. Hobbes, 184.
21. Hobbes, 177.
22. Hobbes, 116.
23. Hobbes, 230.
24. Hobbes, 141.
25. Jean-Jacques Rousseau, *The Social Contract*, trans. Maurice Cranston (London: Penguin Books, 1968), 62–63.
26. Rousseau, 63.
27. Rousseau, 62.
28. Rousseau, 63.
29. Rousseau, 64.
30. Rousseau, 64.
31. Rousseau, 60.
32. Rousseau, 74.
33. Rousseau, 84–85.
34. Rousseau, 95.
35. Rousseau, 89.
36. Rousseau, 87.
37. Carl Schmitt, *Political Theology: Four Chapters on the Concept of Sovereignty*, trans. George Schwab (Chicago, IL: University of Chicago Press, 2005), 5.
38. Schmitt, 5.
39. Schmitt, 6.
40. Schmitt, 7.
41. Schmitt, 7.
42. Schmitt, 7.
43. Schmitt, 15.
44. Schmitt, 30.
45. Schmitt, 31.
46. Schmitt, 31.
47. Schmitt, 31.
48. Schmitt, 46.
49. Schmitt, 46.
50. Schmitt, 36.
51. Schmitt, 37.
52. Schmitt, 37.
53. Schmitt, 66.
54. Michel Foucault, *Society Must be Defended*, trans. David Macey (London: Allen Lane, 2003), 26.
55. Foucault, 37–38.
56. Foucault, 43–45.

57. Foucault, 45.
58. Foucault, 45.
59. Foucault, 46.
60. Foucault, 46.
61. Foucault, 46–47.
62. Foucault, 56.
63. Foucault, 88.
64. Foucault, 126–27.
65. Giorgio Agamben, *Homo Sacer: Sovereign Power and Bare Life*, trans. Daniel Heller-Roazen (Stanford: Stanford University Press, 1998), 5.
66. Agamben, 6.
67. Agamben, 6.
68. Agamben, 15.
69. Agamben, 26.
70. Agamben, 17.
71. Agamben, 24.
72. Agamben, 20.
73. Agamben, 30.
74. Agamben, 31.
75. Agamben, 31–32, italics in original.
76. Agamben, 112.
77. Georges Bataille, *The Accursed Share*, vols. 2 and 3, trans. Robert Hurley (New York: Zone Books), 197.

Chapter Two

1. Georges Bataille, *Erotism: Death and Sensuality*, trans. Mary Dalwood (San Francisco, CA: City Lights, 1986), 32.
2. Bataille, 173.
3. Bataille, 13.
4. Bataille, 18–19.
5. Bataille, 16.
6. Georges Bataille, *The Unfinished System of Non-Knowledge*, trans. Michelle Kendall and Stuart Kendall (Minneapolis, MN: University of Minnesota Press, 2001), 229.
7. Bataille, 228.
8. Jacques Derrida "Force of Law: The Mystical Foundation of Authority," in *Acts of Religion*, ed. Gil Anidjar, trans. Mary Quaintance (New York: Routledge, 2002), 293.
9. See Georges Bataille, *The Trial of Gilles de Rais*, trans. R. Robinson (New York: Amok Books, 2004).

10. Bataille, *Erotism*, 180.
11. Bataille, 62, italics in original.
12. Bataille, *The Accursed* Share, 2–3:285.
13. Bataille, 239.
14. Bataille, 239.
15. Bataille, 240.
16. Bataille, 240.
17. Bataille, 254.
18. Bataille, 214.
19. Bataille, 221.
20. Bataille, 203.
21. Bataille, 204.
22. Bataille, 215.
23. Bataille, 216.
24. Bataille, 200.
25. Bataille, 221.
26. Bataille, 221–22.
27. Georges Bataille, *Literature and Evil*, trans. Alistair Hamilton (London: Calder & Boyars, 1973), 30.
28. Bataille, 194, italics in original.
29. Georges Bataille, *On Nietzsche*, trans. Bruce Boone (New York: Paragon House, 1992), 96.
30. Bataille, *The Unfinished System of Non-Knowledge*, 161.

Chapter Three

1. Benjamin, "Critique of Violence," 300.
2. Benjamin, 300.
3. Derrida, "Force of Law," 298.
4. Benjamin, "Critique of Violence," 288.
5. Benjamin, 293.
6. Benjamin, 293.
7. Benjamin, 294.
8. Benjamin, 294.
9. Benjamin, 295.
10. Benjamin, 296.
11. Benjamin, 297.
12. Benjamin, 297.
13. Benjamin, 297.
14. Benjamin, 297.
15. Benjamin, 297.

16. Benjamin, 297.
17. Benjamin, 298.
18. Benjamin, 297.
19. Benjamin, 299.
20. Benjamin, 299.
21. Benjamin, 300.
22. Benjamin, 300.
23. Benjamin, 300.
24. Derrida, "Force of Law," 234.
25. Derrida, 233, italics in original.
26. Derrida, 239.
27. Derrida, 241.
28. Derrida, 242.
29. Derrida, 242.
30. Derrida, 242.
31. Derrida, 239.
32. Derrida, 242.
33. Derrida, 244.
34. Derrida, 244.
35. Derrida, 244.
36. Derrida, 248.
37. Derrida, 248.
38. Derrida, 243.
39. See Giorgio Agamben, *State of Exception*, trans. Kevin Attell (Chicago, IL: University of Chicago Press, 2005), 64.
40. Derrida, "Force of Law," 251.
41. Derrida, 253.
42. Derrida, 258.
43. Derrida, 260.
44. Derrida, 298.
45. Derrida, 262.
46. Derrida, 262.
47. Derrida, 262.
48. Derrida, 276, italics in original.
49. Derrida, 286, italics in original.
50. Derrida, 286.
51. Derrida, 286.
52. Derrida, 287.
53. Derrida, 287.
54. Derrida, 287.
55. Derrida, 288.
56. Derrida, 288.

57. Derrida, 288.
58. Derrida, 288.
59. Derrida, 289.
60. Derrida, 289.
61. Derrida, 289.
62. Derrida, 290.
63. Derrida, 290.
64. Derrida, 290–91.
65. Derrida, 291.
66. Derrida, 298.
67. Derrida, 260.
68. Derrida, 291.
69. Derrida, 291.
70. Derrida, 291.
71. Derrida, 291.
72. Derrida, 290.
73. Derrida, 243.
74. Derrida, 291–92.
75. Derrida, 293.
76. Derrida, 293.
77. Derrida, 293.
78. Derrida, 293.
79. Bataille, *The Trial of Gilles de Rais*, 41.
80. Bataille, 28.
81. Bataille, 33.
82. Bataille, 17.
83. Bataille, 196.
84. Bataille, 250.
85. Bataille, 20.
86. Bataille, 41.
87. Bataille, 102.
88. Bataille, 34.
89. Bataille, 42.
90. Bataille, 40.
91. Bataille, 89.
92. Bataille, 16.
93. Bataille, 16.
94. Bataille, 17.
95. Bataille, *Accursed Share*, vols. 2 and 3, 302.
96. Jacques Derrida, *The Gift of Death*, trans. David Wills (Chicago, IL: University of Chicago Press, 1995), 66.

97. Derrida, 114.
98. Derrida, 109.
99. Derrida, "Force of Law," 293.

Chapter Four

1. Jacques Derrida, *The Beast and the Sovereign*, trans. Geoffrey Benington (Chicago, IL: Chicago University Press, 2011), 2:7–8.
2. Derrida, 21.
3. Martin Heidegger, *The Fundamental Concepts of Metaphysics: World, Finitude, Solitude*, trans. William McNeill and Nicholas Walker (Bloomington: Indiana University Press, 1995), 26.
4. Derrida, *The Beast and the Sovereign*, 2:40.
5. Derrida, 9.
6. Heidegger, *The Fundamental Concepts of Metaphysics*, 177.
7. Heidegger, 247.
8. Heidegger, 284.
9. Heidegger, 360.
10. Heidegger, 361.
11. Heidegger, 361.
12. Heidegger, 361.
13. Heidegger, 361.
14. Heidegger, 361.
15. Heidegger, 361.
16. Heidegger, 361.
17. Heidegger, 361.
18. Heidegger, 362.
19. Heidegger, 362.
20. Heidegger, 363.
21. Heidegger, 363.
22. Heidegger, 363.
23. Heidegger, 363.
24. Heidegger, 364.
25. Heidegger, 364.
26. Heidegger, 364.
27. Heidegger, 365.
28. Heidegger, 364.
29. Derrida, *The Beast and the Sovereign*, 2:283.
30. Derrida, 280.
31. Derrida, 40.

32. Derrida, 123.
33. Derrida, 39.
34. Derrida, 191.
35. Jacques Derrida "Différance," in *Margins of Philosophy*, trans. Alan Bass (Chicago, IL: University of Chicago Press, 1982), 22.
36. Derrida, 18.
37. Derrida, 19, italics in original.
38. Derrida, 22.
39. Derrida, 23.
40. Derrida, *The Beast and Sovereign*, 2:41.
41. Derrida, 123n17.
42. Derrida, 246.
43. Derrida, 278–79.
44. Derrida, 279.
45. Derrida, 286n57.
46. Derrida, 286.
47. Derrida, 286–87.
48. Derrida, 288.
49. Derrida, 287.
50. Derrida, 289.
51. Derrida, 88.
52. Derrida, 288–89.
53. Derrida, 288.

Chapter Five

1. Derrida, "Force of Law," 298.
2. Jacques Derrida, *Of Hospitality: Anne Dufourmantelle Invites Jacques Derrida to Respond*, trans. Rachel Bowlby (Stanford, CA: Stanford University Press, 2000), 77.
3. Derrida, 77.
4. Derrida, 75.
5. Derrida, 77.
6. Derrida, 75.
7. Derrida, 79, italics in original.
8. Derrida, 79–81, italics in original.
9. Derrida, 149.
10. Derrida, 155.
11. Cited in Derrida, 153.
12. Derrida, 151.
13. Cheryl J. Exum, *Fragmented Women: Feminist (Sub)Versions of Biblical Narratives* (Sheffield, UK: JSOT Press, 1993), 177.

14. See Martin Noth, *A History of Pentateuchal Traditions* (Englewood Cliffs, NJ: Prentice-Hall, 1972).

Chapter Six

1. Jacques Derrida, "Violence and Metaphysics," in *Writing and Difference*, trans. Alan Bass (Abingdon, Oxford: Taylor & Francis, e-Library, 2005), 134.
2. Derrida, 112.
3. Derrida, 113.
4. Derrida, 113.
5. Derrida, 117–18, italics in original.
6. Derrida, 122.
7. Derrida, 129.
8. Derrida, 142.
9. Derrida, 144.
10. Derrida, 145.
11. Derrida, 145.
12. Derrida, 145–46.
13. Derrida, 146.
14. Derrida, 146.
15. Derrida, 146.
16. Derrida, 146.
17. Derrida, 146.
18. Derrida, 157.
19. Derrida, 158.
20. Derrida, 160, italics in original.
21. Derrida, 160.
22. Derrida, 160.
23. Derrida, 160, italics in original.
24. Derrida, 162, italics in original.
25. Derrida, 162.
26. Derrida, 162.
27. Derrida, 162.
28. Derrida, 162.
29. Derrida, 162.
30. Derrida, 162.
31. Derrida, 184.
32. See Alain Badiou, *Ethics: An Essay on the Understanding of Evil*, trans. Peter Hallward (London: Verso, 2001), 18ff.
33. Jacques Derrida, *The Death Penalty*, Vol. 2, trans. Elizabeth Rottenberg (Chicago, IL: Chicago University Press, 2016), 114.

34. Derrida, "Force of Law," 291–92.

35. Derrida, *The Death Penalty*, 2:5.

36. Jacques Derrida, *On the Name*, ed. Thomas Dutoit, trans. David Wood, John P. Leavey, and Ian McLeod (Stanford: Stanford University Press, 1995), 90.

37. Derrida, 91, italics in original.

Conclusion

1. Jaques Derrida, *The Death Penalty*, 2:45.

2. Derrida, 2:46.

3. Derrida, 2:47.

BIBLIOGRAPHY

Agamben, Giorgio. *Homo Sacer: Sovereign Power and Bare Life.* Translated by Daniel Heller-Roazen. Stanford, CA: Stanford University Press, 1998.
Agamben, Giorgio. *State of Exception.* Translated by Kevin Attell. Chicago, IL: University of Chicago Press, 2005.
Arendt, Hannah. *On Revolution.* Harmondsworth, UK: Penguin, 2006.
Badiou, Alain. *Ethics: An Essay on the Understanding of Evil.* Translated by Peter Hallward. London: Verso, 2001.
Barbour, Charles. "The Sovereign Without Domain: Georges Bataille and the Ethics of Nothing." In *The Politics of Nothing: On Sovereignty*, edited by Clare Monagle and Dimitris Vardoulakis, London and New York: Routledge, 2013, 37–49.
Bartelson, Jens. *A Genealogy of Sovereignty.* Cambridge: Cambridge University Press, 1995.
Bataille, Georges. *The Accursed Share: An Essay on General Economy.* Vol. 1. Translated by Robert Hurley. New York: Zone Books, 1991.
Bataille, Georges. *The Accursed Share: An Essay on General Economy.* Vol. 2 and 3. Translated by Robert Hurley. New York: Zone Books, 1993.
Bataille, Georges. *Erotism: Death and Sensuality.* Translated by Mary Dalwood. San Francisco, CA: City Lights, 1986.
Bataille, Georges. *The Impossible.* Translated by Robert Hurley. San Francisco, CA: City Lights Books, 1991.
Bataille, Georges. *Inner Experience.* Translated by Leslie Anne Boldt. Albany: State University of New York Press, 1988.
Bataille, Georges. *Literature and Evil.* Translated by Alistair Hamilton. London: Calder & Boyars, 1973.
Bataille, Georges. *On Nietzsche.* Translated by Bruce Boone. New York: Paragon House, 1992.
Bataille, Georges. *The Trial of Gilles de Rais.* Translated by R. Robinson. New York: Amok Books, 2004.

Bataille, Georges. *The Unfinished System of Non-Knowledge*. Translated by Michelle Kendall and Stuart Kendall. Minneapolis: University of Minnesota Press, 2001.

Bataille, Georges. *Visions of Excess: Selected Writings: 1927–1939*. Edited and translated by Allan Stoekl. Minneapolis: Minnesota University Press, 1985.

Beardsworth, Richard. *Derrida & the Political*. London: Routledge, 1996.

Benjamin, Walter. "Critique of Violence." In *Reflections*, translated by E. Jephcott. New York: Schocken Books, 1978.

Biles, Jeremy, and Kent L. Brintnall, eds. *Negative Ecstasies: Georges Bataille and the Study of Religion*. New York: Fordham University Press, 2015.

Black, Matthew, ed. *Peake's Commentary on the Bible*. London: Thomas Nelson, 1962.

Blumenthal-Barby, Martin. "Pernicious Bastardizations: Benjamin's Ethics of Pure Violence." *MLN* 124, no. 3 (April 2009): 728–51.

Bodin, Jean. *On Sovereignty*. Edited and translated by Julian H. Franklin. Cambridge: Cambridge University Press, 2015.

Botting, Fred, and Scott Wilson, eds. *Bataille: A Critical Reader*. Oxford: Blackwell, 1998.

Brown, Wendy. *Walled States, Waning Sovereignty*. New York: Zone Books, 2010.

Buonamano, Roberto. "The Economy of Violence: Derrida on Law and Justice." *Ratio Juris* 11, no. 2 (1998): 168–79.

Butler, Judith. "Critique, Coercion and Sacred Life in Benjamin's 'Critique of Violence.'" In *Political Theologies: Public Religions in a Post-Secular World*, edited by Hent de Vries and Lawrence E. Sullivan. New York: Fordham University Press, 2006.

Derrida, Jacques. *Aporias*. Translated by Thomas Dutoit. Stanford, CA: Stanford University Press, 1993.

Derrida, Jacques. *Archive Fever: A Freudian Impression*. Translated by Eric Prenowitz. Chicago, IL: Chicago University Press, 1996.

Derrida, Jacques. *The Beast and the Sovereign*. Vol. 1. Translated by Geoffrey Bennington. Chicago IL: Chicago University Press, 2009.

Derrida, Jacques. *The Beast and the Sovereign*. Vol. 2. Translated by Geoffrey Bennington. Chicago, IL: Chicago University Press, 2011.

Derrida, Jacques. *The Death Penalty*. Vol, 1. Translated by Peggy Kamuf. Chicago, IL: Chicago University Press, 2013.

Derrida, Jacques. *The Death Penalty*. Vol. 2. Translated by Elizabeth Rottenberg. Chicago, IL: Chicago University Press, 2016.

Derrida, Jacques. "Différance." In *Margins of Philosophy*, translated by Alan Bass. Chicago, IL: University of Chicago Press, 1982.

Derrida, Jacques. "Force of Law: The Mystical Foundation of Authority." In *Acts of Religion*, edited by Gil Anidjar and translated by Mary Quaintance. New York: Routledge, 2002.

Derrida, Jacques. *Given Time 1: Counterfeit Money*. Translated by Peggy Kamuf. Chicago, IL: University of Chicago Press, 1992.

Derrida, Jacques. *The Gift of Death*. Translated by David Wills. Chicago, IL: University of Chicago Press, 1995.

Derrida, Jacques. *Learning to Live Finally: An Interview with Jean Birnbaum*. Translated by Pascale-Anne Brault and Michael Naas. New York: Palgrave Macmillan, 2010.

Derrida, Jacques. *Of Hospitality: Anne Dufourmantelle Invites Jacques Derrida to Respond*. Translated by Rachel Bowlby. Stanford, CA: Stanford University Press, 2000.

Derrida, Jacques. *On the Name*. Edited by Thomas Dutoit. Translated by David Wood, John P. Leavey, and Ian McLeod. Stanford, CA: Stanford University Press, 1995.

Derrida, Jacques. *Positions*. Translated by Alan Bass. Chicago, IL: Chicago University Press, 1981.

Derrida, Jacques. *Rogues: Two Essays on Reason*. Translated by Pascale-Anne Brault and Michael Naas. Stanford, CA: Stanford University Press, 2005.

Derrida, Jacques. *Specters of Marx: The State of the Debt, the Work of Mourning & The New International*. Translated by Peggy Kamuf. New York: Routledge, 1994.

Derrida, Jacques. "Violence and Metaphysics." In *Writing and Difference*, translated by Alan Bass, London: Taylor & Francis e-Library, 2005, 97–192.

Exum, J. Cheryl. *Fragmented Women: Feminist (Sub)versions of Biblical Narratives*. Sheffield: JSOT Press, 1993.

Fohrmann, Jürgen. "Enmity and Culture: The Rhetoric of Political Theology and the Exception in Carl Schmitt." *Culture, Theory & Critique* 51, no. 2 (2010): 129–44.

Foucault, Michel. "A Preface to Transgression." In *Language, Counter-Memory, Practice*, translated by Donald F. Bouchard and Sherry Simon. Ithaca, NY: Cornell University Press, 1977, 29–52.

Foucault, Michel. *Society Must Be Defended*. Translated by David Macey. London: Allen Lane, 2003.

Friedlander, Eli. "Assuming Violence: A Commentary on Walter Benjamin's 'Critique of Violence.'" *Boundary 2* 42, no. 4 (2015): 159–85.

Gasché, Rodolphe. *Deconstruction, Its Force, Its Violence*. Albany: State University of New York Press, 2016.

Gasché, Rodolphe. *Georges Bataille: Phenomenology and Phantasmatology*. Translated by Roland Végs. Stanford, CA: Stanford University Press, 2012.

Gratton, Peter. *The State of Sovereignty: Lessons from the Political Fictions of Modernity*. Albany: State University of New York Press, 2012.

Greenberg, Udi E. "Orthodox Violence: 'Critique of Violence' and Walter Benjamin's Jewish Political Theology. *History of European Ideas* 34, no. 3 (2008): 324–33.

Guzman, Luis. "Benjamin's Divine Violence: Unjustifiable Justice." *CR: The New Centennial Review* 14, no. 2 (2014): 49–64.

Hackett, Jo Ann. "Violence and Women's Lives in the Book of *Judges*." *Interpretation* 58 no. 4 (2004): 356–64.

Heidegger, Martin. *The Fundamental Concepts of Metaphysics: World, Finitude, Solitude.* Translated by William McNeill and Nicholas Walker. Bloomington: Indiana University Press, 1995.

Hobbes, Thomas. *Leviathan.* Oxford: Oxford University Press, 1996.

The Holy Bible, English Standard Version. ePub edition.

Kakoliris, Gerasimos. "Jacques Derrida on the Ethics of Hospitality." In *The Ethics of Subjectivity: Perspectives Since the Dawn of Modernity*, edited by Elvis Imafido, 144–56. Houndmills: Palgrave Macmillan, 2015.

Kantorowicz, Ernst H. *The King's Two Bodies: A Study in Medieval Political Theology.* Princeton, NJ: Princeton University Press, 1957.

Kellogg, Catherine. "Walter Benjamin and the Ethics of Violence." *Law, Culture and the Humanities* 9, no. 1 (2011): 71–90.

Kotsko, Adam. "On Agamben's Use of Benjamin's 'Critique of Violence.'" *Telos* 145 (Winter 2008): 119–29.

Krell, David Farrell. *Derrida and Our Animal Others: Derrida's Final Seminar, "The Beast and the Sovereign."* Bloomingtion: Indiana University Press, 2013.

Leitch, Vincent B. "Late Derrida: The Politics of Sovereignty." *Critical Inquiry* 33, no. 2 (Winter 2007): 229–47.

Levinas, Emmanuel. *Totality and Infinity: An Essay on Exteriority.* Translated by Alphonso Lingis. Pittsburgh, PA: Duquesne University Press, 1969.

Martel, James R. *Divine Violence: Walter Benjamin and the Eschatology of Sovereignty.* London: Routledge, 2012.

McNulty, Tracy. "The Commandment Against the Law: Writing and Divine Justice in Walter Benjamin's 'Critique of Violence.'" *diacritics* 37, no. 2–3 (Summer–Fall 2007): 34–60.

Mitchell, Andrew J., and Jason Kemp Winfree, eds. *The Obsessions of Georges Bataille: Community and Communication.* Albany: State University of New York Press, 2009.

Monagle, Clare. "A Sovereign Act of Negation: Schmitt's Political Theology and Its Ideal Medievalism." *Culture, Theory & Critique* 51, no. 2 (2010): 115–27.

Morgan, Benjamin. "Undoing Legal Violence: Walter Benjamin's and Giorgio Agamben's Aesthetics of Pure Means." *Journal of Law and Society* 34, no. 1 (March 2007): 46–64.

Noth, Martin. *A History of Pentateuchal Traditions.* Englewood Cliffs, NJ: Prentice-Hall, 1972.

O'Gorman, Kevin D. "Jacques Derrida's Philosophy of Hospitality." *Hospitality Review* 8, no. 4 (2006): 50–57.

Peeters, Benoit. *Derrida: A Biography.* Translated by A. Brown. Cambridge: Polity Press, 2013.

Procyshyn, Alexei. "Manifest Reason: Walter Benjamin on Violence and Collective Agency." *Constellations* 21, no. 3 (2014): 390–400.

Ross, Alison. "The Distinction Between Mythic and Divine Violence: Walter Benjamin's "Critique of Violence" from the Perspective of "Goethe's Elective Affinities." *New German Critique* 41, no. 1 (121) (Winter 2014): 93–120.

Rousseau, Jean-Jacques. *The Social Contract*. Translated by Maurice Cranston. London: Penguin Books, 1968.

Schmitt, Carl. *The Concept of the Political*. Translated by George Schwab. Chicago, IL: University of Chicago Press, 2007.

Schmitt, Carl. *Political Theology: Four Chapters on the Concept of Sovereignty*. Translated by George Schwab. Chicago, IL: University of Chicago Press, 2005.

Schmitt, Carl. *Theory of the Partisan*. Translated by G. L. Ulmen. New York: Telos Press Publishing, 2007.

Sherwood, Yvonne, ed. *Derrida's Bible: Reading a Page of Scripture with a Little Help From Derrida*. New York: Palgrave Macmillan, 2004.

Sinnerbrink, Robert. "Deconstructive Justice and the 'Critique of Violence': On Derrida and Benjamin." *Social Semiotics* 16, no. 3 (2006): 485–97.

Smith, Mark S. *God in Translation: Deities in Cross-Cultural Discourse in the Biblical World*. Grand Rapids, MI: William Eerdmans, 2010.

Still, Judith. *Derrida and Hospitality: Theory and Practice*. Edinburgh, UK: Edinburgh University Press, 2013.

Stoekl, Allan. *Bataille's Peak: Energy, Religion and Postsustainability*. Minneapolis: Minnesota University Press, 2007.

Surya, Michel. *Georges Bataille: An Intellectual Biography*. Translated by Krzysztof Fijalkowski and Michael Richardson. London: Verso, 2002.

Vardoulakis, Dimitris. *Sovereignty and Its Other: Toward the Dejustification of Violence*. New York: Fordham University Press, 2013.

White, Jessica. *Catastrophe and Redemption: The Political Thought of Giorgio Agamben*. Albany: State University of New York Press, 2013.

Zacharias, Robert. "'And yet': Derrida on Benjamin's Divine Violence." *Mosaic: A Journal for the Interdisciplinary Study of Literature* 40, no. 2 (June 2007): 103–10.

INDEX

Abraham, 8, 96–97, 127–32. See also under Derrida
Abyss, 4, 9, 36, 39, 40, 63, 70, 75, 103, 139. See also under Bataille; Derrida; Schmitt
Agamben, Giorgio, 2, 34, 37, 75, 76, 79; on Bataille, 39; on doubleness, 37; on exceptionality, 36–38; on justice, 39; on law, 36–38; on power, 35–36, 40; on sovereignty, 35–41; on violence, 38, 39, 40
Animality, 56, 58, 61, 101. See also under Derrida; Heidegger

Badiou, Alain, 157
Bataille, Georges, 2, 5, 13, 35, 39, 40, 41, 43–68, 76, 113, 114, 139, 159, 165; *The Accursed Share*, 92; and deconstruction, 47; influence on Derrida, 7, 47–48; on the abyss, 50, 51, 89, 102; on Christianity, 45, 51, 67, 89, 92, 96; on communication and community, 59, 61, 62; on continuity and discontinuity, 45–47, 50, 51–52, 53, 54, 64, 116; on death, 7, 50, 51, 53, 54, 61, 63, 65, 92; on economy, 45–49, 53, 54; on energy, 7, 60, 64, 116–17; on excess, 7, 45–50, 52, 53, 56, 57, 59, 63, 65, 87; on freedom, 65, 87, 88, 92; on Gilles de Rais, 87–93, 122; on God, 57, 66, 88, 97; on impossibility, 48–51, 55, 58, 60; on killing, 65; on master/slave dialectic, 59; on nothingness, 62–65; on otherness, 48, 49; on religion, 45, 51, 67, 88, 89, 91, 93; on the sacred, 50, 51, 61, 64, 71, 92; on sacrifice, 45, 65; on sex, 7, 45, 50, 53, 54, 65; on sovereignty, 55–68, 91, 99–101; on subjectivity, 89, 93; on taboo and transgression, 52–55, 65, 66, 92; on violence, 50, 51, 61–62, 67, 88; on war, 65
Beardsworth, Richard, 154
Being and beings. See ontological difference
Benjamin, Walter, 2, 132, 143; "Critique of Violence," 71–77, 159–60; on divine violence, 5, 7, 71–77, 160, 162; on God, 72–75, 76; on Judaism, 75; on justice, 73; on law, 10, 71–77; on mere life, 74–76, 83, 98; on myth, 72–74, 76, 82; on revolution, 5, 7, 27, 76; on violence, 73–76. See also under Derrida
Bible, the, 9, 135–38
Biopolitics, 32

Bodin, Jean, 2, 6, 19, 20, 21, 40, 60, 64, 113, 162; on justice, 15, 16; on law, 13, 14, 15, 16; on nature, 14; on power, 13–17; on sovereignty, 13–18

Christianity, 38, 115. *See also under* Bataille; Schmitt
Clausewitz, Carl von, 33
Climate change 1, 2, 4, 9, 122, 157, 161
Community, 165–166. *See also under* Bataille

Decisionism, 139. *See also under* Derrida; Schmitt
Deconstruction, 2, 40, 103, 104, 112, 114, 163. *See also under* Derrida
Democracy, 98. *See also under* Derrida
Derrida, Jacques, 2, 3, 43, 70; *The Beast and the Sovereign*, 4, 8, 102, 110–19; *Death Penalty*, 172–73; "Force of Law," 77–87, 121, 148; *The Gift of Death*, 8, 93–97; *Given Time*, 147; "Khora," 168; *Of Grammatology*, 114; on Abraham, 8, 90, 93–97, 122, 127–32; on the abyss, 78, 81, 86, 132; on the animal, 117–18; on auto-immunity, 168; on Bataille, 112, 147, 160; on Benjamin, 8, 75–87, 90, 98, 172–73; on calculation, 78, 80, 84; on Dasein, 117–19; on the decision, 32, 80, 83, 84, 86, 94, 95, 158; on deconstruction, 79, 84; on democracy, 4, 5, 9, 98, 122, 157, 159; on doubleness, 5, 6, 9, 80, 148, 156, 158–59; on ethics, 142–46, 152; on excess, 79, 82, 95, 110, 115, 155; on the gift, 94, 147; on God, 51, 81–82, 84, 86, 93–98, 113, 114, 121–22, 125, 127–38, 143, 145; on Heidegger, 6, 8, 9, 103, 110–19, 154; on history, 154–55; on hospitality, 4, 5, 9, 97, 121–40; on impossibility, 9, 79, 103, 166–68; on justice 4, 5, 8, 48, 77–87, 97, 114, 121–22, 147, 157; on law, 8, 78, 80, 95, 97, 114, 121–22, 157; on Levinas, 10, 142–54; on the Levite of Ephraim, 9, 123, 125, 132–38; on Lot, 9–10, 123, 125–32, 133, 136; on the messianic, 81; on ontological difference, 110–17, 154, 158; on openness, 32, 157, 166; on otherness, 8, 28, 79, 142–54, 157; on patriarchy, 125–27, 135, 138–39; on politics, 5, 114, 115, 155, 157, 160; on possibility, 110, 167; on *Robinson Crusoe*, 102; on sacrifice, 94, 95; on Schmitt, 28; on sovereignty, 101–4, 110–19; on subjectivity, 95; on the trace, 112; on undecidability, 80; on violence, 10, 77–87, 125, 127, 139; "Pas d'hospitalité," 125–33; "Violence and Metaphysics," 142–54
De Sade, Marquis, 54, 96
Différance, 9, 101, 103, 104, 110, 112, 115

Excess, 7, 8, 17, 21, 29, 32, 40, 60, 96, 104, 163. *See also under* Bataille; Derrida

Foucault, Michel, 52; on disciplinarity, 34, 35; on power, 32–35; on sovereignty, 32–35; on war, 33–35
Freedom, 10, 11, 61, 62, 67, 86, 87, 92, 96, 121, 161, 165–69, 172

Gilles de Rais, 7, 8, 49, 87–93, 96–97, 98, 113, 117, 148, 153, 155, 164, 165; and Christianity, 51. *See also under* Bataille
God, 2, 10, 19, 20, 63, 92, 96, 98, 117, 163, 164; and human

INDEX

sovereignty, 4, 5, 8, 14–17, 20, 44, 60; covenant with Abraham, 10, 127–32; excessiveness of, 22; law of, 22; name of, 7, 40, 68, 93; unity of, 18. *See also under* Bataille; Derrida; Schmitt; sovereignty; violence

Hegel, G. W. F., 59
Heidegger, Martin, *The Fundamental Concepts of Metaphysics*, 104–10; on animality, 105–6; on Dasein, 8, 9, 101, 106–10, 165; on physis, 104–10; on possibility, 108–10; on Walten, 2, 8, 9, 11, 102, 104–10, 165. *See also under* Derrida
Hobbes, Thomas, 2, 6, 25, 43, 60, 162; on God, 19, 20, 21; on justice, 19, 20; on law, 19, 20; on nature, 21; on power, 18–21; on the social contract, 18, 20; on sovereignty, 18–23
Holocaust, the, 85, 160
Hospitality, 3, 121–40. *See also under* Derrida
Human rights, 170

Ipseity, 49, 52, 101, 118–19, 150

Justice, 4, 10, 11, 60, 67, 98, 161, 165–69, 172. *See also under* Agamben; Benjamin; Bodin; Derrida; Hobbes

Kantorowicz, Ernst, 18
Kierkegaard, Søren, 94, 95
Kingship, 3, 18, 20, 21, 22, 44, 58, 114. *See also* sovereignty, human

Law, 67, 173. *See also under* Benjamin; Bodin; Derrida; Hobbes; Rousseau; Schmitt
Levinas, Emmanuel, 142–54
Liberalism, 2, 8, 66, 79, 81, 86, 121, 122, 165, 166, 171

Marx, Karl, 81, 86

Nature, 14, 20, 24; law of, 21. *See also under* Bodin; Hobbes; Rousseau
Neoliberalism, 1, 2
Nietzsche, Friedrich, 112

Ontological difference, 6, 8, 101, 105–10, 168. *See also under* Derrida; Heidegger
Otherness, 8, 63, 144. *See also under* Derrida; Levinas

Power, 4, 10, 11, 63, 68–69, 72–74, 77, 81, 86, 101, 105, 110, 113–15, 119, 132, 137–38, 158, 167–69, 171–73. *See also under* Agamben; Bodin; Foucault; Hobbes; Rousseau; Schmitt

Religion, 98. *See also under* Bataille; Christianity
Revolution. *See* Benjamin
Rousseau, Jean-Jacques, 7; on law, 25; on the lawgiver, 25–27, 44, 66; on nature, 24, 25, 26; on power, 26; on the social contract, 23, 24; on sovereignty, 23–27

Schmitt, Carl, 2, 35, 75, 162; on the abyss, 27, 28, 30, 31; on the Christian miracle, 28, 30, 38, 115; on the decision, 27, 28, 29, 30, 31; on deism, 30; on exceptionality 5, 7, 23, 27–32, 64, 102, 114; on God, 31; on law, 27, 29, 30, 31, 44, 102; on power, 28–31; on sovereignty, 27–32
Social contract, 18, 44. *See also under* Hobbes; Rousseau
Sovereignty, abyssal nature of, 7, 45, 164 (*see also* Bataille); autonomy of, 6, 102; divine, 6 (*see also* God);

Sovereignty *(continued)*
 exceptionality of, 5, 164 *(see also* Agamben, Schmitt)*; excessiveness of, 99, 164; human or traditional, 6, 13, 14, 60, 91, 115, 137–38, 162 *(see also* kingship); indivisibility of, 6, 102; insistence of, 10, 164–69; laws of 23; self-identity of, 6; unaccountability of, 7, 44, 45, 68, 99, 162, 172, 173 *(see also* Schmitt); unconditionality of, 6, 44, 99; violence of, *see* Violence. *See also under* Agamben; Bataille; Bodin; Derrida; Foucault; Hobbes; Rousseau; Schmitt
Subjectivity, 11, 45, 56, 57, 58, 68, 94, 101; autonomous self, 4, 102; and disciplinarity, 35; and individuality, 59, 60, 62–63, 102, 170; and self-identity, 104, 115, 151, 162–63. *See also* Ipseity

Transgression, 17, 96, 98. *See also under* Bataille

Violence, 35, 37; absolute 6, 7, 9, 49, 51, 61, 62, 67, 68, 88, 139, 150 *(see also* Bataille); divine, 2, 7, 8, 27, 31, 68, 86, 125, 127, 169 *(see also* Benjamin, Derrida, God); economy of, 10, 32; mythical, 73–76, 84, 86, 88; revolutionary, 84, 88 *(see also* Benjamin). *See also under* Agamben

War, 65, 146–47

www.ingramcontent.com/pod-product-compliance
Lightning Source LLC
Chambersburg PA
CBHW020737230426
43665CB00009B/466